KU-498-331

Poets in Their Letters

Poets in Their Letters

by

CECIL S. EMDEN

With Drawings by Lynton Lamb

'It really is of importance, not only what men do,
but also what manner of men they are that do it.'

JOHN STUART MILL, ON LIBERTY

London
OXFORD UNIVERSITY PRESS
1959

*Oxford University Press, Amen House, London E.C.*4

GLASGOW NEW YORK TORONTO MELBOURNE WELLINGTON
BOMBAY CALCUTTA MADRAS KARACHI KUALA LUMPUR
CAPE TOWN IBADAN NAIROBI ACCRA

© OXFORD UNIVERSITY PRESS, 1959

B59 06069

B59 06069

HERTFORDSHIRE
COUNTY LIBRARY

928.215   821.009

1579897

Return to Bishop's Stortford
Telephone

PRINTED IN GREAT BRITAIN

FOR HILDA

PREFATORY NOTE

IN the interests of clarity I have made a few slight modifications in the spelling and punctuation of the extracts from the letters used; and I have also reduced to 'lower-case' many of the capitals at the beginning of ordinary words, to conform with present-day usage, since many people find the typical eighteenth-century profusion of capitals disconcerting. Thomas Gray often adopted the convention of putting 'lower-case' letters at the beginning of his sentences. This, too, can be a source of slight aggravation; and I have therefore substituted capitals.

Mr. H. R. Creswick, the Librarian of the University Library at Cambridge, was most kind and sympathetic in giving me facilities to study some unpublished letters of Edward Fitz-Gerald; and the Master and Fellows of Trinity College, Cambridge, have been so good as to give me permission to print a number of extracts from such letters. The Librarian of the College gave me every possible assistance.

The shrewd counsel of my wife and my brother has been invaluable to me. I have already expressed my gratitude to them; but I am anxious to put it on record here.

C. S. E.

CONTENTS

ACKNOWLEDGEMENTS

Permission to quote copyright material is gratefully acknowledged to the following publishers and editors:

The Correspondence of Alexander Pope, ed. George Sherburn, Clarendon Press

Correspondence of Thomas Gray, ed. Paget Toynbee and Leonard Whibley, Clarendon Press

The Letters of William and Dorothy Wordsworth, ed. Ernest de Selincourt, Clarendon Press

Collected Letters of Samuel Taylor Coleridge, ed. Earl Leslie Griggs, Clarendon Press

Byron: A Self-Portrait, ed. Peter Quennell, Messrs. John Murray, Ltd.

Byron Correspondence, ed. Sir John Murray, Messrs. John Murray, Ltd.

Shelley's Lost Letters to Harriet, ed. Leslie Hotson, Messrs. Faber & Faber, Ltd.

Some New Letters of Edward FitzGerald to Bernard Barton, ed. F. R. Barton, Messrs. Williams & Norgate Ltd.

ABBREVIATED REFERENCES TO COLLECTED LETTERS

P = *Correspondence of Alexander Pope*, ed. G. Sherburn, Clarendon Press, 1956

G = *Correspondence of Thomas Gray*, ed. P. Toynbee and L. Whibley, Clarendon Press, 1935

C = *Correspondence of William Cowper*, ed. T. Wright, Hodder & Stoughton, 1904

E = *Early Letters of William and Dorothy Wordsworth*, ed. E. de Selincourt, Clarendon Press, 1935

M = *Letters of William and Dorothy Wordsworth (Middle Years)*, ed. E. de Selincourt, Clarendon Press, 1937

L = *Letters of William and Dorothy Wordsworth (Later Years)*, ed. E. de Selincourt, Clarendon Press, 1939

CC = *Collected Letters of Samuel Taylor Coleridge*, ed. E. L. Griggs, Clarendon Press, 1956

UC = *Unpublished Letters of Samuel Taylor Coleridge*, ed. E. L. Griggs, Constable, 1932

LC = *Letters of Coleridge*, ed. E. H. Coleridge, Heinemann, 1895

BQ = *Byron, Letters and Diaries, A Self-Portrait*, ed. P. Quennell, John Murray, 1950

BP = *Byron's Works (Letters)*, ed. R. E. Prothero, John Murray, 1898-1901

BM = *Byron Correspondence*, ed. Sir John Murray, John Murray, 1922

S = *Letters of Percy Bysshe Shelley*, ed. R. Ingpen, G. Bell & Sons, 1914

SW = *Complete Works of Percy Bysshe Shelley*, ed. R. Ingpen and W. E. Peck, Julian Editions, Ernest Benn, 1926-30

SLL = *Shelley's Lost Letters to Harriet*, ed. L. Hotson, Faber & Faber, 1933

K = *Letters of John Keats*, ed. M. B. Forman, 4th edn., Oxford University Press, 1952

F = *Letters of Edward FitzGerald*, ed. W. A. Wright, Macmillan, 1894

FM = *More Letters of Edward FitzGerald*, ed. W. A. Wright, Macmillan, 1902

FK = *Edward FitzGerald's Letters to Mrs. Kemble*, ed. W. A. Wright, Macmillan, 1902

FB = *Some New Letters of Edward FitzGerald to Bernard Barton*, ed. F. R. Barton, Williams & Norgate, 1923

FQ = *Edward FitzGerald's Letters to Bernard Quaritch*, ed. C. Quaritch Wrentmore, Bernard Quaritch, Ltd., 1926

FC = MS. letters of Edward FitzGerald in the Cambridge University Library

FT = MS. letters of Edward FitzGerald in the library of Trinity College, Cambridge

INTRODUCTORY REMARKS

IN recent years several admirable editions of the collected correspondence of eminent poets have been published; and, during the same period, it has been increasingly recognized that the study of the minds and characters of poets is calculated to promote a better understanding of their poetry. These new collections of letters, by reason of their scope and expert presentation, open up fresh opportunities for profitable investigation. They can become valuable aids to a more just appreciation of these poets, both as authors and as men.

Some kinds of poetry are manifestly capable of elucidation by reference to biographical particulars; that, for instance, of Cowper and Wordsworth, many of whose poems are concerned with their special susceptibility to the influence of nature and the countryside. Similarly, there are poems of Byron, Shelley, and Keats which cannot be adequately interpreted without a knowledge of their experiences, either in the realms of high romance, or, alternatively, in the ignoble regions of amatory intrigue. One or two investigators into biographical evidence have been censured for allegedly indecorous curiosity regarding the private lives of the poets whose poetry they have been so anxious to subject to every imaginable clarification. It may well be doubted whether some of these assiduous people have not been unduly inquisitive. On the other hand, those who submit to the estimation of the public poetry which is strongly imbued with their personalities, must expect to have their conduct exposed to rigorous scrutiny.

The object of this book is by no means confined to providing aids to the interpretation of the poetry of the nine poets whose characters are to be considered in the chapters that follow. Independently of their poetry, their characters, like their biographies, must naturally be the concern of those who are interested in the study of the art of living. Notable poets have not always been paragons of virtue; some have led lives which impress us by their integrity; others, equally ardent in advocating the pursuit of high ideals, have been less successful in equating principle and practice. But, as men of genius, the poets depicted here all made comments on human behaviour that deserve attention, and have themselves behaved in a manner which, if not uniformly edifying, prompts numerous worth-while speculations.

Sometimes biographies of poets, with their ancillary studies of character, suffer from the disadvantage of deficiency in intimate first-hand material, quoted verbatim, such as letters, diaries, and journals, with the result that the treatment of the subjects of the biographies is apt to be insufficiently realistic. There is little excuse for this where there exists a collection of letters that covers most aspects and periods of a poet's activities. Critics of biographies are constantly insisting on the importance of allowing the subjects to speak for themselves. In the more limited project of providing character-sketches which is undertaken here, it is possible to adopt this principle wholeheartedly.

One of the benefits to be gained from letting poets speak for themselves about themselves is the opportunity that it gives us to appreciate the high literary value of their compositions in prose, at any rate the prose of those poets who wrote in the best period of English letter-writing. Several of the recent scholarly collections of poets' letters enable this to be done in a convincing manner for the first time. It may not be an exaggeration to say that the reputations of some of the poets considered here will, in the long run, rest as firmly on their letters as on their poetry.

When letters written to a poet are available as well as letters written by him, it is obviously a good plan for an editor to include some of these; and this course has the advantage of emphasizing that the practice of friendship is a useful sphere in which to investigate character. Perusal of poets' letters suggests a likelihood that they are particularly intense and zealous in their friendships. As they are mostly persons with a high degree of sensitivity, their letters to their friends display a notable tenderness of expression; and they evidently place much reliance on sympathy and warmth of heart. Wordsworth proved an exception in this respect, partly no doubt owing to inhibitions connected with his self-centred disposition, and partly as a result of the large extent to which he was immersed in his family life. Many of his letters to friends lack the quality of intimacy. He was accustomed to consider friendship as a solemn subject; and his potential friends may have found this standpoint discouraging.

It is sometimes difficult to ascertain a poet's genuine attitude towards friendship from his letters. Pope constantly professed his utter dependence on his friends; and yet our discovery that he put fame before friendship does not necessarily imply that he did not rate friendship at a very high level. Byron, as we shall see, often spoke and acted as if he could be independent of the solace gained from intimacy with friends; but, in this respect as in others, he was adopting a pose. It is natural that the unmarried poets, like Gray, Cowper, Keats, and FitzGerald (for the last-mentioned can hardly be classed as a married man), should show themselves, each in his distinctive way, to be palpably reliant on the support of friendship.

No one can be a poet unless he is acutely sensitive to impressions. It is, therefore, habitual for all poets worthy of the name to pass much of their lives in a state of tension which is peculiar to them, and which is not experienced by the ordinary person. Their behaviour may easily be affected by such proclivities as impetuosity, extreme ardour, or shyness. In one respect, intensity of feeling has excited many poets in similar fashion. Their passionate anxiety for the success of their creations of the imagination has often rendered them painfully susceptible to adverse criticism of their work. When their vulnerability was revealed, they suffered such indignity that their only recourse was to adopt an attitude of disdain. Tennyson was hardly singular in attributing unfavourable reviews either to malignity or to intolerable ignorance. Browning used to characterize reviewers as 'the verminous tribe'. Coleridge was a notable exception; he seems to have been genuinely unmoved by unfriendly comment on his writing. This was perhaps due to his particular faculty for forgetting the past, compromising with the present, and fixing his eyes hopefully on the future.

It is possible that undue notice is taken of the eccentricity of poets, whose singular behaviour is frequently explained as being the result of preoccupation. But, in matters of consequence they are eccentric not so much in the sense of being oddities as in the sense that they are either too visionary or too independently minded to be prepared to conform to conventional standards. The notable inconsistencies in the characters of poets are probably attributable to the tenseness of their emotions. This effect can be noticed in the characters of Pope and Byron; but there can hardly have been a more remarkable incongruity than that between Browning's tender affection and prodigious patience on the one hand, and his outbreaks of rancour and vindictiveness on the other. So extraordinary a contrast can only be explained by an intensity of feeling that filled his breast to bursting, but which might easily be unrecognized by a superficial acquaintance.

Inconsistencies of this kind, though often involving qualities that are distinctly unpleasing, tend to enliven the investigations of the biographer or the student of character. The opposite is also true. Of all the poets who, as men, deserve the epithet of worthy, Robert Southey must stand high. As he was among the worthiest of men, he was also, some would say, among the dullest. He had a formidable sense of duty, many virtues, and no vices—if a mild self-righteousness is not a vice. It is obvious, therefore, that there were few lights and shades in his character. It was flat; and this doubtless explains why it would be so difficult to portray in a character-sketch. He was a conscientious and profuse letter-writer; but the picture of him that emerges from his letters tends to be commonplace and monochrome. Some poet-letter-writers, then, would not seem suitable for inclusion in a gallery such as the present one, because they fail to portray themselves with sufficiently distinctive qualities. This deficiency can hardly be attributable to their letters being unduly concentrated on themselves, for no one would qualify for the title of poet if he were not a person of exceptionally interesting personality.

Egotism is such a common failing that it is not, we may assume, specially prevalent in poets, though there are some aspects of their profession that conduce to an undue prominence of self. Just because they are poets, they may easily believe, and perhaps with reason, that they have an urgent and momentous message to impart to the world. This does not necessarily involve self-importance; and it is easy to recollect poets who have been patterns of modesty. No poet wrote more about himself in his letters than Cowper; and no one could have been less of an egotist. On the other hand, Wordsworth's reputation for egotism is justly notorious. Everything in his life, and much in the lives of his family, had to be subordinated to the sacredness of his mission. He would probably have married Annette, the mother of his natural daughter, if such a course had not threatened to thwart his prospects in his chosen profession. Keats, too, had a sense of vocation that was so insistent and absorbing that it could temporarily blind him to his responsibilities as a man, though it never reduced him to a state of self-conceit. If he had not been subjected to severe emotional strain, he would not have let vocation take precedence over the happiness of Fanny Brawne. Pope, Coleridge, and Byron were all strongly tinged with egotism, but in individual manners, suggestive of the possibility of profitable comparison.

The ability to analyse people's characters is a useful accomplishment for poets; and they have often used their letters for practising it on themselves. Their exploits in self-analysis are interesting in several aspects. We may ask ourselves, for instance, how efficient they are, and, again, how sincere they are, at this pursuit. Pope sometimes anatomized his moral and mental condition, for the benefit of his correspondents; but we must often wonder how far he was acting a part. His letters to Swift frequently illustrate this propensity; and he was more honest with Swift in such matters than with other correspondents. Perhaps the most comprehensive and accurate single self-portraiture in the letters of poets is that provided by Gray, when, as a young man, he wrote to his friend, Richard West, proposing a renewal of their friendship. Gray thought it proper to give West an up-to-date representation of his disposition; and he described himself as being at the same time spirited, and thus fond of banter and drollery, and of a contemplative and unsocial tendency. He claimed also to be imaginative, sympathetic, tolerant, forbearing, and straightforward.* As far as we can judge, this was a notably penetrating analysis, displaying unusual ability in this most delicate undertaking. If all poet-letter-writers had been as gifted in this respect, and as guileless, we should be saved much of the reading between the lines that is required in other instances.

* The passage is quoted verbatim on pp. 31–2, below.

B

Byron and Pope were alike in asserting that they could not 'keep' their resentments. Both of them must have known, or should have known, that this was not true, for they were both, in fact, capable of being vindictive. Byron clearly took a pleasure in the analysis of character, his own and other people's; for instance he used to spend time, not very profitably perhaps, in wondering whether he was essentially of a melancholy or a happy disposition.

The credibility of these self-analyses depends, of course, to a large extent on the persons to whom they were communicated. Keats's earlier letters to his brother George and his sister-in-law Georgiana contain much intimate revelation of his attitude of mind. The relations between the brothers were at this stage so perfectly open and sincere that we need be under no suspicion that he was dissimulating, as we must with Pope in the descriptions of his disposition that he provided for his friends. When, therefore, Keats told his two relations that he enjoyed being self-effacing in company because he found this the most peaceable policy, and when he made the unconventional statement that he was dissatisfied with his standard of unselfishness, we may be assured that he was writing in complete good faith. His self-abasement could, indeed, be quite extraordinary. Sometimes, however, the circumstances in which a poet makes professions of this kind tend to arouse our mistrust, although he may not be dissembling, with self-interested motives, like Pope. Shelley, for instance, who could be capable of prodigious selflessness, especially in his dealings with Claire Clairmont, asserted to her, when trying to reassure her about his health and happiness: 'I have a great desire and interest to live, and I would submit to any inconvenience to attain that object.' This was written towards the end of his life; and there is a good deal that we know about him at that period that makes us sceptical of the genuineness of this affirmation.

In the main, the letters of poets are uniform in observing the distinction between prose and poetical diction; but sometimes, in writing letters, they are carried away by their subject, and break inadvertently into highly imaginative language. This is relatively rare. As is natural enough, poets include in their letters many accomplished and perceptive descriptions of scenery, most of which are worth study, because, among other reasons, these word-pictures are informative about their attitudes of mind. The manner in which a poet interprets a scene of great beauty is bound to tell us something valuable about himself. Pope, in a letter which includes his account of an evening ride from Stonor to Oxford, showed selective skill in depicting the woods, hills, rivers, and waterfalls. As might be supposed, he kept his mode of expression under proper restraint; and his intimation of the melancholy that enveloped him, prompted by such features as the 'gloomy verdure', is truly characteristic of his sensibility.

Gray, with his scholarly propriety, also conscientiously restrained his prose from effervescing into poetry. Only occasionally, in the letters in which he described scenery, did he allow the language of poetry to intrude into his calm, graceful delineations. On one occasion, he amused himself by breaking the rules, or possibly his feelings overmastered him. Anyhow, he pretended to be shocked at his infringement of literary decorum. 'In the East', he wrote, 'the sea breaks in upon you & mixes its white transient sails & glittering blew expanse with the deeper & brighter greens of the woods & corn.' He hastened to add: 'This last sentence is so fine I am quite ashamed. But no matter! You must translate it into prose.'[1] This bewitching type of prospect, of sails seen moving across intervening country, evidently struck a sensitive chord in him, for he had been inclined to ignore his principles on a previous similar occasion in describing a view 'where the sea appears glittering thro' the shade, & vessels with their white sails that glide across & are lost again.'[2] Those people who doubt the depth of Gray's poetical inspiration can have their doubts set at rest by these and other striking instances, in his letters, of his susceptibility to natural beauty. In Borrowdale, he obviously felt as a poet should feel when he described 'that turbulent chaos of mountain behind mountain roll'd in confusion'.[3]

It is to be expected that Coleridge, when enchanted by the beauty of a landscape, would be unable to resist recourse to fantasy and figurative language, even though writing in prose. He could not refrain from describing rocks as 'disdainful of the seasons', and woods as rising 'in a frolic surginess'; he saw 'little hills of an hundred shapes, a *dance* of hills, whose variety of position supplied the *effect* of, & almost imitated motion . . .'.[4] In the same letter, he characteristically digressed to consider descriptions of scenery from the philosophic point of view: 'I could half suspect that what are deemed fine descriptions, produce their effects almost purely by the charm of words, with which & with whose combinations we associate feelings indeed, but no distinct *images*.'

Shelley is another of the poet-letter-writers who behaved typically in describing natural features to his friends. He seemed to have difficulty in finding appropriate language to characterize scenes that moved him deeply, being sometimes reduced to using such epithets as 'unexpressible', 'unutterable', and 'inconceivable'. But what he saw prompted conceptions indicative of his cast of mind and its tendency to subjectivity. The ideas that scenes induced in him are so felicitous that they become as impressive as the phenomena themselves. This effect is specially remarkable in his depiction of the English cemetery at Rome, where 'the whispering of the wind among the leaves', and 'the soil which is stirring in the sun-warm earth', around the graves of women and children, promote an envy for 'the sleep they seem to sleep'.[5] Then, between the wild woods on either side of the ancient tombs of Pompeii, 'you hear the late leaves of autumn shiver and rustle in the stream of the inconstant wind, as it were, like the steps of ghosts'.[6] It is difficult to decide, when we read such descriptions, whether they deserve more attention for themselves or for the information we gain from them about the writer.

Here, however, the poets themselves take precedence. The behaviour of nearly all those discussed in this book afford us intriguing problems for the solution of which we may perhaps make some contribution as a result of a scrutiny of their letters. Pope's disingenuousness, which is apt to be discounted or mitigated by his apologists in recent years, provides an ample and attractive field for speculation; and there is no more propitious material for this purpose than his correspondence. Wordsworth's egotism took a different form from that of Pope, for his circumstances, as well as his character, were entirely different. In some quarters he has gained an unenviable reputation for insisting on his own importance and that of his poetry, to the detriment of the comfort of other people. But, in studying his letters, we can quite easily find passages which incline us to the view that a reputation of this kind cannot be fairly imputed to him. Again, the characters of Byron and Shelley each have aspects which perplex us. To what extent was Byron's behaviour artificial? How far, if at all, was Shelley regardless of involving other people in pain and distress? Poets seem to have a peculiar facility for bringing their personal reputations into discredit, and yet have, as a rule, honestly, and sometimes justifiably, felt aggrieved that this should be so. There are, of course, a number of famous poets whose personal record has been such that we can find little to be disparaged or to need extenuation; for instance, Cowper, Gray, Keats, and FitzGerald, from among those included in the present gallery. Thanks to the full, or nearly full, publication of the letters of most of these, we can find ample ground for admiring their characters without making any large reservations; but, happily, even these poets, coming as they do quite near enough to perfection, have also enigmatical qualities which help to invest their letters with a lasting fascination.

No one can doubt that highly imaginative poets, such as those considered in the following chapters, are in themselves subjects of the liveliest interest. That interest can be extended in various ways. It is the aim of this book to illustrate how pleasurably it can be stimulated by turning to account the most promising means available of improving our acquaintance with these men of genius, their letters.

2

ALEXANDER POPE (1688–1744)
A Subject for Sympathy

WHEN writing of Pope, Dr. Johnson warned us that there are risks in deducing the characters of eminent persons from their letters. Though many such letters are written guilelessly, without thought of publicity or self-glorification, a few of them are the products of more subtle practitioners. Sometimes we may suspect that famous letter-writers, mindful of probable publication, avoid saying anything which may reflect on them adversely. But we may be sure that it is rare for them to be at pains to display only their more agreeable features, and even rarer to magnify them. The assertion of a claim to a standard of morals to which there is no legitimate title is so risky a proceeding that only a foolish or reckless person would indulge in it.

Alexander Pope, though in recent years exonerated from some of the charges of dishonesty and rancour which have been levelled against him, was nevertheless in several respects deceitful. He tampered with the texts of his letters so as to make them reflect to his advantage when published, and he descended to discreditable subterfuges so as to involve other people in responsibility for their publication. W. J. Courthope, in discussing these activities in his *Life of Pope* (p. 294), summarized his conclusions about some aspects of Pope's character in remarks which are still valid. 'The facts', he said, 'speak for themselves. They show that, to exalt his own reputation, Pope, on three occasions, deliberately deceived the public by conniving at the publication of his correspondence, while at the same time protesting that this had been effected without his knowledge and against his wish. They show that he had no scruple whatever in altering and transposing his original letters, and readdressing them to persons to whom they were never sent.'

Less noticed than these regrettable practices was his insincere habit, when writing to his friends, of pretending to a carelessness of fame which was quite inconsistent with his real and predominant attitude of mind. Moreover, though he had some admirable qualities which were manifested in the capacities of son, friend, and helper to those in need, he was apt, in his letters, to lay stress on the high moral standards to which he had attained, a tendency which, if it does not arouse suspicions of imposture, must strike us as a gross transgression of proper modesty and restraint.

All this disingenuousness does not render his letters valueless for the assessment of his character; but it does involve the need for careful appraisal, and for discrimination in drawing inferences. Some of the letters published by Pope are, for various reasons, of little service in gaining an understanding of the real man. On the other hand, there are many which can be assumed to express spontaneously the genuine sentiments of the writer. These factors have been borne in mind in the selection of illustrative extracts included in this chapter, and in the inferences to be drawn from them.

Some writers about Pope have laid what seems to be excessive emphasis on the artificial style of his letters, implying that this provides evidence of insincerity; but this view is too much influenced by present-day standards. Educated people in Pope's time tended to adopt the formal manner of letter-writing affected by the French in the seventeenth century. Especially was this so in literary circles; and, doubtless, Pope's adoption of a mannered style in his letters was encouraged by his correspondence, when a young man, with a notable exponent, William Wycherley. Pope's alleged affectation as a letter-writer has been contrasted with the naturalness and artlessness of Cowper and Southey. But, by their time, the formal style had almost gone out of fashion; and, moreover, Cowper and Southey did not belong to literary coteries in which some degree of mannerism was essential to prestige.*

There is naturally much to be said in vindication of Pope. He has been charged with malevolence; but his outstanding defect was rather a proneness to sharp retaliation for attacks made on him. Occasionally, his contemporaries who practised literary criticism, Dennis for instance, were gratuitously truculent; and Pope had some justification for considering that he was being unfairly persecuted. Often, when he struck at an opponent, he would claim that he only acted in self-defence. Some of his reprisals were, indeed, protracted; but he was usually ready to call a truce on reasonable terms.

It must be admitted, however, that his enmities, which were numerous, were in part the result of his own overweening cleverness. Some contemptuous reference or abusive remark, only slightly veiled perhaps, in a poem of his, provoked the sufferer to counter-attack. Such measures, in the literary circles of those days, were often rough and painful. Pope, with his preternatural susceptibility, would be unable to resist the impulse to continue the struggle; and thus the accumulation of ill-feeling would mount, to the ultimate discomfort of both parties.

The unfortunate man's physical deformity was the indirect cause both of his sensitiveness and the weak points in his character, and thus of the unhappiness resulting from his

---

* A remarkably fine example of Pope's high-flown style in his later years is to be found in a passage of a letter to William Warburton, P. IV, 251.

frequent quarrels. Even the tortuousness of his methods, and his insatiable fondness for intrigue, can be attributed to his ever-afflictive twisted anatomy. It is natural and easy, therefore, to consider his case with tolerant sympathy. A morbid self-consciousness about a condition which was really pitiable, but which seemed to him to be shameful, prompted, by way of compensation, an inordinate ambition which he was always anxious to cloak. He constantly protested his disregard of fame, and insisted on the high value he attributed to virtue and friendship. Fame and friendship are not inconsistent; but, unfortunately for Pope, his concentration on the one was apt to endanger the prosperity of the other. A number of his letters are noteworthy for disclosing the frequency with which he barefacedly disclaimed ambition, and alleged first preference for friendships based on a recognition of his moral worth. He was tireless in the way he persisted in voicing his adherence to these guiding principles. It is perhaps odd that it never occurred to him, shrewd as he was, that, as Dr. Johnson once noticed, 'virtue almost never produces friendship'.

In an early letter to his dear Martha Blount, written at a most exciting moment in his literary career, about the time of the publication of the first volume of his translation of Homer's *Iliad*, he alleged: 'Whatever some may think, fame is a thing I am much less covetous of, than your friendship; for that I hope will last all my life, the other I cannot answer for.'[1] His affection for Martha Blount was strong and enduring; but no careful student of Pope, the man, can doubt that the appetite for celebrity was so predominant in his mind as to amount to an infatuation which left other emotions lagging behind it.

In 1716, soon after this letter to Martha, he wrote, while still at the height of his career, to his intimate friend, John Caryll, in a strange medley of hypocrisy and immodesty: 'As for myself who . . . have no interests at my heart but those of mankind, a general good will to all men of good will, I shall be content to wear away a life of no importance in any safe obscurity. The old conceits of fame and idle pleasures of poetry are seriously over with me, and I think of nothing but entire indolence, resignation, or something between both, which I want [i.e. lack] a name for. I am really a greater philosopher than I have the vanity to describe to you; and perhaps a better Christian than is consistent with Christian humility to pretend to be.'[2] In fact, his translation of *The Iliad* was still occupying his active attention; and the only justification for the misrepresentation about indolence and resignation could be a mood of depression, due to physical causes.

Nearly ten years later, when his customary intrigues had landed him in an awkward quandary, he wrote self-consciously to William Broome, his literary assistant: 'I know myself to be an honest man, and, I will add, a friendly one; nor do I in my conscience think I have acted an unfair or disreputable part with the public, if my friends will do me justice. This indeed is my sore place; for I care not what they say of my poetry, but a man's morals are of a tenderer nature, and higher consequence. . . . The people whose friendship I have wished, and endeavoured all the ways I could to deserve, have generally allowed it to me, and that is all the solid pleasure I ever received from the partiality the world has shown my character.'[3]

After passing the height of his literary career, Pope still persisted in his assumed disdainful attitude to fame. In a letter to Swift, in 1733, he posed as being detached from the turmoil of the literary arena, remarking that 'my whole amusement is in reviewing my past life, not in laying plans for the future', adding, 'I wish you cared as little for popular applause as I'.[4] But he had, in fact, interests that engaged him much more closely than the dubious diversion of reviewing his past life; and he was far from retiring into obscurity, for, in 1733, his *Moral Essays* appeared; and, in 1735, his masterpiece the *Epistle to Arbuthnot*.

Three years after this letter to Swift he again wrote to him in the same feigned posture of languid disinterest in literary distinction. 'Pray whose esteem or admiration should I desire now to procure by my writings? whose friendship or conversation to obtain by 'em? I am a man of desperate fortunes, that is a man whose friends are dead: for I never aimed at any other fortune than in friends. . . .'[5]

He continued in these canting protestations until the end of his days. Not long before his death he asserted to the Earl of Marchmont: 'I never had any uneasy desire of fame, or keen resentment of injuries, & now both are asleep together: other ambition I never had, than to be tolerably thought of by those I esteem'd, and this has been gratify'd beyond my proudest hopes.'[6] And, about the same period, he told Martha Blount: 'I have no sort of ambition nor vanity that costs me an uneasy moment.'[7] It could never have occurred to him that biographical research would disclose that his intricate contrivances for the publication of his letters were aimed primarily at his own glorification, in the sense of depicting him as a paragon of integrity and good nature.

He was particularly insistent, in his letters to his friend, Aaron Hill, regarding his freedom from any keen resentment for injuries. In 1731, he told him: 'I do faithfully assure you, I never was angry at any criticism, made on my poetry, by whomsoever: . . .'[8] And, some seven years later, in defending himself against charges of taking umbrage in respect of criticism directed at him, he wrote, in a letter to the same correspondent: 'I have had two or three occasions to lament, that you seem to know me much better as a *poet*, than as a *man*. You can hardly conceive how little either of pique or contempt I bear to any creature, unless for immoral or dirty actions: any mortal is at full liberty, unanswer'd, to write and print of me as a poet, to praise me one year, and blame me another; only I desire him to spare my character as an honest man, over which he can have no private, much less public, right, without some personal knowledge of my heart, or the motives of my conduct.'[9] When further pressed, he made some limited admissions to Hill: 'In what I said, I gave you a true picture of my own heart, as far as I know it myself. It is true, I have shewn a *scorn* of some *writers*; but it proceeded from an experience that they were bad men, or bad friends, or vile hirelings; in which case, their being authors did not make them, to me, either more respectable, or more formidable. As for any other pique, my mind is not so susceptible of it as you have seem'd, on each occasion, too much inclin'd (I think) to believe.'[10]

It was fairly common knowledge in Pope's lifetime that he was painfully sensitive to criticism; and, as literary critics of the day were sometimes brutally vituperative, the agonies he suffered must have been severe. Dr. Johnson described Pope in the act of reading one of Cibber's abusive strictures on his

work. 'These things are my diversion,' said Pope, with pretended nonchalance. But his features were seen to writhe in
anguish, as he read the pamphlet. Dr. Johnson, who had
excellent opportunities to obtain intimate knowledge of Pope's
character, thus summed up this aspect of it: 'He pretends in-
sensibility to censure and criticism, though it was observed by
all who knew him that every pamphlet disturbed his quiet, that
his extreme irritability laid him open to perpetual vexation;
but he wished to despise his criticks, and therefore hoped that
he did despise them.'

Nearly all the poets whose characters are considered in this
book were highly susceptible to adverse criticisms of their
works. If they tried to pretend that it was otherwise, this
pretence was rarely convincing. But Pope evidently assumed
that a frequent repetition of his assertions would make for their
acceptance. In this, as in other respects, he manifested a
characteristic combination of self-complacency and self-
deception.

These defects in his character are particularly conspicuous
in the efforts he made, in his letters, to establish a reputation
for virtue. In these efforts, he displayed an almost indecent
satisfaction in his moral rectitude. He was a man of many kindly
instincts; and, reading between the lines of his letters, we can
notice a number of instances of generous behaviour to friends
and acquaintances. It may well be, then, that he did not
greatly exaggerate the extent of his beneficence. But this cannot
free him from reproach in this matter, for those who adhere to
the normal canons of behaviour do not advertise their kind-
heartedness in their letters to their friends. In his younger days,
he told John Gay, to whom he was more frank and straightforward than to some others of his friends: 'I may with honesty
affirm to you, that notwithstanding the many inconveniences
and disadvantages they commonly talk of in the *res angusti domi*,
I have never found any other, than the inability of giving people
of merit the only certain proof of our value for them, in doing
'em some real service.'[11]

His adoption of a moralizing air in addressing such intimate
friends as Caryll became habitual. 'Methinks,' he remarked,
'in our present condition, the more heroic thing we are left
capable of doing, is to endeavour to lighten each other's load,

and (oppressed as we are) to succour such as are yet more oppressed. If there are too many who cannot be assisted but by what we cannot give, our money, there are yet others who may be relieved by our counsel, by our countenance, and even by our cheerfulness.'[12] Pope was referring here to the oppression of the Roman Catholics; and he and Caryll were faithful adherents to that religion. On another occasion, he advertised his self-righteousness when he told Caryll that 'if ever I see a virtue sprung up, or a good action done, it is the only thing that makes me content to live'.[13]

His protestations to Caryll especially strain the reader's credibility. There is something strangely abnormal in a man who could expect the following excuses, for failure to write a promised letter, to carry conviction: 'I find I'm concerned for so many people and love my friends so well that every thing that befalls them interests me so farr in it as to make me seem to forget the rest. Indeed, dear sir, when I'm seeming to do so, I forget none so much as I do myself and attend [no] one's concerns so little.'[14]

It is natural that some of his remarks in this strain startle the reader whose standards are conventional, and raise suspicions about their sincerity, as, for instance, in a letter to Martha Blount with birthday wishes, in which he adds: 'Every year that passes, I wish some things more for my friends, and some things less for myself.'[15] Again, in a letter to Hugh Bethel, he thus concludes a discourse on the practical difficulties of active benevolence: 'But still I affirm, those very disappointments of a virtuous man are greater pleasures, than the utmost gratifications and successes of a mere self-lover.'[16] In reading such passages as these, we must conclude that some of Pope's friends, who were doubtless ordinary, sensible people, can hardly have felt complimented at his confident assumption of their credulity.

His letters to Swift include some of his more intimate thoughts; but it seems doubtful whether, even in these letters, he does not sometimes transgress the standard of reserve which should limit the proper expression of benevolent principles. In a letter where he seems to declare his readiness to endow Swift with £100 a year, he remarked: 'Don't be angry; I will not live to be very old. I have revelations to the contrary. I would not crawl upon the earth without doing a little good when I have a mind to do it: I will enjoy the pleasure of what I give, by giving it, alive, and seeing another enjoy it. When I die, I should be asham'd to leave enough to build me a monument, if there were a wanting friend above ground.'[17]

Alas! there is no escape from the conclusion that most of these letters were written with an eye to publication, and with the object of establishing for him a widespread reputation for moral perfection. Pope's exceeding cleverness doubtless met with a considerable measure of success during his lifetime. Many readers of his published letters must have been strongly impressed by the picture of a poet of such elevated sentiments. It did not seem to have occurred to them that there was a discrepancy between the model of benevolence disclosed in the letters and the relentless satirist of some of the poems. The fact remains that his letters when published gained him eligible admirers seeking his friendship. In particular, his close, and, in the main, happy friendship with Ralph Allen arose in this way; and Allen was by no means a gullible person. He was an astute man, of sterling character, and justifiably the prototype of Fielding's Squire Allworthy. But, as the years passed by, Pope's intrigues and subtleties were increasingly exposed; and his character, after being ruthlessly dissected, was bluntly denounced, until at last, towards the end of the nineteenth century, the process went too far; and it has required modern research to redress the balance and demonstrate that the poet's defects of character had in some respects been exaggerated.

*   *   *

So far in this chapter Pope's character, as interpreted chiefly by means of extracts from his letters, has suffered from the implication of undue subtlety. It is probable that his persistent endeavour to represent himself as a man of outstanding virtue was largely concerned in attracting desirable friendships with eminent people, though his personal reputation at the bar of history was doubtless also a factor. In spite of his considerable foibles, some of which amount to serious defects, it is not fair to use them as the main basis for an assessment of the real man. Owing to his physical deformity, he was specially reliant on the consolation of friendship. And, although his own fame as an author, and his acceptance by society and by posterity as a man of worth, came first in his plans, he had a genuine reverence for friendship; and he proved himself in several instances to be a faithful and conscientious friend. He could number some half a dozen close friends with whom unbroken relations lasted into decades. Dr. Johnson's remark that he does not appear to have lost a single friend by coldness or by injury may well be nearly sustainable. This is a record not to be attained by a persistent hypocrite. Nevertheless, the constant intrigues in which he involved himself, sometimes to the detriment of innocent people, must in some degree lower his prestige as an exponent of friendship.*

A large number of extracts from Pope's letters could be quoted to substantiate his reputation as a true friend, extracts, that is to say, which have a genuine ring of spontaneity about them. A few will be sufficient here. A letter to Pope's friend, Charles Jervas, the painter, displays such a sensible philosophy of friendship that it can hardly be make-believe. It looks for no extravagant results from friendship, but is so modest and reasonable in its outlook that it has a convincing air of sincerity. The letter is evidently written with special care, and may well have been composed with some thought of publication later; but it is not necessary to suspect it of hypocrisy on that account. It must be quoted at some length: 'I fancy no friendship is so likely to prove lasting as ours, because I am pretty sure there never was a friendship of so easie a nature. We neither of us demand any mighty things from each other; what vanity we have expects its gratification from other people. It is not I, that am to tell you what an artist you are, nor is it you that are to tell me what a poet I am; but 'tis from the world abroad we hope (piously hope) to hear these things. At home we follow our business, when we have any; and think and talk most of each other when we have none. 'Tis not unlike the happy friendship of a stay'd man and his wife, who are seldom so fond as to hinder the business of the house from going on all day, or so indolent as not to find consolation in each other every evening. Thus well-meaning couples hold in amity to the last, by not expecting too much from human nature; while romantic

* Especially is this so in regard to his deceitful treatment of Swift, when planning the publication of Swift's letters.

friendships, like violent ones, begin with disquiets, proceed to jealousies, and conclude in animosities. I have liv'd to see the fierce advancement, the sudden turn, and the abrupt period, of three or four of these enormous friendships, and am perfectly convinc'd of the truth of a maxim we once agreed in, that nothing hinders the constant agreement of people who live together, but meer vanity; a secret insisting upon what they think their dignity or merit, and an inward expectation of such an overmeasure of deference and regard, as answers to their own extravagant false scale; and which no body can pay, because none but themselves can tell, exactly, to what pitch it amounts?'[18] This essay on friendship obviously owes something to predecessors writing in the same vein; but it also represents some individual thought and experience. Pope, in fact, spent considerable periods living with Jervas in the latter's town house.

Like many other letter-writers, Pope often took the opportunity of a lapse in correspondence with a friend to protest the continuing validity of their friendship. On such an occasion, he made earnest assurances to Caryll: 'I beg you at all times, to believe me as zealous to continue our friendship, as I was at the first moment I began it: and that as it has increased ever since that time, so it shall never suffer any abatement by any intervals of absence or fortune.'[19] Five years later, he repeated assurances of this kind to Caryll, but perhaps with less conviction: 'I preserve with great constancy all the regards I ever had to my friends, and in particular yourself. I rarely see any of 'em, but often recollect there are some such in the world, and that recollection renders me the better satisfied to be in it.'[20]

For reasons at which we can only guess, Pope evidently became disappointed in the satisfaction to be gained from his more intimate friendships. This is hardly to be attributed to his increased attention to friendships with titled people, though it may have been a minor factor. A more likely explanation is to be gathered from Swift's complaint that Pope was never at leisure for conversation, because he had 'always some poetical scheme in his head'. He gained the reputation of having so little taste for company that he would prefer even a book of moderate quality to the most agreeable conversation.[21] In fact, he became more and more absorbed in his own literary concerns to the exclusion of social activity. This development may explain the ineffectual and apparently futile terms in which he mentioned friendship in a pathetically phrased letter to his close friend, John Gay, in 1730: 'Are we never to live together more, as once we did? I find my life ebbing apace . . . Companions I have enough, friends few, and those too warm in the concerns of the world for me to bear pace with; or else so divided from me, that they are but like the dead whose remembrance I hold in honour. Nature, temper, and habit, from my youth made me have but one strong desire; all other ambitions, my person, education, constitution, religion &c. conspir'd to remove far from me. That desire was to fix and preserve me a few lasting, dependable friendships: and the accidents which have disappointed me in it, have put a period to all my aims.'[22] He had obviously lost his hold on, and even his belief in, friendship, and was content to resurrect, in unconvincing terms, some aspirations that had ceased to be real to him.

Swift remained almost the only friend, apart from the aristocracy, on whom he was prepared to expend time and energy. There were special affinities of intellect and principle that bound him and Swift together. One particular characteristic they had in common contributed to their mutual compatibility: they were both said never to have been seen to laugh. Both of them, moreover, had deep insight into the hazards and limitations of friendship. It was about the time that Pope's friendships were withering that Swift wrote to him: 'You are the best and kindest friend in the world, and I know no body alive or dead to whom I am so much obliged; and if ever you made me angry, it was for your too much care about me.'[23]

But whether from disappointment, preoccupation, or weariness, Pope, towards the end of his life, took a decreasing amount of trouble to maintain a sympathetic correspondence with his friends. His deficiencies were sufficiently obvious to require apology; and he made a succession of unconvincing excuses to such friends as Ralph Allen and William Fortescue. He told Allen, in 1736: 'I do not write too often to you for many reasons, but one which I think a good one is, that friends should be left to think of one another for certain intervals without too

c

frequent memorandums, it is an exercise of their friendship, &
a tryal of their memory: and moreover to be perpetually
repeating assurances is both a needless & a suspicious kind of
treatment, with such as are sincere.'[24] These are words which
it is impossible to accept as honestly meant; and they attest a
loss of faith in the principle, or at least in the practice of friendship. His excuses to Fortescue, in 1739, for his increasing
remissness, are even more specious and transparent: 'The whole
purpose of it [friendly correspondence] is only to tell, now and
then, one is alive; and to encourage one's friends to tell us the
same, in the consciousness of loving and being loved by each
other. All news, if important, spreads itself; and, if unimportant,
wastes time and paper; few things can be related as certain
truths, and to hunt for pretty things belongs to fops and
Frenchmen.'[25] Finally, he told Warburton, in 1741: 'I am
always naturally sparing of my letters to my friends, for a
reason I think a great one; that it is needless, after experience,
to repeat assurances of friendship and no less irksome to be
searching for words, to express it over and over.'[26] The com-
pleteness of the change in Pope's attitude to friendship is
certainly very puzzling. In his younger days, he devoted a
great deal of energy to advertising his moral perfection so as to
attract desirable friends; and then, later in life, wasted that
energy by treating his friends cavalierly.

Even as he grew older and, it would seem, more self-sufficient,
he could open his mind and his heart when moved to do so.
Swift was, as we have suggested, one of Pope's friends with
whom he adopted particular standards of behaviour; and, as
late as 1739, Pope wrote him a cordial, communicative letter,
containing his personal news, with a picture of his everyday
activities; in fact the kind of letter which should pass from time
to time between good-humoured friends, living apart. 'Having
nothing more to tell you of my poetry', he wrote, 'I come to
what is now my chief care, my health & amusement: the first
is better, as to headakes, worse as to weakness & nerves; the
changes of weather affect me much, otherwise I want not
spirits, except when indigestions prevail. The mornings are my
life; in the evenings I am not dead indeed but sleep, and am
stupid enough. I love reading still, better than conversation;
but my eyes fail; and at the hours when most people indulge in

company, I am tired, & find the labour of the past day sufficient to weigh me down: so I hide my self in bed, as a bird in his nest, much about the same time, & rise & chirp the earlyer the next morning . . . In the summer I generally ramble for a month, to Lord Cobham's, the Bath, or elsewhere. In all those rambles, my mind is full of the images of you and poor Gay, with whom I travell'd so delightfully two summers.'[27]

Conforming to the practice of many exemplary correspondents, Pope claimed that he was constantly thinking of his friends and imagining their activities, and even imagining conversation with them. He told Swift once, in a letter, that 'every day I talk with you, and of you, in my heart'.[28] At his prime, Pope showed a remarkably lively sympathy in imagining the situations in which his correspondents might be placed, and a happy faculty for genial, and even sentimental, recollections of past experiences. In such passages in his letters, he proved himself to be a genuine exponent of the art of friendship. He wrote to Henry Cromwell, in 1711: 'The news you tell me of the many difficulties you found in your return from Bath gives me such a kind of pleasure as we usually take in accompanying our friends in their mixt adventures; for methinks I see you labring thro all your inconveniences, of the rough roads, the hard saddle, the trotting horse, and what not?'[29] To Caryll, about 1713, he wrote: 'I have just now stolen myself from a tumult of acquaintance at Will's [coffee-house], into my chamber, to enjoy the pleasing melancholy of an hour's reflection alone. There is an agreeable gloominess which instead of troubling, does but refresh and ease the mind, and has an effect upon it not unlike the relief a sudden cloud sometimes gives the eye, when it has been aching and too much distended with the glaring of a summer's day. In one of these moments I have past over the pleasures I last tasted in your company.'[30] Perhaps the best example of this sympathetic relationship between Pope and his friends occurs in a letter to an old friend of his youth, living in his home country, in Windsor Forest, Thomas Dancastle. 'I hope', wrote Pope, 'you are arisen from the gout with which I hear you were laid up, & that your brother is also well. The memory of our old neighbors yet lives in me; I often give a range to my imagination, & goe a strolling with one or other of you, up & down Binfield Wood, or over

Bagshot Heath. I wish you all health, not you only, but your horse, your dog Lilly, &c. May your gun never fail, and your aim never miss. May your pouch come swagging home, laden with woodcocks, and may those woodcocks be so fatt & good as to please Mr. Philips [Dancastle's chaplain].'[31]

Pope's kindness and loyalty to friends and acquaintances is well established by his more tolerant biographers. His friend, Aaron Hill, had, at an early stage of their friendship, been suspicious of Pope's bona fides; but when Hill's wife died, in 1731, he became convinced of Pope's authentic friendship, and wrote to him: 'It will never be in my power to forget, how compassionate you have been, in *calling* and *sending* so often—It is plain, you have none of the *fashionable want of feeling, for the calamities of others*; and when I reflect, that you are kind enough to *concern* yourself for *mine*, it brings me nearer to *comfort*, than either resignation, or philosophy.'[32] The practical loyalty and unshakable fidelity he demonstrated in regard to several of his friendships is fully appreciated and well substantiated by Norman Ault, in his *New Light on Pope* (pp. 23-4), who mentions, in support of Pope's reputation as a faithful friend, incidents relating to the first Earl of Oxford, Bishop Atterbury, Swift, and Viscount Bolingbroke.

Numerous instances could be quoted where famous authors have displayed a great deal of patience and good humour in satisfying the requests of tyros in the literary profession for advice and assistance in their early endeavours at writing poetry. Pope was most generous in spending himself in helping deserving aspirants, and would even write letters of recommendation for them so as to support their efforts to pursue their chosen careers. The amount of trouble to which he would go is well illustrated by the extensive activities he undertook on behalf of the youthful Samuel Johnson, after reading, and being much impressed by, his early poem, *London*. It was natural, and evidently pleasurable, for Pope to expend energy in overlooking the poetry and other writings of his close friend, John Gay, and in canvassing for the patronage of his plays.

The charity by which Pope helped needy friends and acquaintances is notable because it did not consist merely in gifts of money, but also in exercising sympathetic discrimination, and sometimes placability. There was perhaps no compassion, any more than there was large financial risk, in lending money to Robert Dodsley, to set up in the bookseller's and publisher's business. But he shewed an impressive degree of forbearance when dispensing charity to the wayward and exasperating Richard Savage;[33] and remarkable freedom from resentment in helping his one-time enemy, John Dennis, when he was old and in want.[34] His goodness of heart is manifested in several small incidents which are noticeable occasionally in his correspondence, and which he did not, as far as we know, disclose to his acquaintance. He took considerable pains to help suffering people in a humble way of life; and evidently had an instinctive feeling of kindliness for the poor.[35]

It might perhaps be supposed that so ambitious a person as Pope would have treated his undistinguished relations slightingly or with some remissness. On the contrary, his reverence and solicitude for his parents is plainly evident from his letters. To suspect his genuineness in this respect would be to rank him as a despicable hypocrite. For many years he shewed exemplary devotion and patience in nursing and comforting his mother during the protracted invalidism of her old age. He never complained about this considerable hindrance to his literary activities, and to his ability to enjoy social contacts with his friends. 'It is my mother only', he wrote to a friend, 'that robs me of half the pleasure of my life, and that gives me the greatest at the same time.' He treated his half-sister, Mrs. Rackett, with kindly consideration, and we can notice, in his letters to her, his habit of advising her in her troubles, and of lending her money when in need.

An ambitious man is often incapable of self-effacement and self-sacrifice; but Pope had the sagacity, as well as the disposition, to eschew, when writing to his friends, such of his personal troubles as might be wearisome. He never burdened them with particulars of his physical distresses which must have been frequent and vexatious. Two extracts from his letters illustrate how lightly he touched on his ailments and illnesses. About 1719, he told Martha Blount: 'As to my health, I'm in a very odd course for the pain in my side: I mean a course of brickbats and tiles, which they apply to me piping hot, morning and night and sure it is very satisfactory to one who loves architecture at his heart, to be built round in his very bed. My body may properly at this time be called a human structure.'[36] When he was forty years old, he wrote to his friend, William Fortescue: 'I am in the condition of an old fellow of threescore, with a complication of diseases upon me; a constant headake; ruin'd tone of the stomach; the piles, a vomiting and looseness; & an excess of wind. Some of these succeed, the moment I get quit of the others: & upon the whole, indeed I am in a very uncomfortable way.'[37] Nothing could be more objective and concise. This restraint, this obvious refusal to be tempted into pouring forth details of personal troubles on his friends, is in notable contrast with the practice of another famous letter-writer, whose sufferings were also severe, Dr. Johnson. Pope's sustained sprightliness of manner in the large majority of his letters is highly praiseworthy, in view of the persistent depression from which he suffered as a result of his ill-health.

No consideration of his character should fail to give due weight to the severity of his handicaps. These were specially grievous to him when he contemplated his relations with Martha Blount. There is ample evidence of his being in love with her, and yet he feared that he could not make her happy, even if she would let him try. At one stage he seems to have contemplated offering her his hand. But the project became a hopeless one, largely no doubt because he became increasingly conscious of his inadequacy as a prospective husband. Whatever may have been the predominant cause of his abandoning the project, Pope must surely have our abundant compassion. Three letters of his, written to Martha Blount about 1717 to 1719, are suggestive of the enactment of a tragic drama, and speak for themselves in disclosing not only his chagrin, and even his anguish, but also his patient submission to compulsive circumstances, and his loftiness of purpose. 'Let me open my whole heart to you', he wrote. 'I have some times found myself inclined to be in love with you: and as I have reason to know from your temper & conduct how miserably I should be used in that circumstance, it is worth my while to avoid it: it is enough to be disagreeable, without adding fool to it, by constant slavery. I have heard indeed of women that have a kindness for men of my make; but it has been after enjoyment, never before; and I know to my cost you have no taste of that talent in me,

which most ladies would not only like better, but understand
better, than any other I have.

'I love you so well that I tell you the truth, & that has made
me write this letter. I will see you less frequently this winter,
as you'll less want company. When the gay part of the world is
gone, I'll be ready to stop the gap of a vacant hour whenever
you please. Till then I'll converse with those who are more
indifferent to me, as you will with those who are more entertaining.'[38]

Another letter, written to Martha and her sister about a year
later, again proves the extent to which Pope was capable of
magnanimity: 'Pray think me sensible of your civility & good
meaning in asking me to come to you.

'You will please to consider that my coming or not is a thing
indifferent to both of you. But God knows, it is far otherwise to
me, with respect to one of you.

'I scarce ever come but one of two things happens which
equally afflicts me to the soul. Either I make her uneasy, or I
see her unkind.

'If she has any tenderness, I can only give her every day
trouble and melancholy. If she has none, the daily sight of so
undeserved a coldness must wound me to death.

'It is forcing one of us to do a very hard and very unjust
thing, to the other.

'My continuing to see you, will, by turns, teize all of us. My
staying away can at worst be of ill consequence only to myself.

'And if one of us is to be sacrific'd, I believe, we are all three
agreed, who shall be the person.'[39]

It is possible, but hardly likely, that these letters were
intended to draw from Martha a declaration, induced by an
access of pity for the unfortunate victim of a well-nigh hopeless passion. We shall never know the truth about this; but, by
the end of another year, Pope's feelings were assuaged, as
appears from a third letter from him to Martha: 'I do sincerely,
and from my soul, wish you every pleasure and contentment the
world can give; and do assure you at the same time, the greatest
I can receive will always be in hearing of yours, and in finding,
by your communicating it to me, that you know how much I
partake of it. This will satisfy my conscience better, than if I
continued to trouble you daily; though there is really no day of

my life that I don't long to see you.'[40] His deep affection for Martha Blount remained steadfast to the end of his life. Though he could not marry her, he was piteously anxious not to lose her intimate friendship and sympathy.

*　　*　　*

Many of the disparaging views of Pope's character that were prevalent in his lifetime, and have sometimes influenced his biographers, can probably be traced to his unfortunate propensity for making enemies; and his enemies were assiduous in disseminating ill-natured and exaggerated accounts of his imperfections. A much more satisfactory source of information is a level-headed friend. One of Pope's friends on whose opinion we can most safely rely is Joseph Spence, a conscientious, sensible man, and an accomplished scholar, who, in his introduction to his anecdotes about Pope, supplied the following tribute: 'All the people well acquainted with Mr. Pope looked on him as a most friendly, open, charitable, and generous-hearted man;—all the world almost, that did not know him were got into a mode of having very different ideas of him. . . .'

Nowadays it is quite generally allowed that Pope's career, though punctuated by repeated acts of chicanery and deception, should be regarded as less blameworthy than has sometimes been supposed. He was probably not so much a trickster as an unhappy mortal impelled by an insidious spirit within him to cloak the seeming shame of his physical inferiority by the demonstration of his moral and intellectual superiority to most of his fellow-men. If he could hear around him eulogies of his pre-eminent reputation as a poet and a friend, the bitterness of his plight, his sense of humiliation at having to live his life in so pitiable a frame, would doubtless be mitigated.

3

THOMAS GRAY (1716–1771)
Delicate Sensibility

I T would be surprising if men with such sublime qualities as
poets conformed to the pattern of the average man. And yet,
when poets display curious characteristics, those who discuss
their behaviour are apt to consider their disconformities to be
unfortunate. People who make it their business to comment
upon Thomas Gray's conduct as a man sometimes conclude
that he was much handicapped by a shy manner and secluded
habits. He was, indeed, remarkably diffident; and, in his chosen
life as a scholar, he naturally took pleasure in considerable
periods of solitude, or at least of tranquillity. But these features
by no means amount to imperfections of character; nor do they

bulk so largely in his make-up as to justify a charge of oddity.

On making Gray's close acquaintance through the medium of his letters, we find that he is not so singular a person as a common view of him implies. He was not unsocial or aloof, though, as we shall have occasion to notice, he had, like many academical persons, his whims and unconventionalities. In order to substantiate a picture of him as a kindly, genial man, we may first concern ourselves with such of his qualities as are typical of the normal person, especially his sociability. Thereafter it will be fair and proper to remark on some of the aspects of his character that are more distinctive.

Like most of the other poets discussed in this book, Gray placed a high value on friendship. It was a subject that engaged his thoughts from his schoolboy days. An unhappy atmosphere in his home intensified his need for human sympathy; but, luckily for him, he formed one of a small group of congenial companions at Eton, with whom he was able to experiment in the art of friendship under propitious conditions. In this group was included Horace Walpole, the son of Sir Robert Walpole, the First Minister of the Crown. Even in those days, school-life could, in particularly favourable circumstances, enable a boy coming from a middle-class home, like Gray, to enjoy an unaffected and at the same time a profitable friendship with another of a more elevated station in society. But, as early as the schoolboy stage of this friendship, Gray was diffident, partly owing to the effect on him of the disadvantages of his distasteful home life, and to a large extent owing to the disparity between the social strata of Walpole and himself. During his undergraduate career at Cambridge, he wrote to Walpole: 'You can never weary me with repetition of any thing that makes me sensible of your kindness: since that has been the only idea of any social happiness that I have ever received almost, & which (begging your pardon for thinking so differently from you in such cases) I would by no means have parted with for an exemption from all the uneasinesses mixed with it.'[1]

The friendship with Walpole developed so favourably that Gray was taken as his friend's guest and companion on the European Grand Tour. As is well known, after some months of pleasant travel, differences of taste and temperament between the two young men became intensified until they culminated in a quarrel and a separation. It has been generally agreed that the cause of this rift was partly Walpole's arrogant assumption that Gray would be prepared to subordinate his views on sight-seeing and other activities, and partly to Gray's touchiness in regard to his dependent relationship. A complaint made by Gray in a letter to a mutual, but perfidious friend may have been the immediate cause of the breach.

A few days before the quarrel broke out, but when it was imminent, Gray wrote to another of his Eton friends, Richard West. In this letter it is easy to remark, in reading between the lines, how considerably Gray's susceptible nature had been shaken, and how much he felt the need for steadfastness and solace from a school-friend of more equal social standing than Walpole, so as to appease and tranquillize him in his rough disillusionment. Gray was not in the least suited to be a mere hanger-on to someone in a more affluent and exalted situation than himself. He was a young man with obvious charm, wit and intellect, entitling him to generous and whole-hearted appreciation on his own merits. He evokes our sympathy, therefore, in opening his mind to West with an almost excessive modesty, not in any way disguising his need for consolation. It is thus that he wrote from Florence: 'I know not what degree of satisfaction it will give you to be told that we shall set out from hence the 24th of this month, and not stop above a fort-night at any place in our way. This I feel, that you are the principal pleasure I have to hope for in my own country. Try at least to make me imagine myself not indifferent to you; for I must own I have the vanity of desiring to be esteemed by somebody, and would choose that somebody should be one whom I esteem as much as I do you. As I am recommending myself to your love, methinks I ought to send you my picture (for I am no more what I was, some circumstances excepted, which I hope I need not particularize to you); you must add then, to your former idea, two years of age, reasonable quantity of dullness, a great deal of silence, and something that rather resembles, than is, thinking; a confused notion of many strange and fine things that have swum before my eyes for some time [?poetry], and a want of love for general society, indeed an inability to it. On the good side you may add a sensibility for what others feel, and indulgence for their faults or weaknesses, a love of truth, and detestation of every thing else. Then you are to deduct a little impertinence, a little laughter, a great deal of pride, and some spirits. These are all the alterations I know of, you perhaps may find more. Think not that I have been obliged for this reformation of manners to reason or reflection, but to a severer schoolmistress, experience. One has little merit in learning her lessons, for one cannot well help it; but they are more useful than others, and imprint themselves in the very heart.'[2]

In this remarkably frank review, Gray displayed a considerable ability for self-analysis. It is surely rare for a young man to gauge his merits and demerits so discerningly. The shock of the breach with Walpole was especially severe for anyone of his delicate sensibility, and had the result of inducing him to turn for satisfaction to less brilliant friendships. It was more than three years before Walpole suggested a reconciliation, and more than four years before Gray called on him, and relations were restored, or at least renewed. Gray describes this meeting, when writing to a friend, in delightful, elegant, eighteenth-century language: 'I went the following evening to see *the party* (as Mrs. Foible says). Was something abash'd at his confidence: he came to meet me, kiss'd me on both sides with all the ease of one, who receives an acquaintance just come out of the country, squatted me into a fauteuil, begun to talk of the Town & this & that & t'other, & continued with little interruption for three hours, when I took my leave very indifferently pleased, but treated with wondrous good breeding.'[3] The dissatisfaction that Gray felt as a result of this meeting was due to Walpole's failure to be frank about their quarrel and the causes of it. He had mentioned to West that he had 'a great deal of pride'. This was clearly evidenced by his slow response to Walpole's advances, and in his sceptical attitude after the reconciliation.

Relations between them were never the same as when they set out on the Grand Tour. Even if they had tried, they could not have recovered the earlier candour and open-heartedness characteristic of unsuspicious and confiding youth. They hardly tried; and the friendship was re-established on terms of respect and liking; and, to some extent, on terms of mutual advantage. Walpole gained genuine pleasure from Gray's comprehensive erudition and entertaining whimsicality. As an amateur author he learnt, too, to value Gray's help in historical research. Contrariwise, Gray, though by no means a snob, enjoyed an occasional entrée into the world of power and prestige. He derived a good deal of pleasure from observing Walpole's experiments in Gothic art, and in discussing with him his association with his accomplished or fashionable friends. Above all, perhaps, he liked to be 'in the know' about public affairs, for he became, as we shall notice, an inveterate trader in the gossip of high politics.

There was, in the renewed friendship, a slight undercurrent of constraint; and we can sometimes discern an inclination to correctitude, if not formality, in Gray's letters to Walpole, even when they had passed middle age. At times, they each spoke to their friends about the other in terms that were disdainful or derogatory. As Walpole's character developed, he showed himself to be ill-qualified for confidential friendship with Gray, who, with all his drollery, needed a basis of sincerity. Although Walpole, in his maturity, gained some reputation for good nature, it was suspect in some quarters as being only on the surface. Nevertheless, the two saw a good deal of each other, and corresponded freely.

Two or three remarks in Gray's letters indicate that, in retrospect, he sincerely regretted that his quarrel with Walpole was not adjusted by a quick and frank explanation of the points of view of both parties. He actually told Walpole, within two years of the renewal of their friendship, in relation to another instance, that 'it is a tenet with me . . . that if ever two people, who love one another, come to breaking, it is for a want of a timely éclaircissement, a full and precise one, without witnesses or mediators, and without any one disagreeable circumstance for the mind to brood upon in silence'[4]. The problem involved in such a situation lingered in his mind throughout his life. Many years later he gave a friend advice which was obviously based in part on his own early experience. He observed 'how many idle suspicions a sensible mind, naturally disposed to melancholy, & depress'd by misfortune, is capable of entertaining, especially if it meets with but a shadow of neglect or contempt from the very (perhaps the only) person, in whose kindness it had taken refuge'.[5]

Gray learnt much and painfully from his breach with

Walpole. He not only learnt how to avoid a repetition of it, but he evidently came to the conclusion that it would be wise in future for his friendships to be set in a lower key. He wanted something less elegant, less superficial; something more steady and serviceable. It is true that he had not a large range of choice; but the cool manner in which he regarded a possible rapprochement with Walpole proves that he had no particular anxiety to re-establish himself in high society.

Soon after his return to England, after the Grand Tour, he resumed residence at Cambridge, but now in the role of a devotee of learning; and, as may be gathered from his published correspondence, his three chief friendships originating in the University were with Thomas Wharton, James Brown, and William Mason. Happily for his success in the kind of career to which he was best suited, he renewed an old friendship, that with Wharton, and found some advantageous new ones to fill the painful void left by his quarrel with Walpole. When he first returned from the Continent, he hoped for a deepening of his congenial friendship with West, his old Eton companion; but he suffered a grievous blow by West's death at a youthful age.

To Wharton, above all, he owed a debt for the re-establishment of his composure and self-esteem; and Wharton is undoubtedly entitled to be described as Gray's best friend. They had been companions as undergraduates; and their friendship became very active from the time that Gray returned to Cambridge after his tour abroad. Wharton (who, in his prime, was a distinguished physician), after ceasing to reside in Cambridge as a Fellow of Pembroke, lived in London, and later in County Durham, where Gray visited him. He was a sterling character, utterly reliable, with an obvious desire to satisfy the highest ideals of friendship. Numerous incidents recorded in Gray's letters prove how successful Wharton was in these aspirations. In Gray's younger days, at a period when his finances were sometimes strained, he asked Wharton for a loan of £40, but only if convenient, for he could himself raise the money by a visit to London. Wharton immediately produced the money; but Gray was horrified to discover that it was only possible for Wharton to do so by borrowing the money himself.[6] On another occasion, when Gray was in financial difficulties owing to some house property in London being burnt down, other friends of his contented themselves by commiserating with him, and tendering superfluous advice, while Wharton spontaneously offered a loan of money.[7] He would put himself to any amount of personal trouble on behalf of his friend. When Gray was getting on in years, he had to undergo an operation for piles. Wharton well knew how agitated Gray would be; and he offered to come from County Durham to Cambridge to give his moral support.[8] He was constantly advising Gray in regard to all sorts of personal questions, medical and otherwise; and Gray turned to him in a variety of problems, many of which he might quite well have disposed of himself, for they only needed a little common sense for their solution.

For his part, Gray did all in his power to reciprocate. He constantly made thoughtful suggestions to Wharton, in the period when the latter was residing away from Cambridge, in regard to books for general reading. He was, at one period, assiduous in sending Wharton reports based on his observations of natural history phenomena, a subject of intense interest to them both. He advised about family troubles, and other personal matters; and he took infinite pains regarding the choice of furniture and decorations for Wharton's new home in the North. But, doubtless, Gray's part in the friendship was made most effective by the distinctive way in which his glowing sincerity warmed the heart without leaving any sense of embarrassment.

This happy association lasted from student days to Gray's death with scarcely a flutter on the serene surface of its gently flowing progress. On one occasion, Wharton suspected that he might have been supplanted in Gray's affections by a lady; but Gray assured him that his heart was no less his friend's than it had long been.[9] A few years later, Wharton somehow got it into his head that all was not well between them; and Gray wrote: 'Pray don't suspect me of any such *suspicions*, as you mention. I would hardly believe you were tired of me, tho' you told me so yourself, sensible as I am nevertheless that you might have reason enough to be so. To prove what I say I have thoughts of coming to you for three days in April. . . .'[10]

Gray's letters have been criticized by Lord David Cecil, who observed:[11] 'That they were reserved was to be expected; but they were also unspontaneous and a little impersonal.' It is hoped that a number of extracts from his letters, quoted in this chapter, will be proof to the contrary. In particular, there are many passages in his letters to Wharton in which he opened his heart on intimate personal questions without formality or reserve. It is true that most of his letters to Wharton are on general subjects, news, gossip, natural history, and books; but a genuine and profound good-fellowship pervades them all.

When Wharton vacated his Fellowship at Pembroke Hall, on his marriage, he left Cambridge; and his place as frequent companion to Gray was taken by James Brown, Fellow, President (i.e. Vice-Master), and later Master of Pembroke. Brown was a quiet, retiring, conscientious man, small in stature, and with no obvious social gifts. Punctual and precise, he lacked ambition, and had no palpable force of character. Nevertheless, his natural dignity made it impossible for anyone to take a liberty with him; and, in spite of his slight physique, he was resolute in formidable situations. The most notable features about him were his loyalty to his College, his natural modesty, and his impressive integrity.

An entertaining episode illustrates Brown's modesty. When the headship of the College became vacant, Gray tried to use his influence in high places to ensure that Brown, the most obvious claimant to the office, should be appointed; and he was tickled, and a little embarrassed, to find that Brown had, at the same time, been plotting his (Gray's) own elevation to the headship. Brown had no self-importance, and would undertake numerous menial tasks for Gray without ever thinking them beneath him. He gladly made detailed arrangements about parcels, letters, bills, and the cleaning of rooms. If unobtrusive altruism is an essential quality in friendship, Brown deserves a high place as an exponent of the art. Some endearing mannerisms of his can be inferred from sundry casual references in Gray's letters, such as his looking benignly over his spectacles, and his ending his negative pronouncements with 'at all, at all'. Particulars of this kind help us to gain a visual impression of this simple-minded, kindly don, on whom Gray largely relied for companionship and sympathy for the greater part of his adult life. So closely were the two of them associated in their daily affairs, their relationship was as easy and unconstrained as that of brothers. Various remarks in Gray's letters indicate that Brown was constantly dropping in at Gray's rooms. It is significant that Gray, with his

lively wit and brilliant intellect, should choose this trusty, un-
assuming little scholar for his friend at the time when he did.

The friendship with Mason (for some time Fellow of Pembroke) was of a different order. Mason was eight years younger
than Gray, who was inclined to treat him rather as a pupil
than a complete equal. Although Mason was warm-hearted
and good-humoured, with some slight ability as a poet, and a
general veneer of culture, he was a weak character, with an
over-insistent ambition, and several minor traits which tended
to make him a subject of ridicule. It was perhaps inevitable that
Gray should be constantly teasing him, and treating him in a
way which made a properly balanced friendship impossible.
Although Mason was incapable of the inspiriting companionship that Gray so often needed, it is obvious that Gray, who
enjoyed calling him by the nickname of 'Skroddles', had a
strong affection for him. There must have been some un-
apparent but excellent grounds for respecting him, for Gray
named him as his literary executor.

When writing to Wharton soon after the establishment of his
friendship with Mason, Gray summed up Mason's character
in a remarkably penetrating manner considering the limited
opportunities he had then of forming a judgement. He observed
that Mason 'grows apace into my good graces, as I know him
more. He is very ingenious with great good-nature & simplicity.
A little vain, but in so harmless & so comical a way, that it
does not offend one at all; a little ambitious, but withall so
ignorant of the world & its ways, that this does not hurt him in
one's opinion. So sincere & so undisguised, that no mind with a
spark of generosity would ever think of hurting him, he lies so
open to injury. But so indolent, that if he cannot overcome this
habit, all his good qualities will signify nothing at all. After all
I like him so well, I could wish you knew him.'[12] We can learn
almost as much about Gray as about Mason in this passage, for
it discloses very plainly his combination of shrewdness with a
tolerance that cannot help warming into benevolence.

A number of Gray's letters to Mason are concerned with
criticisms of drafts of the latter's poetry. These letters illustrate
not only the degree of Gray's patient care expended for his
friend, but also his quick discernment, latent humour, and ready
tact. A few extracts will give an impression of these features,

D

but they cannot communicate any adequate idea of the extent and thoroughness of Gray's scrutiny and expert helpfulness. 'I am charmed', he once wrote, 'with the idea you give me of your 4th Ode. It is excellently introduced, & the specimen you send me, even sublime. I am *wrap'd* in it; but the last line of the stanza falls off; & must be changed, . . . but as to trickling *runlet*, I never heard of such a thing, unless it were a runlet of brandy.'[13] On another occasion he was more constructive in his suggestions: 'I do not see how one person can *lift* the voice of another person. . . . A dragon *pecks*, why a cock-sparrow might do as much! . . . A ghost does not fall. These are all my little objections, but I have a greater. Extreme conciseness of expression, yet pure, perspicuous, & musical, is one of the grand beauties of lyric poetry. This I have always aim'd at, & never could attain. The necessity of rhyming is one great obstacle to it. Another & perhaps a stronger is that way you have chosen of casting down your first ideas carelessly & at large, and then clipping them here and there and forming them at leisure. This method after all possible pains will leave behind it in some places a *laxity*, a diffuseness. The frame of a thought (otherwise well invented, well-turned, & well-placed) is often weaken'd by it. Do I talk nonsense? or do you understand me?'[14]

These sensible comments on the craftsmanship of poetry, made by such a poet, are worthy of quotation for their own sake, apart from the light they throw on Gray as the generous friend. There is a further extract of this kind which must be included, because its phrasing is particularly lively and even poetical. In concluding his criticisms on an elegy of Mason's, Gray remarked: 'All I can say is, that your elegy must not end with the worst line in it. It is flat, it is prose, whereas that above all ought to sparkle, or at least to shine. If the sentiment must stand, twirl it a little into an apophthegm, stick a flower in it, gild it with a costly expression, let it strike the fancy, the ear, or the heart, & I am satisfied.'[15]

Although Mason attained some moderate reputation as a poet, literary critics soon decided that even that slight distinction was hardly deserved. Probably he would never have qualified for the title of poet at all without Gray's help. Austin Dobson, when making a judicious assessment of Mason's work, remarked: 'What is best in him he owes to Gray and Gray's criticism.'

There is ample evidence of Gray's kindness to friends apart from his generous advice to them in regard to their literary compositions. He seems to have enjoyed employing himself as adviser in a general way, and to have prided himself on being something of a man of the world, especially in his relations with Wharton and Mason, and, later, with younger friends, like Norton Nicholls. He would undertake the giving of advice on such subjects as the adoption of a profession, attitudes to superiors, and even matrimonial complications, in which his qualifications were not conspicuous. Sometimes his kindness was extremely practical, and involved much more patience and inconvenience than might be expected from a man of his susceptible and fastidious disposition. On four or five occasions we learn, in his letters, of his being assiduous in nursing his relations and friends when they were ill; notably his close friend, Brown, whom he tended for three weeks after an operation on his leg.[16] Minor instances of his kindness emerge casually from his correspondence.

It is only too seldom that Gray is depicted as a tender-hearted, affectionate man; but he evidently was so. When he was within five years of his end, he wrote to his friend, Norton Nicholls, about the latter's mother who was ill, begged him to take all possible care of her, and added: '. . . I had discover'd a thing very little known, wch is, that in ones whole life one never can have any more than a single Mother. You may think this obvious, & (what you call) a trite observation. You are a green gossling! I was at the same age (very near) as wise as you, & yet I never discover'd this (with full evidence & conviction, I mean) till it was too late. It is 13 years ago, & seems but yesterday, & every day I live it sinks deeper into my heart.'[17]

In his frequently attributed role of recluse, Gray is doubtless often pictured as having no more than a small number of acquaintances who were supposedly treated in a formal and pedantic manner. In fact, he must have had, in middle age, at least a dozen friends in the University with whom he was on intimate and familiar terms, some of whom he addressed by their Christian names or nick-names; and this at a period when Christian names were less freely used than today. There were Jemmy Bickham, Dick Forester, Tom Lyon, and 'Delly' Delaval, all Fellows of Pembroke; Billy Robinson, Fellow of

St. John's, Tom Neville, Fellow of Jesus, as well as other Cambridge residents, and others educated at Cambridge who returned to the University on occasional visits. His genial relationships with such as these imply something quite distinct from aloofness or inability to mix with his fellow-men.

Evidently Gray entered wholeheartedly into the convivial activities enjoyed by the Fellows of Pembroke. He wrote to Mason about the delightful evenings they were spending. One of the Fellows, Delaval (above-mentioned) played on the musical glasses 'that sing like nightingales, & we have concerts every other night'. He added that there was 'a vast deal of good company'.[18] On another occasion, he begged Mason to come and visit Pembroke, 'for our copuses [spiced ale] and Welch rabbets are impatient for you'.[19] One or two references to Cambridge coffee-houses suggest that Gray was a habitué.

But it was in London that his festive habits were given fullest rein. Some of his letters to Wharton bear witness to his gaieties. 'My evenings have been chiefly spent at Ranelagh & Vauxhall. . . .'[20] 'I have been in town (I suppose you know) flaunting about at publick places of all kinds with my two Italianized friends.'[21] 'I have been this month in town . . . diverting myself among my gay acquaintances; & return to my cell [at Cambridge] with so much the more pleasure.'[22] An account of an incident, given by him to Brown, enables us to gain a realistic impression of his ability to be unconstrainedly frivolous, even when he had passed the age of fifty. 'I have seen his lordship of Cloyne often [i.e. the bishop]. He is very jolly, and we devoured four raspberry-puffs together in Cranbourn-Alley standing at a pastry-cook's shop in the street; but he is gone, and Heaven knows when we shall eat any more.'[23] Visits in the provinces also provided opportunities for light-hearted recreation. Gray was in the habit of visiting the local Assembly Rooms; this he did at Durham, when on a visit to Wharton; and, on the same visit, he went twice to the Races.[24]

He was undoubtedly a lively companion in the right company. When staying in Kent with Billy Robinson, a party of them visited Ramsgate. The stone pier had just been built; and a cross-grained member of the party enquired: 'For what did they make this pier?' Gray immediately replied: 'For me to walk on'; and proceeded, with long strides, to claim possession

of it. He could be delightfully facetious when in the mood;
and that mood was not infrequent. Even Walpole admitted
that 'Humour was his natural and original turn'. Gray sometimes, when describing his visits to various parts of England,
adopted a neat means of making a turn of humour effective.
For instance: 'I have one of the most beautiful vales here in
England to walk in, with prospects that change every ten steps,
& open something new wherever I turn me, all rude & romantic,
in short the sweetest spot to break your neck or drown yourself
in that ever was beheld.'[25] Again: 'I have been for two days at
Hartlepool to tast the water, & do assure you, nothing can be salter,
& bitterer, & nastier, & better for you. . . . I am delighted with
the place: there are the finest walks & rocks & caverns, & dried
fishes, & all manner of small inconveniences a man can wish.'[26]

His sprightly humour was well sustained into his fifties. He
wrote at this stage to Mason: 'I am afraid something is the
matter with you, that I hear nothing from you, since I pass'd
two days with you *in your absence* [i.e. at his house when he was
away]. I am not in Ireland, as you perhaps might imagine by
this natural sentence: but shall be glad to hear from you, as if
I were.'[27] Finally, he could laugh at himself, a critical test of
the authentic humorist, for he told Mason: 'I keep an owl in
the garden as like me, as it can stare; only I don't eat raw meat,
nor bite people by the fingers.'[28]

He was not merely diverting by reason of his whimsicality.
He was among the most active of the purveyors of sensational
news. When in Cambridge, he made it his business to provide
Wharton and Mason, in the provinces, with particulars of
passing events in University politics, with the addition of some
pungent comments. But he chiefly prided himself on his inside
information about doings in high quarters in London. He made
little attempt to exclude the element of scandal from these
reports. Some of his picturesque descriptions of famous scenes
of national history are highly entertaining, such as the trial of
the Scottish Lords in 1746, the death of George II, and the
coronation of George III.[29]

It was his great ambition to send inside information from
London, when he was staying there, to Brown at Cambridge
for the delectation of the Fellows of Pembroke. Cambridge
dons (like Oxford dons) used then to indulge in an appetite for

scandal. Gray wrote to Brown: 'I hope to send you the first intelligence of the Church preferments tho' such is your eagerness there for this sort of news, that perhaps mine may be stale before it can reach you.'[30] His anxiety to stand well with his Cambridge colleagues, as being 'in the know', is illustrated by a letter of his to Walpole: 'Do oblige me with a change in the Ministry: I mean something one may tell, as if it were near at hand; or if there is no truth to be had, then a good likely falsehood for the same purpose.'[31] In default of public matters, he would sometimes insert a sprightly story, the point of which struck closer home.

As may easily be assumed, the diverting quality of his letters was often enhanced by the introduction of an ironical or sardonic strain. He could thus put a sharp edge on his critical remarks. When discussing Boswell's recently published *Account of Corsica*, he wrote: 'The pamphlet proves what I have always maintained that any fool may write a most valuable book by chance, if he will only tell us what he heard and saw with veracity. Of Mr. Boswell's truth I have not the least suspicion, because I am sure he could invent nothing of this kind.'[32] Perhaps Gray's caustic manner was most effective when his personal feelings were aroused. Like everyone else, he had his prejudices; and one of them was against footnotes. When preparing his *Odes* for publication, he was pressed to explain some allusions in them which might not be plain to all his readers. He remarked: 'I would not have put another note to save the souls of all the *owls* in London. It is extremely well, as it is. Nobody understands me, & I am perfectly satisfied.'[33] A number of years afterwards, when he was bringing out a second edition, and the question recurred, he yielded so far as to add 'certain little notes'; and he explained, in a letter to a friend, that this was 'partly from justice (to acknowledge the debt, where I had borrowed any thing), partly from ill-temper, just to tell the gentle reader, that Edward I was not Oliver Cromwell, nor queen Elizabeth the witch of Endor'.[34]

There are singularly few supercilious remarks about the defects of Gray's friends to be found in his letters; and that is highly meritorious at a time when dons spent much of their leisure in pulling each other's reputations to pieces. An instance of his tolerant good-nature is to be noticed in his mention of a wearisome friend of Mason's who was lavish in imparting to his companions the details of his numerous ailments. 'I shall be very ready', Gray remarked, 'to take as much of Mr. D:ᵖˢ [Delap's] dullness as he chuses to part with, at any price he pleases, even with his want of sleep & weak bowels into the bargain.'³⁵

*   *   *

Up to this point we have used Gray's letters to depict him as possessing the qualities of the normal man, his reliance on friendship, his clubbability, tolerance, kindliness, and his capacity to amuse, both himself and his friends. This picture has been essayed so as to modify some prevailing views of Gray, the man. But we have not yet taken account of his peculiarities; and there is no disguising their existence or the fact that his character cannot be justly estimated without considering them, though none of them is so flagrant or so fundamental as to shake our respect and affection for him.

His excessive shyness in uncongenial society is well known. It is questionable whether this was not to some extent due to what he once described (see below) as 'the sulkiness of my disposition'. If he did not like his company, he was apt to withdraw into himself, and to exclude himself from his surroundings. A household of high-spirited and excitable women (or men and women) was more than he could bear, especially when, as frequently happened, he felt a little out of health. In circumstances such as these, he could hardly be thought to be peculiar if his sense of discomfort became apparent. He described his feelings in this kind of situation with pathetic realism: 'I have been obliged to go every day almost to Stoke-house, where the Garricks have been all the last week. They are now gone, & I am not sorry for it, for I grow so old [he was only forty-two at the time] that, I own, people in high spirits and gayety overpower me, & entirely take away mine. I can yet be diverted with their sallies, but if they appear to take notice of my dullness, it sinks me to nothing.'³⁶ (This passage, like several others quoted in this chapter, illustrates convincingly how intimate and open-hearted Gray's letters can be. The frankness of this self-analysis, in which he lays bare his inner thoughts and feelings, is indeed remarkable according to any standards.)

On another occasion, a few years later, his experiences were much the same. 'For me, I am come to my resting place

[Cambridge], and find it very necessary after living for a month in a house with three women that laughed from morning to night, and would allow nothing to the sulkiness of my disposition. Company and cards at home, parties by land and water abroad, and (what they call) *doing something*, that is, racketting about from morning to night, are occupations, I find, that wear out my spirits, especially in a situation where one might sit still, and be alone with pleasure. . . .'[37] Our sympathy must surely go out to the contemplative scholar who rashly involved himself in such a *ménage*. On the other hand, if he had been 'alone with pleasure', it is to be feared that dire depression would have set in, as it often did when he lacked company. Such, alas, are the dilemmas of the sensitive mind.

Contact with eminent and elevated personages disconcerted Gray, as it does the majority of people; but it disconcerted him more acutely. The Chancellor of the University, the Duke of Newcastle, was a favourite subject of his scorn, being described by him opprobriously as 'that old fizzling Duke' or 'that owl Fobus'. Nevertheless, when he was to be presented to the Chancellor, he was in a fever of apprehension. After the event, he wrote a charming avowal to Wharton: 'I did not run away from his Grace, but follow'd your advice, had a very affectionate squeeze by the hand, & a fine compliment in a corner. Many people here have been curious to know what it was; but I have kept my own secret, for indeed I do not know myself: only remember it [the Duke's hand] felt warm, & sweated a little.'[38]

Some of Gray's peculiarities are doubtless attributable to his liability to depression, to which he made numerous references in his letters, from his youth to his last years. It is to his credit that he generally contrived to discuss the matter in a light vein. As early as his undergraduate days, he discoursed on the subject to his friend, West: 'Low spirits are my true and faithful companions; they get up with me, go to bed with me, make journeys and returns as I do; nay, and pay visits, and will even affect to be jocose, and force a feeble laugh with me; but most commonly we sit alone together, and are the prettiest insipid company in the world. However, when you come, I believe they must undergo the fate of all humble companions, and be discarded.'[39]

In middle life, he told Brown: 'My health I can not complain of, but as to my spirits they are always many degrees below

changeable, & I seem to myself to inspire every thing around me
with ennuy & dejection; but some time or other all these things
must come to a conclusion, till which day I shall remain very
sincerely. . . .'[40] It is likely that the prevalence of a depressed
state of mind among eighteenth-century notables was often
caused by a combination of an excessive or ill-advised diet with
insufficient bodily activity; but Gray's liability to this affliction
is more probably due to periods of loneliness or lack of congenial
amusement, especially during the Cambridge vacations. While
his mother and his aunts were alive, he spent much of his
vacations with them at Stoke Poges, where he often felt the lack
of male companionship.

In later life he hit upon a means of warding off his bugbear
without involving himself in frivolities of an exhausting kind.
His summer expeditions to various parts of the kingdom raised
his spirits miraculously. He found that 'motion & change of
the scene is absolutely necessary to me'.[41] 'I am convinced I
owe my late & present ease to my little expeditions I always
make in the summer.'[42] He went so far as to assert to Wharton:
'travel I must, or cease to exist'.[43] It is sad to notice that his
assumption that the state of his finances would not permit him
to indulge in travel had deterred him from undertaking
peregrinations in middle life. Even within about five years of his
death, he supposed that he could not afford quite modest
expeditions. He must either have underestimated the extent
of his fortune, or else have been excessively circumspect.

Gray's acceptance of the principle of the need for relaxation
and change emphasizes the advisability for its general adoption,
for he was a scholar of such unusual versatility that it might be
thought that he could have maintained a cheerful outlook from
the fascination of his learned pursuits alone. Without them, he
would doubtless have fallen by the way quite early in life. The
subjects he studied included literature, English and foreign
(especially French literature); history, both classical and
medieval; art, music, architecture, heraldry, antiquities, and
natural history. He was an omnivorous reader from his childhood. As a young man, he told West: 'I learn Italian like any
dragon and in two months am got through the 16th book of
Tasso, whom I hold in great admiration.'[44] About the time of
his return to Cambridge, after the Grand Tour, he again wrote

to West giving particulars of his achievements in reading: 'My life is like Harry the fourth's supper of hens. "Poulets à là broche, poulets en ragôut, poulets en hâchis, poulets en fricasées." Reading here, reading there, nothing but books with different sauces.'[45] Later on, he told Wharton, with genuine modesty, no doubt: 'My works are not so considerable as you imagine. I have read Pausanias and Athenaeus all thro', & Aeschylus again. I am now in Pindar & Lysias: for I take verse and prose together, like bread & cheese.'[46]

Music, including occasional performance on the harpsichord, was his diversion almost all his life. But, in his later years, natural history occupied much of his attention, and was a sure solace. He collected specimens, recorded observations (some of which were transmitted to Wharton), he executed the most delightful and delicate drawings of birds, insects, and shells, to illustrate his copy of Linnaeus's *Systema Naturae*; and he carried out intricate experiments with insects. It might well be thought that this wide range of activities, some of which could fairly be described as recreational, might soothe his solitary hours, and serve to fend off the clouds of depression that frequently threatened to descend on him.

His standard of scholarship and literary accomplishment was high, so high that, as sometimes happens in such cases, his publications were remarkably few. He had all the fastidiousness and even finicalness of the perfectionist scholar. When his poems were being printed at Walpole's private printing press, he was much disturbed at the risk of misprints. He even charged Walpole with being incapable of correcting proofs. On another occasion, he remarked caustically to Walpole: 'Tho' I admire rapidity in writing, & perseverance in finishing, being two talents I want; yet I do not admire rapidity in *printing*, because this is a thing that I or any body can do.'[47]

He always required his rooms in College to be kept in scrupulous order, and immaculately clean. On the occasion of his return to Cambridge after an absence, everything had to be carefully dusted, and the bedclothes aired. He made it a principle to try and provide against all conceivable risks. When, for instance, some crates of furniture and household effects were to arrive at his rooms in Cambridge in his absence, he wrote to Brown to ask for his assistance in the matter: 'Those

marked with a cross [in an accompanying list] are easier to
break [he marked 24 out of 28, including articles as unfragile as
a fire-grate and fire-irons, and pillows and cushions], & therefore pray observe if they appear to have received any damage in
coming . . . they may all stand pack'd up as they are, till I
come . . . : in the mean time I beg no fire may be made, nor
any body go flaunting in with a candle, for so many mats &
so much packing will make it very dangerous.'[48]
His terror of conflagrations was intense, and not without
reason, for he lost a house by fire in London; and he was nearly
involved in an extensive fire at Pembroke Hall. Though he
made light of this affair in a letter, he must have been considerably startled by being roused at night and being told the
College was ablaze. At the time when, at an earlier period, he
lived in Peterhouse at Cambridge, he had reason to apprehend
that some unruly undergraduates in rooms below his might
inadvertently set the building on fire; and he therefore asked
the ever-helpful Wharton to procure him a rope-ladder.[49]
So cloistered a life as Gray's did not qualify him to face dangerous situations, or even situations that seemed to him to involve
danger. He was certainly not of an adventurous or even enterprising disposition; and he evidently had a particular aversion
to crossing large rivers. But he was by no means chicken-
hearted. On one of his summer expeditions in and around the
Lake District, when he was over fifty, he pressed on with his
travels through pouring rain, and at the end of them reported
that he was charmed with his journey.[50] Two years later, when
at Keswick, he fell down on his back 'across a dirty lane . . .
but broke only my knuckles: stay'd nevertheless, & saw the
sun set in all its glory'.[51]
Gray's extreme apprehensiveness about the reception of his
poetry is, indeed, regrettable, for it is one of the main causes of
his limited output. A quite tentative criticism of the draft of
his youthful play, Agrippina, caused him to abandon it. A little
later, Mason, while admiring his draft of an Ode on the Progress
of Poetry, made an ill-considered remark about the risk of not
hitting the public taste. Gray, without a word, abandoned the
project; and, when Mason remonstrated with him later on,
replied glumly: 'You have thrown cold water on it.'
The publication of his Odes in 1757 aroused in him the most

hopeful expectations. He obviously regarded them as his finest work; and his pride even allowed him to enquire from various friends what comments were being made in their circles of acquaintance. He questioned Walpole about the reception of the *Odes* in London. 'I am going to add to the trouble I have given you by desiring you would tell me, what you hear any body say (I mean, if any body says anything).'[52] To another friend he applied for information 'what the North says either in good or bad'. And he added disconsolately: 'As to the South, it is too busy & too fastidious to trouble its head about any thing that has no wit in it.'[53] But, above all, he wanted to know what was being said in Cambridge; so he wrote to Brown: 'You will not wonder therefore at my curiosity, if I enquire of you, what you hear said? For tho' in the rest of the world I do not expect to hear, that any body says much, or thinks about the matter, yet among *mes confreres*, the learned, I know there is always leisure to find fault, if not to commend.'[54]

By the spring of 1758 it became clear to Gray that the reception of the *Odes* was, in spite of a number of flattering remarks, disappointing. His high hopes had failed; his spirits were dashed; and depression seized upon him with particular severity. He hastily came to the forlorn conclusion that he would never practise as a poet again. Such was the effect of a questionable set-back on a man whose confidence in himself was too easily shaken. As an expression of his disgust at the futility of trying to please the public in that métier, he turned to humdrum, plodding occupations. One of these was an archaeo-logical handbook or guide-book. He wrote to Wharton: 'Would you know, what I am doing? I doubt, you have been told already, & hold my employment cheap enough: but every one must judge of his own *capabilities*, & *cut* his amusements accord-ing to his disposition.'[55] A few days later he explained further to Wharton. 'It is indeed for want of spirits, as you suspect, that my studies lie among the cathedrals, the tombs, and the ruins. . . . At present I find myself able to write a catalogue, or to read the peerage book, or Miller's Gardening Diction-ary, and am thankful that there are such employments and such authors in the world. Some people, who hold me cheap for this, are doing perhaps what is not half so well worth while. As to posterity, I may ask (with some body whom I have forgot) what has it ever done to oblige me?'[56]

Various explanations have been given for Gray's small output in poetry, such as Matthew Arnold's suggestion of his incompatibility with the 'proseness' of the age in which he lived. But surely the predominant reasons are, first, his fastidiousness in publishing work which he feared might not gain a favourable reception; and, secondly, his lack of ideas, or of what is often called inspiration. A number of the most striking images in his masterpieces can hardly be called original. Other poets, such as Cowper, have lacked ideas; but Cowper was lucky in having friends to suggest them. There was no one among Gray's friends who was able to help him in this respect; and perhaps he was incapable of being so helped. His muse was always apt to be shy; and many remarks in his letters attest this. After telling Mason about one of his attacks of depression, he remarked: 'You will not expect therefore I should give you any account of my *verve*, wch is at best (you know) of so delicate a constitution, & has such weak nerves, as not to stir out of its chamber above three days in a year.'[57] He tried to analyse his state of mind to Wharton: 'I by no means pretend to inspiration, but yet I affirm, that the faculty in question is by no means voluntary. It is the result (I suppose) of a certain disposition of mind, wch does not depend on oneself, & wch I have not felt this long time. You that are a witness how seldom this spirit has moved me in my life, may easily give credit to what I say.'[58] A good deal later, he made a frank disclosure of his inmost feelings on this subject, when writing to Walpole, in whom he did not usually repose his confidences. 'I will be candid (for you seem to be so with me), and avow to you, that till fourscore-and-ten, whenever the humour takes me, I will write, because I like it; and because I like myself better when I do so. If I do not write much, it is because I cannot.'[59]

Dr. Johnson, in his superior way, described Gray's inability to write but at certain times, or at happy moments, as 'a fantastic foppery'. It was certainly not that, but rather, as we have suggested, a mixture of inhibitions, attributable in part to the dread of the humiliation that might follow from adverse criticism, and in part to a disposition that was only poetical in a limited degree. It was, indeed, impossible for Dr. Johnson, with his contempt for the more delicate sensibilities, to understand the intensity of feeling of so highly strung a person as Gray. This feature in his make-up is excellently disclosed in a letter of his to Walpole, protesting against a proposal to include an engraving of his portrait in his collected poems shortly to be published. He wrote: 'Sure you are not out of your wits! This I know, if you suffer my head [i.e. portrait] to be printed, you infallibly will put me out of mine. I conjure you immediately to put a stop to any such design. . . . I do assure you, if I had received such a book with such a frontispiece without any warning, I believe, it would have given me a palsy. . . .'[60]

Circumstances seldom induced him to break out into such extravagant expressions as these, for his life was singularly free from agitating incidents. But his excitability must have often been active, though cloaked. It was exhibited in a very interesting fashion towards the end of his life. His friend, Norton Nicholls, introduced to him a young Swiss, named Bonstetten, who was in England studying social life and similar subjects. Bonstetten's charm and engaging manner completely captivated Gray, who enjoyed his company with an intensity of pleasure that is astonishing. After a few weeks' acquaintance, Gray spoke as if this companionship meant more to him than any other he had experienced. And, when Bonstetten left England to return to his native land, Gray wrote to him in terms not very different from those of a love-letter. This remarkable transformation from behaviour that had always erred rather on the side of sedateness and self-restraint opens up the possibility of latent features in Gray's constitution. We have emphasized that Gray was extremely sensitive in certain respects. Was the Bonstetten episode a natural extension and an outstanding example of this prominent trait in his character, or was some new factor becoming operative? Did he feel so old that he thought that it did not matter if he failed to observe his usual standards of restraint? Or was it some strange yearning to be compensated for the void in his experience, due to the lack of family life?

Gray's character has been described as inscrutable; but, in a broad view, it is probably more correct to regard it as complex, involving a number of intriguing inconsistencies. We can certainly derive much pleasure from studying such questions; and, in this task, his letters are indispensable.

———— 4 ————

WILLIAM COWPER (1731–1800)
Gentle, Troubled Spirit

IN the preceding chapter Gray's ability for self-analysis
proved to be a valuable aid to the assessment of his character.
William Cowper will be found to be even more co-operative in
this respect. He discloses himself to us in his letters in liberal
measure, with ingenuous simplicity, and without a shade of
simulation. This remark is not in the least intended to imply
that Gray's letters are either pretentious or artificial. No one
could be more scrupulous and straightforward, in spite of his
proneness to drollery and clever turns of phrase. But there is
something conspicuously artless in Cowper's self-analysis. He
certainly did not imagine that he was placing on record the

materials for a portrait of himself. And it is with himself, as we shall see, that his letters chiefly deal. Other poet-letter-writers of distinction have tended in this direction, but Cowper outstrips them all. His case is specially remarkable because he was much addicted to elaborate discussion of his personal problems, and yet was notably self-effacing in his disposition. It might be expected that his correspondents would be wearied at this one-sided intercourse. But this was not so, for no one could be more truly modest. He knew instinctively that his friends wanted to learn all that he could tell them about himself. Moreover, his letters were never wearisome because the undercurrent of affection flowing through them touched the hearts of the recipients.

There are, then, excellent reasons why Cowper, especially, should be allowed to disclose his character in his own words, in fact to speak for himself; not only because of the large extent to which his own experiences formed the subject-matter of his letters, but also because he wrote with such candour and lack of artifice. He can be implicitly trusted as his own interpreter, as will be obvious from the extracts from his letters which illustrate this chapter.

In any biography of Cowper, the central theme must be the tragic drama of his struggle to avoid mental breakdown. But, in a character-sketch based on his correspondence, particulars of his sufferings during his periods of insanity can be largely neglected. Especially is this so where the intention is, as here, to depict him against the background of his home and his surroundings, where the amiability of his disposition is evoked by his relations with the select number of friends suitable to his circumstances. Admiration of Cowper as the poet of the home is generally based on the charm of his interpretations of tranquil rural life. His readers have, therefore, a particular interest in learning what kind of life he led in his retired corner of the countryside. But, even if we do not read much of his poetry, his character has so much in it that is gentle and endearing that we may gladly seize the opportunity the letters give us of coming into close relationship with him.

Although we need not investigate the history of Cowper's periods of insanity, it must be remembered that he very often underwent intense strain even when his mind was free from acute disease, suffering as he did from distressing delusions, and agonizing apprehensions of renewed insanity. In middle life he explained to a correspondent that a feeling of despair was almost constantly in his mind, though he often contrived to appear cheerful, and maybe succeeded temporarily in being so.[1] Even in the periods between his mental breakdowns, he talked in the most deplorable way of God's 'departure' from him or 'abandonment' of him, or of God's casting him off for ever. He once said that he often spent his nights under a constant sense of God's contempt and abhorrence.[2] It is, indeed, sad to reflect that anyone, while supposedly sane, should undergo such pitiable experiences.

In his efforts to manage his life so as to avoid mental crises, Cowper enjoyed support and assistance from a succession of friends. No one can have had more completely devoted allies than he had. Their practical sympathy for him, and their self-sacrifice on his behalf, were unfailing. Why was this so? It was not primarily because of his social qualities, though these were delightful in congenial conditions. It was partly, no doubt, to be explained by their compassion for a man of such marked innocence and natural gaiety being subjected to experiences of so grievous a kind. But there is surely another and more convincing explanation—namely, the obviousness of his warm-hearted, tender affection for them. This affection, by its calm intensity, induced a strong reciprocal feeling. His gratitude for their kindness ensured them the deepest pleasure that life is said to hold, that of endowing others with happiness.

*   *   *

Cowper's mother died when he was only six years old. She typified for him all that was safe and consoling in a perilous world. He never forgot his reliance on her, and the intensity of his love for her. Ten years before he died, he wrote to a niece bearing witness to his undiminished tenderness more than fifty years after her death. 'Every creature', he said, 'that bears any affinity to my mother is dear to me, and you, the daughter of her brother, are but one remove distant from her: I love you, therefore, and love you much, both for her sake, and for your own. The world could not have furnished you with a present so acceptable to me, as the picture which you have so kindly

E

sent me. I received it the night before last, and viewed it with a trepidation of nerves and spirits somewhat akin to what I should have felt, had the dear original presented herself to my embraces. I kissed it, and hung it where it is the last object that I see at night, and, of course, the first on which I open my eyes in the morning. She died when I completed my sixth year; yet I remember her well, and am an ocular witness of the great fidelity of the copy. I remember, too, a multitude of the maternal tendernesses which I received from her, and which have endeared her memory to me beyond expression. . . .'[3]

Of all the tragic circumstances in Cowper's life, perhaps the most tragic happened soon after his mother's death, when he was sent to a small private school. The occurrence was appalling enough at the time; but it seems likely to have had most grievous consequences. He was subjected to horrible cruelty by a brutal fellow-schoolboy; and the terror thus struck into his very being probably provided the explanation of his mental instability in later life. The vividness of this maltreatment may well have been relegated to the back of his mind a few years later, when Cowper went to Westminster School, where he was happy in his work, his play, and his friendships. But the seed of weakness had been sown.

Both at Westminster, and afterwards as a law student, he benefited by a widening of his social and intellectual experiences. This student period included light-hearted associations between young people; and these in turn involved a failure to apply himself seriously to his legal studies. He wrote one or two articles for periodicals, but he made no real advance towards becoming an efficient lawyer. His interests tended to be literary rather than legal. Bonnell Thornton and George Colman (the elder) were among the literary friends that he acquired as a young barrister. Two other friends of importance in his life were companions in his law studies, Edward Thurlow (afterwards Lord Chancellor) and Joseph Hill. The latter showed him remarkable constancy and practical kindness for many years, especially in regard to the management of his slender finances.

But the greatest social happiness he experienced in his early life was that he enjoyed with his two young cousins, Theodora and Harriet, the daughters of his uncle whose home was in

Southampton Row. He spent much of his time there, fell in love with Theodora, and would have fallen in love with Harriet too, if it had been possible to be in love with two persons at the same time. This period as a young barrister, with little responsibility and a good deal of frivolity, was the pleasantest in his life. But circumstances put an end to it. He felt, or perhaps was made to feel, that he must embrace a remunerative career with proper resolution. He had very little private means; and it may be assumed that his desire to marry Theodora prompted him to try to gain a satisfactory livelihood. Round about thirty years of age, however, he exhibited a tendency to morbid depression. Doubtless there was a mental weakness in his constitution, only hidden slightly below the surface of his superficial normality. He was offered an unexacting legal appointment by an influential cousin; but the apprehension of his incapacity to satisfy the necessary standards broke him down. He tried to commit suicide, and then spent eighteen months in a private asylum.

When this attack of madness was allayed, he wisely determined to settle quietly in the country. Soon after taking rooms at Huntingdon, he was adopted into the family of an Evangelical minister in that town, Morley Unwin. After Mr. Unwin's death two years later, he lived with the widow, Mary Unwin, who cared for him devotedly for nearly thirty years, till, in fact, her health broke down completely as the result of the strain of her self-imposed task.

From the time of his first recovery, Cowper became a keen Evangelical, and practised religion with intense devoutness. Though it was not sufficiently realized at the time, the emotional excitement of these practices had a harmful effect on his delicately poised mental structure. The dangers so involved were increased when he and Mrs. Unwin moved to Olney, in Bucks, to be under the guidance of a minister of notable religious zeal, John Newton, a dynamic personality with inclinations towards fanaticism. Newton, who became a lifelong and faithful friend, induced Cowper to act as his assistant in parochial work, to compose hymns, to preach, and to bear witness to the effectiveness of his conversion. This well-meaning enthusiast was so ardent in his interpretation of Evangelicalism that he was incapable of understanding that Cowper's need

was for relaxation, and not agitation. Emotional excitement
was a feature in Newton's conception of the proper expression
of Evangelical principles; and he regarded spiritual conflict
as a normal experience for the converted. Cowper could hardly
have hit upon a more unpropitious friendship.

After some years of this inexpedient mode of life, the almost
inevitable result followed, and Cowper again lost his reason.
Newton, though wrong-headed in his role of guide, proved to be
beyond all praise as a helper in distress. He took the utterly
demented man and the faithful Mrs. Unwin into his house and
looked after him with extreme tenderness and forbearance for
more than a year.

Relaxation, combined with occupations that would not
disturb his equanimity, was the only regimen by which Cowper
could be saved from a succession of mental breakdowns.
Happily for him, Newton moved to London; and he was able,
with the advice and help of more discerning friends, to understand how best to aim at a placid and imperturbable way of
living.

Mary Unwin's son, William, became a close friend of
Cowper's from the time of his first connexion with the Unwin
family. William Unwin was then an undergraduate at Cambridge, where he had a distinguished academic career. He later
became a parson, with a living in Essex. Both these friends had
shy and affectionate natures; and their friendship was one of
delightful intimacy. Cowper's letters to John Newton, William
Unwin, and his old friend, Joseph Hill, written after his
recovery from his second attack of madness, include a series of
revealing descriptions of his home life and the means now
adopted to maintain mental composure.

A letter to John Newton gives a realistic impression of the
parlour at the house, 'Orchard Side', where Cowper and Mrs.
Unwin settled at Olney, and the cramped conditions in which
his daily avocations were pursued: 'You will wonder, no doubt,
when I tell you that I write upon a card-table; and will be still
more surprised when I add, that we breakfast, dine, sup upon a
card-table. In short, it serves all purposes, except the only one
for which it was originally designed. . . . The round table,
which we formerly had in use, was unequal to the pressure of
my superincumbent breast and elbows. When I wrote upon it,

it creaked and tilted, and by a variety of inconvenient tricks, disturbed the process. The fly-table was too light and too small; the square dining-table too heavy and too large, occupying, when its leaves were spread, almost the whole parlour; and the sideboard-table, having its station at too great a distance from the fire, and not being easily shifted out of its place and into it again, by reason of its size, was equally unfit for my purpose. The card-table, therefore, which had for sixteen years been banished as mere lumber; the card-table, which is covered with green baize, and is, therefore, preferable to any other that has a slippery surface; the card-table that stands firm and never totters,—is advanced to the honour of assisting me upon my scribbling occasions; and, because we choose to avoid the trouble of making frequent changes in the position of our household furniture, proves equally serviceable upon all others. It has cost us now and then the downfall of a glass: for when covered with a table-cloth, the fish-ponds [hollows for counters] are not easily discerned; and not being seen, are sometimes as little thought of. But, having numerous good qualities which abundantly compensate that single inconvenience, we spill upon it our coffee, our wine, and our ale, without murmuring, and resolve that it shall be our table still to the exclusion of all others.'⁴ Some readers who are not in sympathy with the letter-writer's temperament may characterize this information as trivial and humdrum. Possibly the pace of this letter, and one or two others of Cowper's, may seem unduly leisurely. But it must be remembered that he delighted in that kind of mood, and knew subconsciously at least, that his mental health depended on his maintaining it. Moreover, he, like one or two famous essay-writers, had a partiality for discoursing on inanimate objects; and he had such confidence in the attachment to him of his intimate friends that it would never have occurred to him that any description with a personal bearing could be wearisome to his correspondent.

It was not until some years after his recovery from his second attack of madness that he renewed correspondence with his cousin, Harriet, who had married and become Lady Hesketh. She had been previously, and remained until the end, a most sensible, reliable, and generous friend. She had been specially perspicacious in disapproving of the harassing nature of

Cowper's exploits into Evangelicalism. Naturally enough, he soon suggested that she should come and stay with Mrs. Unwin and himself at 'Orchard Side'. But he wondered whether his house, plain, tall, rectangular, brick-built, with its front immediately on a noisy street, would be dignified enough for his visitor. A redeeming feature was the small, secluded garden at the back. Cowper described to Lady Hesketh the modest entrance to the house and his sitting-room improvised from a greenhouse, in a letter discussing her projected visit: 'My dear, I will not let you come till the end of May, or beginning of June because before that time my greenhouse will not be ready to receive us, and it is the only pleasant room belonging to us. When the plants go out we go in. I line it with mats, and spread the floor with mats; and there you shall sit with a bed of mignonette at your side, and a hedge of honeysuckles, roses and jasmine; and I will make you a bouquet of myrtle every day. . . . And I will tell you what you shall find at your first entrance. *Imprimis*, as soon as you have entered the vestibule, if you will cast a look on either side of you, you shall see on the right hand a box of my making. It is the box in which have been lodged all my hares, and in which lodges Puss at present: but he, poor fellow, is worn out with age, and promises to die before you can see him. On the right side stands a cupboard, the work of the same author; it was once a dove-cage, but I transformed it. Opposite to you stands a table, which I also made: but a merciless servant having scrubbed it until it became paralytic, it serves no purpose now but of ornament; and all my clean shoes stand under it. On the left hand, at the further end of the superb vestibule, you will find the door of the parlour, into which I will conduct you, and where I will introduce you to Mrs. Unwin, unless we should meet her before, and where we will be as happy as the day is long.'[5]

Cowper had already described, in a letter to William Unwin, the charms of the room improvised from a greenhouse, situated well away from 'the incessant barking of dogs and the scream- ing of children' which discomposed the occupants of the parlour facing the street. There he could look with delight on his beloved myrtles and favourite flowers in his small garden. He could enjoy quiet comfort and the companionship of nature at the same time.[6] Some of Cowper's local acquaintances probably discovered how to find him in his greenhouse; and it ceased to be a safe refuge from intrusion. Accordingly, a few years later, after he had started writing poetry, he adapted a tiny hut at the end of the garden; and he gave a description of this retreat to his old friend, Joseph Hill: 'I write in a nook that I call my *Boudoir*. It is a summerhouse not much bigger than a sedan-chair, the door of which opens into the garden, that is now crowded with pinks, roses, and honeysuckles, and the window into my neighbour's orchard. . . . Having lined it with garden mats, and furnished it with a table and two chairs, here I write all that I write in the summer-time, whether to my friends, or to the public. It is secure from all noise, and a refuge from all intrusion; for intruders sometimes trouble me in winter evenings at Olney. But (thanks to my *Boudoir!*) I can now hide myself from them.'[7]

We can assume that even before Newton left Olney, Mrs. Unwin discouraged Cowper from undertaking the strain of further parochial activities, and counselled a tranquil habit of life. At first he did not attempt to do more than fill up his time by keeping pets, or by some manual occupation, such as carpentry; but he soon found that these pursuits gave his mind opportunity to concern itself with the melancholy subjects that were likely to bring about his downfall. He learnt that it was essential to deflect his attention from such vexatious influences. What he required was some interesting undertaking, sufficiently absorbing to engross him, yet not so absorbing or so exciting as to put an undue strain on the brittle texture of his mind. He wrote a number of letters describing to his friends his experiences in search of the right kind of relaxation; and these letters throw much light on the character of the writer.

The problem, then, was, on the one hand, to forget the morbid delusions that were ready to engulf and unman him. On the other hand, he needed a kind of relaxation that, by inducing a sense of tranquillity, would serve to diminish the unremitting strain to which he was exposed. Somehow or other, it was bruited abroad, in the parts of Olney near 'Orchard Side', that poor 'Sir Cowper', as he was often respectfully, and even affectionately, called, found consolation in keeping pets. He was given three hares, and offered many more. The variety of his other pets at this period is extraordinary. Of birds, there were a tame linnet, two robins, a magpie, a jay, a starling, two goldfinches (which occupied the greenhouse in summer), two canaries, and, outside in the garden, eight pair of tame pigeons. Of animals, besides the famous hares, there were five rabbits, two guinea-pigs, three dogs, occasional cats and kittens, and a squirrel which sometimes played with the hares. Looking after this menagerie must have been almost a full-time occupation; and it is permissible to wonder whether it entailed some labour also for the devoted Mrs. Unwin.

The keeping of all these pets also naturally involved the necessity of housing them; and it was in this way that Cowper started practising the trades of carpenter and handyman. He made hare-houses, a squirrel-house, rabbit-hutches, and bird-cages, as well as stools and other furniture for domestic use.

The intense pleasure, and, indeed, the solid intellectual satisfaction he gained in studying his pets is well disclosed in several of his letters about them, but in particular in the long letter he wrote for publication about his three pet hares.[8] This letter manifests lively powers of observation, a little reminiscent of the great Gilbert White, combined as it was with some scientific ability. His investigations led him to sensible deductions; and his detailed study of the factors relating to the dietary of the hare reflects an unexpected light on his personality. Among various qualities exemplified, patience, gentleness, and ingenuity are outstanding; there is, in fact, so much of Cowper in this long letter that a large portion of it must be reproduced here:

'In the year 1774, being much indisposed both in mind and body, incapable of diverting myself either with company or books, and yet in a condition that made some diversion necessary, I was glad of any thing that would engage my attention without fatiguing it. . . . I undertook the care of three [hares], which it is necessary that I should here distinguish by the names I gave them, Puss, Tiney, and Bess. Notwithstanding the two feminine appellatives, I must inform you that they were all males. Immediately commencing carpenter, I built them houses to sleep in; each had a separate apartment so contrived that their ordure would pass thro' the bottom of it; an earthen pan placed under each received whatever fell, which being duly emptied and washed, they were thus kept perfectly sweet and clean. In the daytime they had the range of the hall, and at night retired each to his own bed, never intruding into that of another.

'Puss grew presently familiar, would leap into my lap, raise himself upon his hinder feet, and bite the hair from my temples. He would suffer me to take him up and carry him about in my arms, and has more than once fallen asleep on my knee. He was ill three days during which time I nursed him, kept him apart from his fellows that they might not molest him . . . and, by constant care and trying him with a variety of herbs, restored him to perfect health. No creature could be more grateful than my patient after his recovery; a sentiment which he most significantly expressed, by licking my hand, first the back of it, then the palm, then every finger separately, then between all the fingers, as if anxious to leave no part of it unsaluted, a ceremony which he never performed but once again upon a similar occasion. Finding him extremely tractable, I made it my custom to carry him always after breakfast into the garden, where he hid himself generally under the leaves of a cucumber vine, sleeping or chewing the cud till evening; in the leaves also of that vine he found a favourite repast. I had not long habituated him to this taste of liberty, before he began to be impatient for the return of the time when he might enjoy it. He would invite me to the garden by drumming upon my knee, and by a look of such expression as it was not possible to mis-interpret. If this rhetoric did not immediately succeed, he would take the skirt of my coat between his teeth, and pull at it with all his force. . . .

'I always admitted them into the parlour after supper, when, the carpet affording their feet a firm hold, they would frisk and bound and play a thousand gambols, in which Bess, being remarkably strong and fearless, was always superior to the rest. . . .

'These creatures have a singular sagacity in discovering the minutest alteration that is made in the place to which they are accustomed, and instantly apply their nose to the examination of a new object. A small hole being burnt in the carpet, it was mended with a patch, and that patch in a moment underwent the strictest scrutiny. They seem too to be very much directed by the smell in the choice of their favourites; to some persons, though they saw them daily, they could never be reconciled, and would even scream when they attempted to touch them; but a miller coming in, engaged their affections at once; his powdered coat had charms that were irresistible.

'You will not wonder, Sir, that my intimate acquaintance with these specimens of the kind has taught me to hold the sportsman's amusement in abhorrence; he little knows what amiable creatures he persecutes, of what gratitude they are capable, how cheerful they are in their spirits, what enjoyment they have of life, and that, impressed as they seem with a peculiar dread of man, it is only because man gives them peculiar cause for it. . . .

'I take it to be a general opinion that they graze, but it is an erroneous one, at least grass is not their staple; they seem rather to use it medicinally, soon quitting it for leaves of almost any kind. Sow-thistle, dent-de-lion, and lettuce are their favourite vegetables, especially the last. I discovered by accident that fine white sand is in great estimation with them; I suppose as a digestive. It happened that I was cleaning a bird-cage while the hares were with me; I placed a pot filled with such sand upon the floor, to which being at once directed by a strong instinct, they devoured it voraciously; since that time I have generally taken care to see them well supplied with it. They account green corn a delicacy, both blade and stalk, but the ear they seldom eat; straw of any kind, especially wheat-straw, is another of their dainties; they will feed greedily upon oats, but if furnished with clean straw never want them; it serves them also for a bed, and, if shaken up daily, will be kept sweet and dry for a considerable time. . . .

'I cannot conclude, Sir, without informing you that I have lately introduced a dog to his [Puss's] acquaintance, a spaniel that had never seen a hare to a hare that had never seen a spaniel. I did it with great caution, but there was no real need for it. Puss discovered no token of fear, nor Marquis the least symptom of hostility. There is, therefore, it should seem, no natural antipathy between dog and hare, but the pursuit of the one occasions the flight of the other, and the dog pursues because he is trained to it: they eat bread at the same time out of the same hand, and are in all respects sociable and friendly.'

People who keep pets often do so in order to compensate for

the loss or lack of human society, as well as to provide them with objects on which to lavish affection. Cowper was doubtless influenced by both these motives; and there was a special applicability for the former, since he could not at that time bear the strain of much social activity. His pets were excellent company, but quite unexacting: they never agitated or irritated him.

At about the same time that he set about keeping pets, he undertook by degrees a number of gardening enterprises, starting with lettuces, cabbages, and cauliflowers, and becoming more proficient as he grew cucumbers and melons, and cultivated fruit-trees. This involved the further employment of his skill as a carpenter and handyman, in the construction, for instance, of a cucumber-frame and a greenhouse, and in the manufacture of cabbage-nets in which he prided himself on his expertness.

In the course of his keeping pets and his gardening, he was operating on the borders of natural history; and he wrote some remarks on the subject, especially in relation to his hares, which indicate that he might well have disclosed a notable talent in that direction. Natural history might have proved as engrossing and as satisfying as poetry, and, what was of special importance to him, less harassing, for, as we shall see, when revisions of his compositions were pressed on him, and when adverse criticism was levelled at him, he became so agitated that his friends began to wonder whether some other type of occupation than poetry would not be more appropriate to his case.

During some four years after his recovery from his second attack of madness, and until he took up the art of poetry as an eligible occupation, he found the garden and his pets adequate to keep obnoxious thoughts at bay, and to ward off the incursions of mental disease. But as the daily round of manual work grew more familiar, he found that his mind was apt to stray to afflictive subjects. His lively intelligence required something more arresting. He explained to Lady Hesketh: 'I find constant employment necessary, and therefore take care to be constantly employed. Manual occupations do not engage the mind sufficiently, as I know by experience, having tried many. But composition, especially of verse, absorbs it wholly.'[9] He likewise told Newton: 'While I am held in pursuit of pretty images, or a pretty way of expressing them, I forget everything that is irksome.'[10]

Although Cowper often described the composition of poetry as a recreation, he did not always find it so. He soon discovered that his stock of subjects was only a small one. His social contacts were so limited that he had little opportunity of watching, say, the clash of temperaments, or of gaining suggestive ideas casually in the course of conversation. Moreover, his disinclination to move far from home hampered him in what some poets have described as the acquisition of images, or, in other words, the ability to use imagery with freshness and variety. Mrs. Unwin was of help to him in proposing subjects for some of his early poems; but her range of experience, too, was necessarily limited. He explained in a letter to a relation that he often found himself reduced to the necessity of writing about himself.[11] As it proved, this was a subject of ample scope, which enabled him to develop a distinctive *genre* of poetry. He mentioned his predicament to his dear friend, William Unwin, in terms which indicate how timid he felt his muse to be: 'Alas! what can I do with my wit? I have not enough to do great things with, and these little things are so fugitive, that while a man catches at the subject, he is only filling his hand with smoke. I must do with it as I do with my linnet; I keep him for the most part in a cage, but now and then set open the door, that he may whisk about the room a little, and then shut him up again.'[12]

John Newton was always in a special class among Cowper's friends. Besides being among his intimate confidants, he was his spiritual adviser; and Cowper felt that he could unburden himself of his most lively hopes and pressing fears to this warm-hearted enthusiast who had played so unselfish a part in rescuing him from the horrors of mental breakdown. It was to Newton, therefore, that he expressed his doubts whether the strength of his nervous system would enable him to undertake the role of poet: 'If I had the strength of mind, I have not the strength of body for the task which, you say, some would impose upon me. I cannot bear much thinking. The meshes of that fine network, the brain, are composed of such mere spinner's threads in me, that when a long thought finds its way into them, it buzzes, and twangs, and bustles about at such a rate as seems to threaten the whole contexture.'[13]

At first he was innocent of any object beyond recreation.

'I never write but for my amusement', he told William Unwin, 'and what I write is sure to answer that end, if it answers no other. If, besides this purpose, the more desirable one of entertaining you be effected, I then receive double fruit of my labour. . . .'[14] Gradually, however, ambition insinuated its baleful influence, though at first in a very mild form; and he began to write, in his letters, as if approbation from friends, or even from a wider set of readers, was of importance to him: 'I am pleased with commendation, and though not passionately desirous of indiscriminate praise, or what is generally called popularity, yet when a judicious friend claps me on the back, I own I find it an encouragement.'[15] 'You ask me how I feel on the occasion of my approaching publication. . . . I have had in view two principal objects; first, to amuse myself,—and secondly, to compass that point in such a manner that others might possibly be the better for my amusement.'[16] 'If the world approve me not, so much the worse for them, but not for me. I have only endeavoured to serve them, and the loss will be their own. And as to their commendations, if I should chance to win them, I feel myself equally invulnerable there.'[17]

Two years passed, and Cowper became increasingly involved in the toils of ambition, as he was indeed bound to be. He confessed as much, with complete frankness, to William Unwin: 'Before I had published, I said to myself—You and I, Mr. Cowper, will not concern ourselves much about what the critics may say of our book. But having once sent my wits for a venture, I soon became anxious about the issue, and found that I could not be satisfied with a warm place in my own good graces, unless my friends were pleased with me as much as I pleased myself. Meeting with their approbation, I began to feel the workings of ambition. It is well, said I, that my friends are pleased, but friends are sometimes partial, and mine, I have reason to think, are not altogether free from bias; methinks I should like to hear a stranger or two speak well of me. I was presently gratified by the approbation of the *London Magazine*, and the *Gentleman's*, particularly that of the former, and by the plaudit of Dr. Franklin. . . .'[18]

Four years later, he had surrendered to ambition without any qualification at all. Indeed, he became enthralled by it; and this was by no means for his comfort and peace of mind. He was, it seems, more beguiled than he was prepared to admit, though his admissions to Lady Hesketh were considerable. 'I am not', he told her, 'naturally insensible, and the sensibilities that I had by nature have been wonderfully enhanced by a long series of shocks, given to a frame of nerves that were never very athletic. I feel accordingly, whether painful or pleasant, in the extreme; am easily elevated, and easily cast down. The frown of a critic freezes my poetical powers, and discourages me to a degree that makes me ashamed of my own weakness. . . . I am not ashamed to confess that having commenced author, I am most abundantly desirous to succeed as such. I have (what, perhaps, you little suspect me of) in my nature an infinite share of ambition. But with it I have at the same time, as you well know, an equal share of diffidence. To this combination of opposite qualities it has been owing that, till lately, I stole through life without undertaking any thing, yet always wishing to distinguish myself. At last I ventured, ventured, too, in the only path that at so late a period was yet open to me; and am determined, if God have not determined otherwise, to work my way through the obscurity, that has been so long my portion, into notice.'[19]

There are some passages in Cowper's letters which seem to suggest that when he undertook the task of translating Homer's *Iliad* and *Odyssey*, he was burdening himself with a more exacting task than was prudent for a man of his vulnerable constitution. This, of course, cannot be proved; and Cowper was apt to refer to the pleasant recreation he enjoyed from his daily translation of forty lines or so. It is clear, however, that, in the course of his draft translations being submitted to voluntary critics, he suffered exasperations which demonstrate both the high degree of his susceptibility to irritation, and the unwisdom of his being exposed to any criticism but of the most temperate and diplomatic kind. It was to Lady Hesketh once more that he confided his sensations: 'The vexation, the perplexity, that attends a multiplicity of criticisms by various hands, many of which are sure to be futile, many of them ill-founded, and some of them contradictory to others, is inconceivable, except by the author, whose ill-fated work happens to be the subject of them. . . . I speak thus, my dear, after having just escaped from such a storm of trouble, occasioned by endless remarks, hints, suggestions, and objections, as drove me almost to despair, and to the very verge of a resolution to drop my undertaking for ever. . . . My beloved cousin, trust me for it, as you safely may, that temper, vanity, and self-importance, had nothing to do in all this distress that I suffered. It was merely the effect of an alarm, that I could not help taking, when I compared the great trouble I had with a few lines only, thus handled, with that which I foresaw such handling of the whole must necessarily give me. I felt beforehand that my constitution would not bear it.'[20] This letter indicates, from its perplexed language, that the writer was acutely perturbed. We may at least suspect that this extreme sensitiveness and apprehension at the need of dealing peremptorily with some teasing amateur critic of his translation arose from a condition of over-strain due to excessive application to this immense project.

In the early stages of Cowper's entry into the profession of poet, his mental health was evidently so much improved that he was ready to modify the rule of seclusion from social activity which he had imposed on himself as a safeguard against imprudent mental exertion. He doubtless came to realize, as time went by, that he could not be a normal man with a normal man's mental health, unless he was a normally sociable person. Moreover, he must also have discovered that attempts at relaxation, in which sociality played no part, were impractical, if continued beyond a reasonable period of convalescence.

Having come to these conclusions, he suddenly broke out from his self-imposed constraint, and enjoyed the society of a vivacious, enterprising, impressionable, and, as far as we can guess, well-favoured and engaging young widow. A Lady Austen came to stay with relations at Olney; and an acquaintanceship with Cowper rapidly developed into an intimate friendship. She, Mrs. Unwin, and Cowper enjoyed many delightful pastimes together, and came to spend much of every day in each other's company. Lady Austen was evidently a most delightful companion, with considerable natural intelligence, full of delicate sympathy, and, what was specially valuable to Cowper, full of excellent ideas for his amusement—amusement, of course, in which she would participate.

It must soon have become obvious to the lady that she was in love with Cowper; and a recognition of this fact by him may have contributed to a temporary rupture in their friendship which was, however, quickly healed. He certainly acted with indiscretion, for he wrote verses to her which served to stimulate her romantic disposition; and she was then, not unnaturally, tempted to display her feelings more clearly. Events thus moved to a dénouement, in which Mrs. Unwin doubtless played a part. Cowper had to choose between them. Before his second madness, he had been engaged to Mrs. Unwin; but his mental instability forbad the marriage. Mrs. Unwin, however, was, we may be sure, not now prepared to lose him. She had sacrificed herself on his behalf in a way that must rival any records of this kind of devotion. She had nursed him tenderly when he was most perverse and unlovable, and had shown forbearance and practical sympathy of the highest order. When, therefore, Cowper saw the choice plainly exhibited before him, he could not hesitate; and the friendship with Lady Austen was finally broken.

Lady Austen was an important factor in his career, for she demonstrated to him that he needed not merely diversion, but social diversion. Her usefulness to him was considerable. When she saw him struggling to find subjects for his poetry, she, by means of her lively intellect and sympathetic understanding of the man, was able to suggest to his mind the ideas or the germs of some of his most famous poems. After tasting the benefits of this friendship, he must have realized that the inspiration of a poet may be better stimulated through the social intercourse of congenial companionships than by the speculations of the solitary mind.

Not long after Lady Austen disappeared out of Cowper's life, he found some new and delightful friends who were not in the least likely to involve him in romantic embarrassments—namely, the Throckmortons, of Weston Park, near Olney. This was a most desirable attachment. The Throckmortons, modest, genuine, cultivated people, were most welcoming to Cowper and Mrs. Unwin. Nothing could be kinder than the way they put their park, their gardens, their produce, and their library at the disposal of their new friends. There was no hint of condescension. They invited them to family meals and to meals at which local people were also guests. Cowper, who was now a poet of considerable reputation, would hardly have been human if he had not enjoyed the deference shown him by the guests at these modest functions. He benefited greatly from the opportunities to be social in this wider, but perfectly congenial environment. It was an ideal situation in which to regain confidence in himself and in his ability to maintain mental health. Thanks to the generous and tactful intervention of Lady Hesketh, Cowper and Mrs. Unwin moved from 'Orchard Side' into the country, to a pleasant house owned by the Throckmortons, in Weston village, a mile from Olney. There, Cowper quite happily renounced his habit of seclusion, and began to lead a life much more like that of a normal member of society. He soon described himself as being 'visited by all around me', and being freely available to callers.[21] Sometimes, when he was suffering from transient mental distress, he found it wise to refuse company, but at other times social activity enabled him to 'recover that elasticity which is able to resist the pressure'.[22]

Soon after moving to Weston, Cowper suffered his third attack of madness, much shorter than the previous ones. Whatever its cause, it was certainly not due to the moderate extent to which he had been mixing with his fellow-creatures. It has been attributed to the sudden death, at the early age of forty-two, of his dear friend, William Unwin; but the strain of his literary occupations, especially his translation of Homer, may well have served to precipitate his collapse.

Frequently, when reading his letters, we realize how delicate was the structure of his mind, and how liable it was to be upset with but slight provocation. A notable instance of his super-sensitiveness is to be found in the mixture of pleasure and misgiving with which he anticipated a visit from Lady Hesketh, the first visit after twenty years. Lady Hesketh evidently became somewhat concerned by his statement that 'when we actually meet, the pleasure, and this unaccountable pain together, will be as much as I shall be able to support'.[23] Cowper, therefore, wrote to allay her anxiety: 'Assure yourself, my dearest cousin, that both for your sake, since you make a point of it, and for my own, I will be as philosophically careful as possible that these fine nerves of mine shall not be beyond measure agitated when you arrive. In truth, there is much greater probability that they will be benefited, and greatly too.

F

Joy of heart, from whatever occasion it may arise, is the best of all nervous medicines; and I should not wonder if such a turn given to my spirits should have even a lasting effect, of the most advantageous kind, upon them. You must not imagine, neither, that I am on the whole in any great degree subject to nervous affections. Occasionally I am, and have been these many years, much subject to dejection; but at intervals, and sometimes for an interval of weeks, no creature would suspect it. For I have not that which commonly is a symptom of such a case belonging to me;—I mean extraordinary elevation in the absence of Mr. Bluedevil. When I am in the best of health, my tide of animal sprightliness flows with great equality, so that I am never at any time exalted in proportion as I am sometimes depressed. My depression has a cause, and if that cause were to cease, I should be as cheerful thenceforth, and perhaps for ever, as any man need be.'[24]

His diffidence and shyness were so extreme as to be almost ridiculous; and he well realized it. Writing to Lady Hesketh about local news at Weston, he said: 'I learn from the Frogs [his playful and familiar name for the Throckmortons: he wrote to Mrs. Throckmorton as 'Mrs. Frog'] that I am somewhat formidable to Mrs. B. Chester, and that she trembles at the thought of encountering a man of my extraordinary consequence. I am glad of this. Nothing could so effectively relieve me from the fears that I should otherwise have of her.'[25] Another letter admits the same weakness: 'When the servant told me that Lady Bagot was in the parlour, I felt my spirits sink ten degrees; but the moment I saw her, at least when I had been a minute in her company, I felt them rise again, and they soon rose even above their normal pitch. . . . I am a shy animal, and want much kindness to make me easy. Such I shall be to my dying day.'[26]

Like a number of shy, retiring people, Cowper had a quiet but playful sense of humour, and a pleasing fantasy. His skill as a story-teller was masterly, with a pre-eminent turn for whimsicality. He knew how to set the scene, and to take advantage of every grotesque incident. One of his most accomplished performances is the account of his being canvassed by the local parliamentary candidate. He told the story to John Newton, to whom he also related other amusing episodes. Newton was rigorous and uncompromising as a spiritual adviser, but he understood humour, and could be humorous himself. Cowper's account runs thus: 'We were sitting yesterday after dinner, the two ladies and myself, very composedly, and without the least apprehension of any such intrusion in our snug parlour, one lady knitting, the other netting, and the gentleman winding worsted, when to our unspeakable surprise a mob appeared before the window; a smart rap was heard at the door, the boys haloo'd, and the maid announced Mr. Grenville. Puss [the hare] was unfortunately let out of her box, so that the candidate, with all his good friends at his heels, was refused admittance at the grand entry, and referred to the back door, as the only possible way of approach.

'Candidates are creatures not very susceptible of affronts, and would rather, I suppose, climb in at the window, than be absolutely excluded. In a minute the yard, the kitchen, and the parlour were filled. Mr. Grenville advancing toward me shook me by the hand with a degree of cordiality that was extremely seducing. As soon as he and as many more as could find chairs were seated, he began to open the intent of his visit. I told him I had no vote, for which he readily gave me credit. I assured him I had no influence, which he was not equally inclined to believe, and the less, no doubt, because Mr. Ashburner, the draper, addressing himself to me at this moment, informed me that I had a great deal. Supposing that I could not be possessed of such a treasure without knowing it, I ventured to confirm my first assertion by saying, that if I had any I was utterly at a loss to imagine where it could be, or wherein it consisted. Thus ended the conference. Mr. Grenville squeezed me by the hand again, kissed the ladies, and withdrew. He kissed likewise the maid in the kitchen, and seemed upon the whole a most loving, kissing, kind-hearted gentleman.'[27]

Cowper was, perhaps, at his most engaging when his droll humour involved him in outlandish flights of fancy which are sometimes incorporated into a story, and sometimes used just to invigorate a passing allusion. The behaviour of a tedious visitor could be admirably caricatured by this means: 'He [the visitor] talks very loud, and when our poor little robins hear a great noise, they are immediately seized with an ambition to surpass it; the increase of their vociferation occasioned an increase in his, and his in return acted as a stimulus upon theirs; neither side entertained a thought of giving up the contest, which became continually more interesting to our ears during the whole visit. The birds, however, survived it, and so did we. They, perhaps, flatter themselves they gained a complete victory, but I believe Mr. —— could have killed them both in another hour.'[28] Another fantastic caricature is that of a diminutive person wearing a hat with a large brim. Here Cowper employs his imagination at its most extravagant: 'He is a very little man, and had he lined his hat with pink instead of yellow, might have been gathered by a natural mistake for a mushroom, and sent off in a basket.'[29]

He could use these quaint conceits equally well to make fun of himself. He was visited by his barber 'who, after having embellished the outside of my head, has left the inside just as unfurnished as he found it'.[30] Perhaps his harmless vanity respecting the due adornment of his head was a little open to pleasantry;* and he was doubtless spry enough to realize this. He wrote to Mrs. Throckmorton (his 'Mrs. Frog') : 'My periwig is arrived, and is the very perfection of all periwigs, having only one fault: which is, that my head will only go into the first half of it, the other half, or the upper part of it, continuing still unoccupied. My artist in this way at Olney has however undertaken to make the whole of it tenantable, and then I shall be twenty years younger than you have ever seen me.'[32]

The grievous trials that Cowper had to undergo throughout most of his life might well have caused him to be egocentric. Doubtless, part of his mental disease, his morbid delusion, was bound up with excessive introspection. But, with due allowance for excusable tendencies of this kind, he was a man of active sympathy for others, especially, of course, his friends. About five years after moving from Olney to the village of Weston, Mrs. Unwin, who had spent a large part of her life and an immense amount of nervous energy in tending, nursing, comforting, and managing for Cowper, suffered from a paralytic stroke, followed later by other strokes. There can be but little doubt that these were due to the strain to which she had been subjected in taking care of him. A few extracts from his letters to his friends at this time enable us to observe that his loyalty

---

* It is pertinent to note his request to William Unwin to buy him a new hat, 'not a round slouch, which I abhor, but a smart well-cocked fashionable affair'.[31]

to his beloved companion never wavered, and to understand in some degree how tenderly he felt and behaved towards her, though this can only be fully possible for those who draw inferences from such poems of his as that entitled 'My Mary'.

'She has been my faithful and affectionate nurse for many years, and consequently has a claim on all my attentions. She has them, and will have them as long as she wants them; which will probably be, at the best, a considerable time to come.

'I feel the shock, as you may suppose, in every nerve. God grant that there may be no repetition of it. Another such stroke upon her would, I think, overset me completely; but at present I hold up bravely.'[33]

'All power to study, all thoughts both of Homer and Milton are driven to a distance, and I can do nothing at present but watch my poor patient, and administer to her, as I do every day, the electrical operation.'[34]

'I have been but once within the Hall door [Weston Hall, the home of the Throckmortons] since the Courtenays came home, much as I have been pressed to dine there, and have hardly escaped giving a little offence by declining it; but though I should offend all the world by my obstinacy in this instance, I would not leave my poor Mary alone.'[35]

'Till she can work and read, and fill up her time as usual (all of which is at present entirely out of her power), I may now and then find time to write a letter, but I shall write nothing more. I cannot sit with my pen in my hand, and my books before me, while she is in effect in solitude, silent, and looking at the fire.'[36]

These were not propitious conditions for the maintenance of Cowper's mental stability. The concluding years of his life, darkened as they were by Mrs. Unwin's physical and then mental decay, as well as by his own increased intensity of despair, are most wretched to dwell upon. It is not necessary to illustrate this final period from his letters, because its history adds nothing to our knowledge of the poet's character. He drifted then into a realm of settled despondency and mental derangement which are outside normal comprehension. In one respect we can learn something significant about him in his last period. Despite the embarrassments and perplexities caused by the sad condition of both Mrs. Unwin and himself, friends, new as well as old, gladly undertook considerable self-sacrifices so as to mitigate their sufferings: Cowper was, in fact, capable of evoking deep devotion to the last.

*   *   *

The numerous extracts from Cowper's letters included in this chapter furnish, owing to his guilelessness, a convincing self-portrait of the man. When we consider this picture, we naturally have the strongest feeling of sympathy for him. How could we feel otherwise towards anyone who suffered such a weight of misery and yet maintained so valiant a front? His letters can, moreover, be enjoyed as literature, for they have features of simplicity, vividness, and refinement which rank them high in standards of artistic expression.

Often, in discussions about literary technique, we are told that simplicity is an essential element; but we seldom find it conspicuous in practice. It is by no means a characteristic to be regarded with condescension. In letter-writing especially, it is cogent evidence of sincerity. As Charles Lamb, who had strong affinities with Cowper, declared, a simple style 'springs spontaneously from the heart'. The modest gracefulness of Cowper's diction is perfectly suited to his intimate themes; and the vicissitudes of his chequered story, depicted as they are with fine courage and restraint, would not be fittingly expressed in high-flown phraseology. One or two literary critics have complained, not only that Cowper's epistolary style suffers from undue homeliness, but also that it lacks vigour and matter. As for matter, what more moving story can we find than that which underlies his unpretending confidences? Lytton Strachey was one of these complaining critics. He remarked that 'Cowper had nothing to say, and he said it beautifully'.[37] We might forgive this pardonable attempt at a *jeu d'esprit*. But he proceeded to add: 'His letters are stricken with sterility; they are dried up; they lack the juices of life.' We could wish that Lytton Strachey's cleverness had not missed so much, in form and substance, especially the significance of the letters in telling Cowper's brave story. Of course, there could be no more unsuitable critic of Cowper than Lytton Strachey in his more epigrammatic and opinionated mood. The two men were leagues apart. Happily, the majority of literary critics take a different and more discerning view.

5

WILLIAM WORDSWORTH
(1770–1850)
Preponderance of Self

SOMETIMES poetry includes a number of the author's personal impressions, or, in the popular term, his reactions. This characteristic may be so extended as to enable the poetry to be described as autobiographical. Very many of Wordsworth's poems are expressive of his feeling for notable scenes; and some of them are predominantly accounts of his own experiences. In such circumstances, a poet's letters are particularly valuable for students of literature, for almost everything that can be known about the writer, his disposition and his character, is of potential usefulness in interpreting his poetry and estimating its worth.

Wordsworth's letters are not so obviously significant of his character as those of several other poet-letter-writers. His tendency to be reserved made him indisposed to share his inner thoughts with his friends, and thus restrained him from outspoken self-revelation. Although he frequently described himself as having a strong dislike for letter-writing, he was a fairly voluminous correspondent. But a large proportion of his letters deal with literary subjects, matters of business, discussions on political and social questions, and family concerns. He wrote but rarely about problems of behaviour, either his own or that of others, in his letters; and yet a general idea of some of his outstanding qualities can be easily gained from an appreciation of his customary attitude to his correspondents. In spite of a rather dry, matter-of-fact style, we can trace in numerous letters a consistent and authentic sympathy in the interests, difficulties, and troubles of his friends and acquaintances. Over and over again, he displayed an anxiety to be helpful; and he never excused himself from obliging a friend by such pretexts as pressure of work. This pervasive good-nature needs to be borne in mind when it becomes necessary to advert to some unattractive qualities which become conspicuous when the contents of his letters are studied.

The disinclination to tell his correspondents about himself that Wordsworth manifested in his letters may seem to be inconsistent with his inescapable reputation for egotism. Perhaps reserve and egotism are not incompatible; but the prominence of self in his disposition must be noticed, if for no other reason than that it has an intimate bearing on his poetry, which is largely dependent for its interest on his personality— some people may say, his intrusive personality. It is often suggested that Wordsworth viewed his experiences and expounded his problems too exclusively from his own personal point of view; that he was too imperious, too authoritative. We have no need to be explicit in any judgement about this; but it is certainly true that his categorical, and even pontifical guise was often evident. His ardent response to the beauties of nature may well excuse the large personal element in his poetry, where so much depends on the way in which a situation or a theme affects the author. But his behaviour in everyday life is said to have been, at times, opinionated and intolerant. In general conversation, he has been described as indulging in lengthy insistence on his own feelings and ideas. This was not necessarily the effect of conceit. He was self-satisfied rather than inflated. Being a man of strong and acute sensibilities, he found it difficult to get outside a question, so as to see it from other people's points of view. He could feel so energetically about a subject under discussion that his whole personality became involved in it. Thus it was that, among a group of companions, he was apt to be self-assertive. He liked to hold the floor, because what he wanted to say seemed to him to be of paramount importance.

Curiously enough, his great friend, Samuel Taylor Coleridge, also liked to hold the floor, for he took a delight, not only in impressing an audience, but in listening to the fluent way in which he could elaborate on any congenial subject. When Wordsworth and Coleridge were together at a party, Coleridge, it seems, by virtue of his matchless eloquence, generally predominated. But, when the two of them talked by themselves, there was no rivalry, for then their mutual affection and respect overcame other inclinations. Coleridge's occasional tendency to be egotistical in conversation was modified by glints of humour and his intense interest in his subject-matter; on the other hand, Wordsworth did not stray far from his own point of view; and he was notably deficient in sprightliness. It is true, he sometimes evinced a quiet humour in his poetry, but in ordinary life his jokes must have been infrequent; and his appreciation of the jokes of other people less frequent still. This was partly due, no doubt, to a constitutional inability to join in general merriment. Like other famous Wordsworths, he was too earnest, and took himself too seriously. It is possible that, where a person is lacking in humour, egotism may easily become a prominent feature in his character; and the converse is, doubtless, also conceivable.

Wordsworth viewed his mission as a poet with immense gravity; and this fact may well explain some puzzling aspects of his behaviour. Much discussion has been expended on the question, why he did not marry Annette Vallon, who had a child by him after a liaison during a visit to France when he was twenty-two. The most likely explanation is that such a marriage would have stirred up so much calumny in his home country that his prospects as a poet would have been impaired. It may even be that Wordsworth's failure to marry Annette some years later, when a further opportunity presented itself, was due to a more intensified sense of his own importance and dignity.[1]

He can hardly have assumed that, even if others must suffer, he was of such supreme value to humanity that he must not suffer too; but he certainly put a very high value on his survival to carry out his mission. His sister, Dorothy, describes an incident in her journals for 1820 which might have shocking implications if he had not been a man of unduly sensitive nerves. He, with his wife and sister, had been for a tour on the Continent, and, shortly after embarking on a ship at Boulogne, on their return journey to England, the ship grounded, a little way from the shore; and the life of all on board seemed in danger. Wordsworth's wife and sister were down below in the ship. Dorothy Wordsworth thus described the situation: 'My brother, thinking it would be impossible to save his wife and me, had stripped off his coat to be ready to swim, but what was our joy and thankfulness when he came into the cabin to tell us that the retreating tide would soon leave the ship bare; and all was safe.'[2] The primary explanation of this extraordinary episode must have been his uncontrollable impulse to seek his own safety, an impulse which was doubtless attributable to an eccentric predominance of self.

Unfortunately for Wordsworth, his family, and posterity, he was 'spoilt' by his sister during the time they kept house together (1795-1802), and by his wife and sister in collaboration for many years after that. Everything centred round William, and the importance of his career as a poet. These two devoted women, with the best of intentions, helped to heighten his egocentricity. For years they relieved him of much minor business of a troublesome kind which he should have undertaken himself. It is, however, fair to say that his sister's journals indicate that he occasionally took a share in the chores of the house and garden at the period when they could afford but little hired labour. A picture of him, therefore, sitting lackadaisically, sucking the end of his pen, while his womenfolk were wrestling with domestic crises, would be an exaggerated one. Perhaps, if he could have enjoyed a few friendships with men and women who were free to treat him with complete sincerity, his character might have developed on more normal lines. But, though he had high ideals on this subject, he had few intimate friends; and these he was apt to lose through lack of proficiency in the art of friendship. At the time when he was writing his best poetry, his attachment to Coleridge meant more to him than any other. His letters to Coleridge are more open-hearted than was his usual style, at least during the earlier part of their friendship. These letters are proof of a strong and unselfish affection, and of his genuine admiration for Coleridge's intellectual abilities. He was at his best in this relationship; and he shewed notable lack of anything like jealousy of Coleridge's poetical genius. The *Lyrical Ballads*, a landmark in the history of poetry, which was published in 1798, was their joint work, but largely that of Wordsworth. It was put about that the whole contents of the volume were written by Coleridge; and Wordsworth wrote to Coleridge, saying: 'Take no pains to contradict the story that the L.B. are entirely yours. Such a rumour is the best thing that can befall them.'[3] These are not the words of a selfish egotist; and his egotism often seemed to recede while he was under Coleridge's influence. But, as we shall see in the next chapter, Coleridge, as his character developed, was not the man to stiffen a friend's resistance against a temperamental but undesirable trend in behaviour.

Another friendship that engaged both his heart and his mind was that with De Quincey, who settled at Grasmere, near Wordsworth's home. Although both Coleridge and De Quincey proved, each in his way, to be difficult associates, it is perhaps significant that Wordsworth quarrelled with them both.

In his middle years, he formed a pleasant relationship with Sir George Beaumont, a benevolent patron of the arts; and this occupied a great deal of Wordsworth's time and attention. It was valuable to both sides: Beaumont enjoyed his contact with an exceptional intellect; and Wordsworth had a genuine respect for a man of artistic ability who stood to him in some degree as a benefactor. This was obviously in part a friendship of convenience, though it was generally managed in a way calculated to sustain the association on healthy and sensible lines. Wordsworth wrote, for instance, about two years after their first acquaintance: 'I know, my dear Sir George, you will give me the credit for speaking without arrogance [about politics]; and I am aware it is not unlikely you may differ greatly from me in these points. But I like, in some things, to differ with a friend, and that he should *know* I differ from him; it seems to make a more healthy friendship, to act as a relief to those notions and feelings which we have in common, and to give them a grace and spirit which they could not otherwise possess.'[4] It might seem doubtful whether a letter written in these stilted terms would be likely to presage the easy procedure that Wordsworth had in mind; but formality was an accepted feature in much correspondence in those days; and, in fact, their intercourse proved to be lasting and pleasurable.

During his later life, Wordsworth enjoyed long and cordial, though hardly intimate, friendships with two well-known figureś, Henry Crabb Robinson and Samuel Rogers. But there could be no question of Wordsworth's disposition being modified as a result of companionship with these friends. By that time his character had become fixed. Crabb Robinson commented, from time to time, on Wordsworth's intolerance and other defects; but never, as far as we know, to his face. He had Crabb Robinson for his companion on a European tour in 1837. Genial relations were maintained superficially; but we learn from Wordsworth's letters to his family that Crabb Robinson tried his patience sorely.

His high, and, indeed, possibly too exalted, ideals were expressed in his first letter to De Quincey, when he remarked: 'My friendship it is not in my power to give; this is a gift which no man can make, it is not in our own power: a sound and healthy friendship is the growth of time and circumstance; it will spring up and thrive like a wild-flower when these favour, and when they do not, it is vain to look for it.'[5] It is surprising that, after this chilly rebuff to the younger man, who had made respectful advances to the older, each was happy in the enjoyment of the other's company during three or four years.

A friendship, like some others, that illustrated the more reticent, unforthcoming aspect of Wordsworth was that with Francis Wrangham, a distinguished classical scholar and a miscellaneous writer. It lasted successfully for very many years, but chiefly by means of correspondence; and the letters that Wordsworth wrote to Wrangham consisted, in the main, of discussions on literary matters. Wrangham sometimes tried to elicit some particulars of Wordsworth's everyday life, but with small success.

The paucity of Wordsworth's intimates is doubtless attributable in some measure to the whole-heartedness with which he identified himself with his family, including, of course, his sister. This implied an admirable trait; but it also involved dangers, for he had scarcely anyone who could act the needful part (especially needful to him) of the blunt, outspoken friend.

The defects in Wordsworth's character, because they are sometimes disagreeable ones, are apt to be made to bulk too large; but they must be frankly acknowledged. He has been described as hard-headed, like many north-countrymen. There was no harm in that, though it was an unusual feature for a poet. But it seems questionable whether he invariably managed to confine his hardness to his head. Here and there in the letters we find traces of a stern and almost harsh strain. When writing to his brother, the solicitor, in 1803, about his business relations with his publishers, he said: 'As soon as this next edition shall be disposed of, the copyright will revert to me, and I shall take care to know precisely upon what terms a bookseller [i.e. publisher] can afford to take it, and he shall not have it a farthing under.'[6] In middle age, he proved himself to have a pretty shrewd ability in business and could deal efficiently with legal questions and with problems relating to the investment of money.[7] When a Welsh poet paid Wordsworth a visit, in 1844, he was impressed by his 'inflexible matter-of-fact manner and spirit', and summed up his shrewdness in picturesque phrases. 'It struck me forcibly at the time,' he said, 'that he would be a capital hand to drive a hard bargain with a Welsh pig-driver at a fair.'

Even in his family, where his virtues shone brightest, and where his deep affection was manifested by frequent acts of kindness, he could be stern and inexorable if his parental authority had been flouted. When his much-loved daughter, Dora, had married against his expressed wishes, he discussed his feelings in the matter with a confidante, Isabella Fenwick, in a letter which certainly convicts him of callousness, perhaps even of a little spitefulness. He wrote: 'To one thing only will I now advert, viz. that I will not bind myself, circumstanced as Dora is, to make her any fixed allowance. I am convinced it would be wrong to do so, as it would only produce in a certain quarter an effect which I should exceedingly deprecate. Be assured I will take care while I live that she should not *suffer* in mind for scantiness of income. That she may be somewhat straitened, acting as she has chosen to do with my strongest disapprobation, I deem fit and right.'[8] Wordsworth can hardly be defended in respect of his attitude in this business. It might be said that it was no more than typical of an outraged Victorian parent. But we should expect a high-minded poet, with pretensions like his, to maintain a loftier standard of benevolence than this.

The egotism in his character is so pervasive that it is apt to divert attention from some good qualities to which he is justly entitled. He was undoubtedly closely wrapped up in himself; but that by no means implies that he was lacking in consideration for others. On the contrary, he was in many respects strongly animated by kindness. This feature in his character clearly appears from some casual references in his own correspondence, and also in remarks in the letters of his wife and his sister. As quite a young man, he wrote a number of letters of careful and thoughtful advice to a contemporary, his friend William Mathews. It is obvious, therefore, that it was an early characteristic of his to take pains to give practical help to those who were in need of it. In 1791, he wrote to this friend: 'I will not employ many words in assuring you of the distress it caused in me to find you so unhappy. It is evident by the manner in which you address me you are persuaded I am deeply interested in whatever affects your happiness.' He then proceeded to tell his friend that 'it is probable my regard for you is greater than your diffidence in your power of winning esteem might encourage you to suppose'.[9] Like several other distinguished poets, he was generous in helping and advising his younger and less experienced confrères; and his help was by no means perfunctory. He did not refrain, as it is so tempting to do in such circumstances, from making pointed criticisms. At the same time, he advanced such comments with delicate tact.

For many years he proved himself to be an ardent sympathizer with the peasantry of the Lake District; and several of his poems attest such feeling. He would spend time and energy in raising funds in cases of distress. There is, indeed, plenty of evidence to show that he treated his neighbouring country-folk generously and helpfully. On the other hand, there are some local reminiscences which suggest that, when past middle age, Wordsworth was considered unconversable and even ungracious by the countrymen in his vicinity. It is, however, in the home that Wordsworth's kindness is best exemplified. Shortly before he married Mary Hutchinson, his sister Dorothy wrote to Mary, describing some effects of a sharp attack of illness from which she was suffering. 'I feel pretty well now', she said, 'except that I have a kind of stupefaction and headache about me. . . . William has slept well these two nights, and he looks well; this is at all times my best joy, and really it is almost a pleasure to be ill, he is so good and loving to me.'[10] This is certainly an impressive testimonial, for Dorothy knew him through and through. A few years after this incident, his much-cherished brother, John, died suddenly at sea; and Wordsworth's wife wrote to a friend: 'Our beloved Wm! my dear friend, you would love him more than ever, could you know how he has exerted himself to comfort us. . . .'[11] His anxiety about the health of his children is not to be characterized as mere fussiness, but was evidently based on sincere affection. The ailments of his son, William, aroused in him 'unconquerable agitation'; and much the same can be said in regard to his solicitude for his favourite child, Dora.

The tributes he paid to his sister's long years of devotion to him were not the perfunctory appreciation of a self-centred man. They were always full and generous; and whenever he mentioned the subject in a letter, the mention was accompanied by affectionate comments, the genuineness of which is unquestionable. After his sister's health had broken down in 1829, these references are particularly tender. He wrote to Charles Lamb in 1833, thanking him for sending his *Last Essays of Elia*: 'I read *Love me and Love My Dog* to my poor Sister this morning, while I was rubbing her legs at the same time. . . . I have been thus particular [i.e. going into details about his sister's condition] knowing how much you and your dear sister value this excellent person, who in tenderness of heart I do not honestly believe was ever exceeded by any of God's creatures. Her loving-kindness has no bounds. God bless her for ever and ever!'[12] Dorothy Wordsworth remained an invalid, with her mind severely affected, for many years. There is not the least sign that her brother displayed any other feelings but those of pity and sympathy. He never for a moment condoled with himself over the trials his sister's condition imposed on him, among others in his household.[13] Some fifteen years after Dorothy became an invalid, when he was seventy-four years old, his wife wrote to Crabb Robinson: 'Our dear sister keeps her usual way—her Br [brother] is at this moment drawing his sister's carriage in the front.'[14]

There are several remarks in Wordsworth's letters which make it evident that he was patient, considerate, and cordial with the servants in the house at Rydal, who were obviously treated as an integral part of the family. He used to send messages to them when writing to his wife from away. On one occasion, when luggage was mislaid through an oversight of a trusted woman-servant, his behaviour was not merely restrained, but entirely sympathetic.[15] Relationships and behaviour such as these are excellent proof of a kindly disposition.

Wordsworth's deep affection for Coleridge has already been mentioned; and the record of his forbearance and practical kindness shown to this wayward and much afflicted friend is impressive. One or two selected instances will be sufficient for notice here. In 1803, when Wordsworth had just married, and was by no means well off, he lent Coleridge £30 so as to enable him to pay a debt which was worrying him. The loan was voluntary, unasked for, a feature which gave it special significance.[16] In the same year, he also 'forced upon him [Coleridge]' a loan of £100 from his hard-earned savings, so as to help him to go abroad for his health. In 1806, Coleridge's relations with his wife were most unhappy; and Wordsworth was determined to do his best to clarify the situation, at whatever cost to himself. He told Sir George Beaumont: 'I have written to him to say that if he does not come down immediately I must insist upon seeing him somewhere. If he appoints London, I shall go. I believe if anything good is to be done for him, it must be done by me.'[17] Here speak the self-assured and the self-sacrificing friend at the same time. Apart from other personal inconveniences in which he would be involved, travelling from the North of England to London was no light matter in those days.

Two years later, after Wordsworth had by his steady moral support upheld his friend, and kept him from despair, he gave him hospitality at Grasmere, apparently intending to shelter him for as long as he wished to remain. This was a heroic undertaking, because Coleridge was a most exacting visitor, moody, exigent, eccentric, unpredictable. While it is obvious that much of the exhausting part of this hospitality fell on his wife and sister, Wordsworth himself took his share in the rescue work. At this time, Coleridge was planning his new periodical, *The Friend*. Wordsworth wrote for it, and in support of it; and even despatched prospectuses advertising it.

Soon after Coleridge terminated his long visit to Grasmere, the two men quarrelled. Coleridge considered that he had been maligned, being represented as an undesirable visitor. Wordsworth denied any culpability. It is not possible to investigate the rights and wrongs of the matter here, but only necessary to remark on the rapid change in Wordsworth from a long record of warm-hearted benevolence to an attitude of callous indifference that was occasionally typical of him in other relationships. Although he could, in favourable circumstances, be unreservedly friendly, he had a tendency to illiberality and bigotry, which, combined with his self-importance, must have circumscribed his capacity for friendship. There were faults on both sides; but Charles Lamb, who knew both parties well, blamed Wordsworth for a coldness which made a rapprochement almost hopeless. Wordsworth adopted a lofty air of detachment about the quarrel, while Coleridge was much distressed, and was genuinely convinced that he was the injured and innocent party. Wordsworth knew quite well that he was dealing with a man whose moral fibre had been seriously debilitated, and who needed all the indulgence available to him. It is true that Coleridge had been inconsiderate; but that was no sudden disclosure; and, after the lapse of a short time, Wordsworth, as the stronger character, might have risked his dignity and made an advance, with the object of reaching an understanding. As it was, the quarrel lasted a year and a half.

G

He displayed an even more uncompromising moral attitude in regard to his friendship with De Quincey, who came to live near the Wordsworths. De Quincey had several children by the daughter of a smallholder in the district, but did not marry her for some years afterwards. Soon after this liaison started, Wordsworth, who was personally in no position to criticize such frailty, refused to continue social relations. In this affair, his attitude was one of moral superiority, which was bad enough; but it was also one of harsh intolerance, which was worse.

Some of Wordsworth's contemporaries and some of his biographers have emphasized his coldness, his reserve, and even his arrogance. Hazlitt, who was by no means his admirer, described him as passing his life 'in solitary musing or in daily converse with the face of nature'. The effect of a number of remarks similar in purport, but less insidious in their intention, is to produce a picture of a glum recluse. Such a picture is undoubtedly a travesty of the man. He was, it is true, at his best in the company of his relations, or a few sympathetic friends. At anything like a soirée or social gathering he was not at his ease; and he was not a success. On the one hand, he was not happy where he had to make himself agreeable to all sorts of people, and to discuss trivialities. On the other hand, his fellow-guests did not enjoy listening to him talking, as if he were talking out of a book; and if they showed their boredom, this spoilt any chance of his enjoyment too.

It is probably a pity, for the sake of accuracy, that most of the testimonials we have for his social charm come from his devoted and highly prejudiced sister. When he was a young man she tried to persuade a friend of hers—and persuasion was evidently required—that her brother was pleasant in company. On one occasion she wrote: 'You do not know him; you do not know how amiable he is.' And, sometime later: 'Indeed William is as chearful as anybody can be; perhaps you may not think it, but he is the life of the whole house.'[18]

The fact is that Wordsworth was only indisposed to social activity in certain moods, and at certain periods in his life. When he lived in the tiny Dove Cottage, there was not much room for hospitality; and the family was being brought up; nevertheless he enjoyed having a few congenial companions around him from time to time. But when he moved to Allan Bank, at Grasmere, there was plenty of room for visitors, and such friends as De Quincey, the Clarksons and Coleridge and his children came to stay, sometimes for considerable periods. This hospitality inevitably interfered with his ability to concentrate on poetical composition; and the fact that we hear of no complaints from him on this score reflects favourably on his capacity to suppress his personal inclinations in the interest of kindliness and sociality.

When his reputation as a poet had begun to achieve its late flowering, he was quite prepared to submit to, and perhaps even to encourage, a round of social festivity at Rydal. A letter to John Kenyon, in 1831, has an air of exhilaration foreign to the poet's usual measured formality; and some phrases in particular reveal the writer in an unaccustomed guise. 'The summer that is over', wrote Wordsworth light-heartedly, 'has been with us as well as with you a brilliant one, for sunshine and fair and calm weather—brilliant also for its unexampled gaiety in regattas, balls, dejeuners, picnics by the lakeside, on the islands, and on the mountain tops—fireworks by night—dancing on the green sward by day—in short a fever of pleasure from morn to dewy eve—from eve till break of day. Our youths and maidens, like Chaucer's Squire "hath slept no more than doth the nightingale", and our old men have looked as bright as Tithonus when his withered cheek reflected the blushes of Aurora upon her first declaration of her passion for him. In the room where I am now dictating, we had, three days ago, a dance—forty beaus and belles, besides matrons, ancient spinsters, and greybeards—and tomorrow in the same room we are to muster for a venison feast. Why are you not here, to enjoy or to philosophize over this dissipation?'[19] This was the period when his children were growing up, and when their parents were expected to provide them with social opportunities. But the warm glow of his belated celebrity was doubtless also a factor. This celebrity involved him, during the 'thirties and early 'forties in the entertainment of successions of respectful pilgrims. As old age came upon him, he found these demonstrations of esteem gratifying, but also exhausting.[20]

In his later years, he was evidently capable of being sociable outside his family. Both his friends, Crabb Robinson and

Samuel Rogers, behaved as if they appreciated his company; and the latter went so far as to describe him at a particular period as being 'so joyous and communicative'. But he could never tolerate social functions in London. 'But O my dear friend', he wrote to Isabella Fenwick in his old age, 'the hollowness of London society—but what an abuse of the term, and not only the hollowness but the tediousness, especially among dabblers in literature—to me their talk, and their flattery above all, is insupportable.'[21]

Wordsworth's firm conviction, steadily held throughout his career, that his poetry was of high and lasting value, was not necessarily an indication of conceit. It was more likely to be an expression of intense confidence in his ability to discharge his vocation, his divinely appointed work in life. Rather in the same way, the considerable degree in which his personality intrudes into his poetry is not, as we have suggested, so much a revelation of egotism as a matter of principle, a conscious means of making his mission effective. Unfortunately, for more than half his career as poet, a majority of those concerned with poetry did not accept his work at his own valuation. Reviews in periodicals were, on the whole, distinctly discouraging. And, what was worse, and highly mortifying, his work was sometimes represented by the reviewers as ridiculous. This scornful kind of disparagement was a sore affliction for so proud a man. But, in public, he succeeded in appearing unmoved, exercising consummate restraint. Instead of railing at his detractors, and publicly protesting against the brutality of the strictures passed on him, he reserved his dudgeon and his remonstrances for his family and near friends.

There is no doubt about the acute suffering he underwent as a result of the taunts and gibes of the reviewers. They made him so ill that his wife and sister found it necessary to hide the reviews from him. Even when the reviewers began to be kinder to his poetry, he affected to treat them with disdain. He preferred the private testimonies 'which I receive very frequently of the effect of my writings on the hearts and minds of men . . . because *they* must be written under *pure* influences . . . '.[22]

In writing to his friends, he persisted in his dogged reiteration that the world would benefit from his poetry, and that one day he would be adequately appreciated. He tried, in these letters, to assume an air of lofty detachment, but his strong feelings on the subject and his latent irritability kept emerging. In 1807, he wrote to Lady Beaumont: 'Trouble not yourself upon their [his poems] present reception; of what moment is that compared with what I trust is their destiny, to console the afflicted, to add sunshine to daylight by making the happy happier, to teach the young and the gracious of every age, to see, to think and feel, and therefore to become more actively and securely virtuous; this is their office, which I trust they will faithfully perform long after we (that is, all that is mortal of us) are mouldered in our graves. I am well aware how far it would seem to many I overrate my own exertions when I speak in this way, in direct connection with the volumes I have just made public. . . . To conclude, my ears are stone-dead to this idle buzz [of adverse criticism], and my flesh is as insensible as iron to these petty stings; and after what I have said I am sure yours will be the same. I doubt not that you will share with me an invincible confidence that my writings (and among them these little poems) will co-operate with the benign tendencies in human nature and society, wherever found; and that they will in their degree, be efficacious in making men wiser, better, and happier.'[23] Many readers of these sentences will disapprove what may seem to be smug self-satisfaction. Many again will find justification for his robust confidence in the pre-eminence of his genius. But, of the latter, there will surely be some who will conclude that he should have expressed his confidence with less presumption. A poet who honestly believed that the improvement of his fellow-men depended on their due appreciation of his poetry is not so much conceited as bigoted. The final sentence in the preceding extract is a relatively modest version of a remark he made at a later date to Crabb Robinson: 'If men are to become better, the poems will sooner or later find admirers.'

Occasionally, Wordsworth was unable to disguise his vexation at adverse criticism. If strictures came from someone he admired or loved, he could not resist disputing their validity; and he sometimes resorted to counter-attack. Naturally enough, anything in the way of detraction that came from Coleridge exasperated him, for he had a particular admiration for his intellectual abilities, besides an eager desire to gain his approval. In 1808, Charles Lamb had ventured to make some critical comments on Wordsworth's *The White Doe of Rylstone*. Coleridge was also involved, so Wordsworth wrote to him in a terse and consequential manner: 'Let Lamb learn to be ashamed of himself in not taking some pleasure in the contemplation of this picture, which supposing it to be even but a sketch, is yet sufficiently made out for any man of true power to finish it for himself—As to the principal characters doing nothing, it is false and too ridiculous to be dwelt upon for a moment. When it is considered what has already been executed in poetry, strange that a man cannot perceive, particularly when the present tendencies of society, good and bad, are observed, that this is the time when a man of genius may honourably take a station upon different ground. If he is to be a dramatist, let him crowd his scene with gross and visible action; but if a narrative poet, if the poet is to be predominant over the dramatist,—then let him see if there are no victories in the world of spirit, no changes, no commotions, no revolutions there, no fluxes and refluxes of the thoughts which may be made interesting by modest combination with the stiller actions of the bodily frame, or with the gentler movements and milder appearances of society and social intercourse, or the still more mild and gentle solicitations of irrational and inanimate nature. But too much of this—of one thing be assured that Lamb has not a reasoning mind, therefore cannot have a comprehensive mind, and least of all, has he an imaginative one.'[24] Some faint outlines of a sustainable vindication of his position are discernible in the confused and irate rumblings of the affronted poet. But, if he had had a livelier human sympathy, he would have realized that he could only convert his critic to his point of view by more genial methods.

A few years later Coleridge was unmannerly enough to make some remarks which indirectly implied that *The Excursion* suffered, as in fact much of Wordsworth's work suffers, from a superfluity of the obvious. Again, Wordsworth wrote to Coleridge with mixed indignation and displeasure: 'One of my principal aims in the Exⁿ has been to put the commonplace truths, of the human affections especially, in an interesting point of view; and rather to remind men of their knowledge, as it lurks inoperative and unvalued in their own minds, than to attempt to convey recondite or refined truths. Pray point out to me the most striking instances where I have failed, in producing poetic effect by an overfondness for this practice, or through inability to realize my wishes.'[25] It is easy to imagine, and to smile at, a picture of the indignant Wordsworth adding aloud to himself: 'There! that will teach him to be presumptuous!'

He wrote a letter in the same strain, but with greater excitability, and consequently with a greater tendency to be ridiculous, to a friend whose friend had made some highly indiscreet comments on *The Excursion*. They probably amounted to no more than amateurish misconceptions which a sensible man would have made light of, or disregarded; but he could not restrain himself from writing a letter in which he attempted to defend himself, and at the same time administered a severe reprimand to the impudent critic. He wrote: 'To talk of the offence of writing *The Excursion* and the difficulty of forgiving the author, is carrying audacity and presumption to a height that I did not think any *woman* was capable. Had my poem been much coloured by books, as many parts of what I have to write must be, I should have been accused (as Milton has been) of pedantry, and of having a mind which could not support itself but by other men's labours. Do you not perceive that my conversations almost all take place out of doors, and all with the grand objects of nature, surrounding the speakers, for the express purpose of their being alluded to in illustration of the subjects treated of? *Much* imagery from books would have been an impertinence, and an incumbrance; where it was required, it is found.

'As to passion, it is to be never lost sight of that *The Excursion* is *part* of a work; that its plan is conversational; and that, if I had introduced stories exciting curiosity, and filled with violent conflicts of passion and a rapid interchange of striking incidents, these things could never have harmonized with the rest of the work; and all further discourse, comment, or reflections must have been put a stop to. This I write for you and not your friend; with whom (if you take my advice) you will neither converse by letters, nor *viva voce*, upon a subject of which she is in every respect disqualified to treat.'[26] The criticism with which Wordsworth was chiefly concerned was, it seems, similar to that made by Charles Lamb in regard to *The White Doe of Rylstone*. It is, perhaps, understandable that he reacted with such vigour, for no criticism of a poem could be more exasperating than one which infers its dullness.

At times he had his modest, and even over-modest moods. These seem to have been exhibited to his acquaintances rather than to his friends. For instance, he wrote to a correspondent whom he had not even met: 'It would be unpardonable were I to conclude without thanking you for not having abstained from expressing your sense of the value of my imperfect, and, comparatively, unworthy writings. The true standard of poetry is high as the soul of man has gone, or can go. How far my own falls below that, no one can have such pathetic conviction as my poor self.'[27] It is natural to draw attention to one's virtues when subjected to criticism, and to be self-depreciatory when saluted with compliments; but Wordsworth went to extremes. Either he was irritated beyond measure, or he affected to be utterly inadequate. The latter mood is more noticeable as he approached old age, when he was apt to indulge in morbid introspection.

No doubt Wordsworth's excessive sensitiveness to criticism, as well as his fretfulness, and his tendency to take small anxieties too seriously, was due in part to physical causes. There is much evidence in his sister's journals and letters, and in his own letters, to prove that the practice of poetical composition played upon his nerves in a peculiar way, especially the nerves of his stomach. This weakness persisted throughout most of his writing career. The following brief extracts from Dorothy Wordsworth's letters and journals deal with incidents in the years from 1800 to 1802:

'. . . he writes with so much feeling and agitation that it brings on a sense of pain and internal weakness about his left side and stomach, which now often makes it impossible for him to write when he is in mind and feelings in such a state that he could do it without difficulty.'[28]

'. . . he is always very ill when he tries to alter an old poem, but new composition does not hurt him so much. I hope he will soon be able to work without hurting himself.'[29]

'Wm. worked at *The Pedlar* all the morning. He kept the dinner waiting till four o'clock. He was much tired.'

'William very nervous. After he was in bed, haunted with altering *The Rainbow.*'[30]

In the following year, 1803, Wordsworth wrote to Sir George Beaumont: 'I have now been more than a fortnight at home, but the uneasiness in my chest has made me beat off the time when the pen was to be taken up. I do not know from what cause it is, but during the last three years I have never had a pen in my hand for five minutes, before my whole frame becomes one bundle of uneasiness; a perspiration starts out all over me, and my chest is oppressed in a manner which I cannot describe.'[31] Nearly twenty years later, his sister mentioned his eye-trouble, which she thought to be connected with his stomach disorder. The latter she attributed to his having worked hard and incessantly, and under great mental excitement.[32]

Still later, in 1837, during a European tour with Crabb Robinson, he wrote letters to his family at Rydal which give some impression of his neurotic tendencies. The inclusion of some lengthy extracts from two letters is justified, because their tone and temper reflect so admirably the disposition of the writer in his later period. The first letter, for the whole family, is written from Salzburg: 'My health has been good, but certainly my frame is weakened by the journey, as I feel in many ways, as for instance the bodily exertion of rummaging in my trunk for something I wanted since I began this letter, has brought a kind of cramp of pain to my stomach such as I have often felt upon like occasions, but never used to have. This stomach weakness may be in part accounted for by the quantity of liquid which from extreme thirst I have been tempted to take, and it has been increased I will confess by the less excusable fault, the labour I have lately undergone in correcting a little poem of 76 lines which I was tempted to write. This work disturbed or rather broke my rest for two or three nights when I might have had the benefit of the cool air of the Alpine country with sound sleep to recruit me. As these verses have cost me in this way more than they ought to have done, I shall be much mortified if you do not like them and think them pretty good. I promise you solemnly that I shall attempt nothing of the kind again during this journey.'[33]

The second letter is addressed to his wife, from Munich:

'. . . My bowels have latterly been in better order and I have no pain anywhere, but my head is often cloudy and my nerves as I have said are much deranged. I sometimes think that the coffee and beer I take, for I have nearly left off wine, are too much for my nerves. If I dared do so I would leave off beer and wine altogether and coffee also, but milk I know is binding. Excuse all this; not a word of which would have been said had not both you and Dora blamed me so much for hurrying. In fact I have not hurried, but been very patient, considering the tiresome way in which when in towns I have been obliged to spend so many hours. . . . Therefore find no more fault; I undertook the journey as a *duty*. I have gone through it as such, and except that as far as concerns my health, having a most unsuitable companion in Mr. Robinson, I have in consequence made many sacrifices of which he is not aware. . . .'[34]

Although he was so highly strung, he does not appear to have had difficulty in controlling his temper, in notable contrast to poets with such diverse characters as Byron, Browning, and Swinburne, who, under suitable provocation, could work themselves up into preposterous passions. There are only one or two instances in his letters where he shows himself to be under the influence of violent feeling. Perhaps the reviewers were most successful in disturbing his equanimity. Hazlitt, with some reason, was among his particular aversions. He wrote to B. R. Haydon: 'The miscreant Hazlitt continues, I have heard, his abuse of Southey, Coleridge and myself, in the *Examiner*—I hope you do not associate with the fellow, he is not a proper person to be admitted into respectable society, being the most perverse and malevolent creature that ill luck has ever thrown in my way. Avoid him—hic niger est—And this, I understand is the general opinion wherever he is known, in London.'[35] Lord Byron, both as author and man, also provoked his violent repugnance and displeasure. Here again, his ire was obviously roused by Byron's scornful opinions on his poetry. But his indignation was overtly based on artistic and moral grounds of a more general kind.[36]

Another effect of Wordsworth's abnormal sensitiveness was a liability to fretfulness and over-anxiety, especially in regard to his children, with whom he had but little cause to be dissatisfied. In writing to Francis Wrangham, in 1816, he said:

'I am happy to hear that your family prospers, and that your children are to your mind. In my own I find much to regret, and something to complain of; faults most of which have probably been created by my own mismanagement.'[37] A few years later, he told his friend, Samuel Rogers: 'Were there no other obstacle, I could not think of leaving England for so long a time till I had disposed of my younger son, who I have just learned from him, is bent on being a beggar either in the honourable character and profession of a soldier or of a farmer. Could you suggest to me anything better for this infatuated youth . . . ?'[38] Even with his much loved daughter, Dora, he could be querulous and captious upon occasion. Such incidents as these hardly imply a lack of easy relations and confidence between parent and child. Moreover these discontents were probably infrequent; and it would be unjustifiable to assume that he consistently played the part of a domestic tyrant.

Towards the end of his life, when his writing and reading activities were perforce limited, he had more time to reflect about the influence of his behaviour, past and present, on others. He evinced an unwholesome proneness to extravagant remorse, and was especially concerned with his past lack of consideration for his wife, his sister, and his daughter. In 1843, he dictated some introductory remarks about many of his poems to his friend, Isabella Fenwick, which were later printed in his collected editions. In one of these, he included, inappropriately enough, apologies to his wife and sister for his inconsiderate behaviour to them. Remarking on *The White Doe of Rylstone*, he said: 'The earlier half of this poem was composed at Stockton-upon-Tees, when Mrs. Wordsworth and I were on a visit to her eldest brother, Mr. Hutchinson, at the close of the year 1807. The country is flat, and the weather was rough. I was accustomed every day to walk to and fro under the shelter of a row of stacks in a field at a small distance from the town, and there poured forth my verses aloud as freely as they would come. Mrs. Wordsworth reminds me that her brother stood upon the punctilio of not sitting down to dinner till I joined the party; and it frequently happened that I did not make my appearance till too late, so that she was made uncomfortable. I here beg her pardon for this and similar transgressions during the whole course of our wedded life. To my beloved sister the same apology is due.' These remarks, like others of his, ultimately prefaced to poems, assume a detailed interest in his personal affairs. Neither the flatness of the country in which the first part of the poem was composed, nor the position of the row of stacks, and still less the moving apologies to his relations, facilitate the interpretation or the enjoyment of the poem. Nor can it be seriously suggested that his intention in making this public apology was to imply a remonstrance to his wife for reminding him of such an episode, for this kind of self-abasement became habitual with him. When he was travelling abroad, in 1837, he wrote to his family: 'Absence in a foreign country, and at a great distance, is a condition, for many minds, at least for mine, often pregnant with remorse. Dearest Mary, when I have felt how harshly I often demeaned myself to you, my inestimable fellow-labourer, while correcting the last edition of my poems, I often pray to God that He would grant us both life, that I may make some amends to you for that and all my unworthiness. But you know into what an irritable state this timed and overstrained labour often puts my nerves. My impatience was ungovernable as I thought *then*, but now I feel that it ought to have been governed. You have forgiven me I know, as you did then, and perhaps that somehow troubles me the more. I say nothing of this to you, dear Dora, though you also have had some reason to complain—But too much of this——' [39]

Some seven years later, in 1844, this distressing aptitude for inordinate contrition must have become embarrassing to his intimates. The special confidante of his old age, Isabella Fenwick, required much patience to submit to some of his more fulsome outbursts in this strain. 'I do feel from the bottom of my heart', he told her, 'that I am unworthy of being constantly in your sight. Your standard is too high for my hourly life;—when I add to what you blame, the knowledge which I bear about all day long of my own internal unworthiness, I am oppressed by the consciousness of being an object unfit to be from morning to night in your presence. Among ten thousand causes which I have to thank God for his goodness towards me is that for more than forty years I have had a companion who can bear with my offences, who forgets them, and enters upon a new course of love with me when I have done wrong, leaving me to the remorse of my conscience.'[40]

In his old age, as in his younger years, Wordsworth's character was notable for having attractive and unattractive features which contrasted with each other more markedly than such features do with most people. His expressions of remorse, though hysterical in tone and preposterous in manner, were evidently not hypocritical. He had, at the same time, a genuine disposition to kindness, which, as we have seen, he exercised freely. This duality is implied in a description of him as an old man, in 1846. An observer, with more than average perspicacity, who saw a good deal of him towards the end of his life, Harriet Martineau, wrote: 'His life is a most serene & happy one on the whole, & while all goes on methodically he is happy and cheery & courteous & benevolent; so that one could almost worship him. But to secure this everybody must be punctual, the fire must be bright & all go orderly as his angel [i.e. his wife] takes care that everything shall as far as depends on her.'[41] We may gather that, if circumstances were propitious— and they generally were—he could, to the end, be affability itself. Occasionally, no doubt, his fractiousness and petulance might be aroused. But, if they were, we may be comforted by the knowledge that, in conformity with his usual behaviour, he would soon be sincerely sorry.

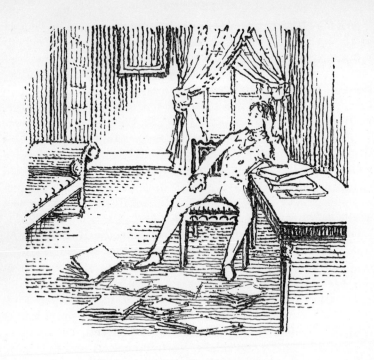

6

SAMUEL TAYLOR COLERIDGE
(1772 – 1834)
Unstable Genius

How far was Coleridge responsible for the weak points in his character, and how far was his character shaped by circumstances beyond his control? Any discussion of the poet as a man must soon be involved in such questions as these. As he suffered acutely from pains and infirmities during much of his life, we should try and learn at the outset what were the facts about his physical condition, since the degree of his blameworthiness for his lamentable frailties must be considered in relation to the extent of his bodily disorders.

We may begin, then, not at the beginning, or even at the end of the story, but after the end, because it was only after an autopsy that it was established that for many years his most vital organs had been radically impaired, as a result of adhesions of the membranes round the heart. His heart proved to be immensely enlarged. The right side of the chest was filled with fluid enclosed in a membrane, so that the lungs on both sides were compressed. It has been conjectured that his suffering would be sufficient to justify the use of narcotics, and that his feeble circulation might well require to be helped by stimulants. The physical derangements which were found to have developed must have originated when he was a young man, as a result, perhaps, of an attack of rheumatic fever. The establishment of the early origin is interesting, because it was when he was in his twenties that he first began to dose himself with opium, though it must be remembered that opium was in those days a normal analgesic.

His experimental doses of opium were probably moderate ones, such as might have been prescribed by a physician to alleviate acute pain. In later years, his addiction became serious, and he took much larger doses than medicinal ones. But whether the doses were large or only moderate, the habitual use of narcotics inevitably undermined his will-power, and a considerable consumption of alcohol, used as a stimulant, during a large part of his life, undoubtedly contributed to the same result.

Recurrent indisposition, and inability to grapple with his responsibilities, became manifest quite early in his career. He was both careless and unfortunate in regard to his health. A silly escapade at school induced his first attack of rheumatic fever; and damp rooms at Cambridge may have caused him further harm. He seemed persistent in his habit of failing to change out of wet clothes and boots, though he should have realized that his abnormal susceptibility made it essential that he should be careful in such matters. He was equally imprudent in the everyday affairs of life. Regularly, year after year, he made plans to earn enough money to maintain his family in a proper manner; and with equal regularity he failed to put the plans into effective operation. He had a self-indulgent tendency to undertake what was pleasant rather than what was necessary,

extending naturally to a selfish lack of consideration for
others, and, even further, under pressure of events, to disingenuousness and even deceit.

There are two conspicuously inconsistent aspects of Coleridge's character, as in the instances of other poets. On the one
hand, we have a man who, as soon as he started talking, proved
himself to be an outstanding conversationalist with towering
intellectual gifts and a vast range of knowledge, anxious to
share his brilliant ideas, and to help his literary colleagues in
promising exploits. During the earlier part of his life at least,
he was undoubtedly a lovable person. That he made a strong
appeal to his friends is proved by the faithful and self-sacrificing
attachment of many of them. Some of these friendships lasted
through most of his life, and through vicissitudes that would
have endangered many less steadfast allegiances. And, even as
he grew older, and, it would certainly seem, less engaging,
new friends came under his spell, and were ready to expend
their time, thought, and money on his welfare. On the other
hand, we have an utterly irresolute man, capricious and self-
centred, regardless of his essential responsibilities, becoming
increasingly enslaved by narcotics and stimulants, and, at a
late stage of his addiction, even bordering on moral degradation. Anyone studying this perplexing personality, with its
contradictory features, must have conflicting feelings. Our
attitude cannot be either that of pity or of aggravation, but
a mixture of the two: in what proportions, his letters can best
help us to decide.

When we contemplate the list of Coleridge's frailties, some of
them, to say the least, most disenchanting, we wonder how his
friends managed to remain as staunch to him as they did. Such
a friend was Thomas Poole, the owner of a tannery, and a
cultivated man, whom he came to know in Somerset shortly
after leaving Cambridge. This invaluable friend helped him to
find a house when he was married, and helped him to finance
some of his early literary ventures. He comforted and advised
him, sustained him both morally and financially, and remained
constant in friendship in spite of numerous provocations.
Daniel Stuart, the newspaper proprietor, who knew him at most
of the stages during which his failings developed into a sad
state of demoralization, never abandoned him, lent him

money when it obviously would not be repaid, and, towards the end, used to give him an annual present to cover the expenses of his holiday by the sea. John Morgan, at one stage, and James Gillman and his wife, at a later period, tended him and helped to restrain him from his grievous addiction in circumstances that would have broken the patience of less virtuous and devoted people. There were several other outstanding instances of loyalty and practical sympathy; and especial mention must be made of Wordsworth's support of Coleridge during the latter's younger days. The forbearance of some of his friends, it is true, gave out under stress; but only after many years of affectionate restraint. Robert Southey was eminent in sacrificing himself in looking after Coleridge's family when he failed to do so himself; but it must be admitted that, after a period in which he exercised notable patience, he did his rescue work rather from a sense of duty than from attachment to Coleridge. He had but small tolerance for a spineless character.

If, then, so many friends could remain constant to him for so many years, we should hesitate before giving rein to our exasperation at his moral debility. They knew him as we cannot know him; and we may be assured that a number of very sensible people, such as nearly all of them were, would not have behaved to him as they did without adequate reason.

One of the most notable testimonials to Coleridge's merits, at the period before his addiction became persistent, was written by his friend, Charles Lamb, who, in spite of occasional disagreements, remained on cordial and intimate terms with him for many years. Lamb wrote to a correspondent in 1800: 'I am living in a continuous feast. Coleridge has been with me now for nigh three weeks, and the more I see of him in the quotidian undress and relaxation of his mind, the more cause I see to love him, and believe him a *very good man*, and all those foolish impressions to the contrary fly off like morning slumbers. . . . He is uncommonly kind and friendly to me. . . . He tends me, amidst all his own worrying and heart-oppressing occupations as a gardener tends his young tulip.'[1]

There is a natural tendency in Coleridge's biographers to give prominence to his abnormalities of behaviour, and to the illustration of the tragic side of his life, for most of the available

H

evidence relates to these aspects. But, in spite of this emphasis, it must not escape our notice that, as a young man, Coleridge had a short period of married happiness, and for several years could be a lively and entertaining companion. One or two of his letters, written soon after he had married and had a son born to him, disclose him as a man with a buoyant, contented frame of mind. 'We have a very pretty garden. . . . We have likewise a sweet orchard. . . . Mrs. Cruickshanks is a sweet little woman, of the same size as my Sara—& they are extremely cordial. T. Poole's mother behaves to *us*, as a kind & tender mother—She is very fond indeed of my wife.—So that, you see, I ought to be happy—& thank God, I am so.'[2] Again: 'I never go to Bristol—from seven to half past eight I work in my garden; from breakfast till 12 I read and compose; then work again—feed the pigs, poultry &c., till two o'clock—after dinner work again till tea—from tea till supper *review*. So jogs the day; & I am happy. I have society—my *friend*, T. Poole, and as many acquaintances as I can dispense with— there are a number of very pretty young women in Stowey, all musical—& I am an immense favorite: for I pun, conundrumize, *listen*, & dance. The last is a recent acquirement—We are *very* happy—& my little David Hartley grows a sweet boy— & has high health—he laughs at us till he makes us weep for very fondness,—You would smile to see my eye rolling up to the ceiling in a lyric fury, and on my knee a diaper pinned, to warm.'[3]

At this time, and for some years after, he delighted in frivolous conversation. 'I laugh more', he said, '& talk more nonsense in a week, than most other people do in a year.'[4] Even after he had passed through some bitter experiences, and life had become far from carefree, this feature persisted. Southey described him as good company, and fond of all kinds of nonsense, like himself.[5]

Coleridge enjoyed being a cynosure, being in fact the central and much admired figure in a lively social scene. Though his health began to break down in 1801, he spent the winter in London trying to earn money in journalism. He evidently found time for some festivity, and he penned a vivid and spirited picture of his activities to his wife: 'I assure you, I am quite a man of *fashion*—so many titled acquaintances

—& handsome carriages stopping at my door—& fine *cards*—
and then I am such an exquisite judge of music and painting—
& pass criticisms on furniture & chandeliers—& pay such very
handsome compliments to all women of fashion that I do verily
believe, that if I were to stay 3 months in town & have tolerable health and spirits I should be a thing in vogue—the very
tonish poet & Jemmy Jessamy fine talker in town. If you were
only to see the tender smiles that I occasionally receive from
the Honorable Mrs. Damer—you would scratch her eyes out,
for jealousy. And then there's the *sweet* (N.B. musky) Lady
Charlotte—nay, but I won't tell you her name, you might
perhaps take it into your head to write an anonymous letter
to her, & disturb our little innocent amour.'[6] It is evident that
he wished to impress his wife with his popularity; and perhaps
he had a mind to enlarge her appreciation of him by inducing a
shade of jealousy. The letter is, of course, more revealing of
his interest in, and approval of, himself than an accurate
account of his life in town. It is also proof that there was a light-
hearted side to his disposition which was not easily damped by
adversity.

Few characters can comprise so incongruous a medley of
features as Coleridge's. It would seem quite unlikely that this
eager, vivacious, self-assertive young man should be, as in fact
he was, sadly lacking in toughness. He proved himself to be
incapable of standing up stiffly to life's trials, large or small.
When faced with any kind of emergency, he was apt to lose all
capacity for concentration and self-control, and to give way to
a self-pity and mawkish sentimentalism that, to a modern way
of thinking at least, is highly distasteful, and indeed almost
nauseating.

His moral instability was signally displayed almost as soon as
he was a free agent, and able to undertake a course of action
affecting his career, for, in a moment of mental turbulence, he
ran away from his College at Cambridge and joined a regiment
of dragoons under an assumed name, causing his brothers,
especially George, much anxiety and trouble. Three brief
extracts from his painfully abject letters to his brother, written
after he had been rescued from his predicament (for he found
the military life utterly intolerable), disclose him at his most
maudlin and sensational:

'My more than brother—What shall I say—what shall I write to you? Shall I profess an abhorrence of my past conduct? Ah me—too well do I know its iniquity—but to abhor! this feeble & exhausted heart supplies not so strong an emotion. O my wayward soul! I have been a fool even to madness. What shall I dare to promise? My mind is illegible to myself—I am lost in the labyrinth, the trackless wilderness of my own bosom. . . .'

'I am indeed oppressed—oppressed with the greatness of your love.—Mine eyes gush out with tears—my heart is sick and languid with this weight of unmerited kindness. . . .'

'Shall I confess to you my weakness, my more than brother! I am afraid to meet you—When I call to mind the toil and wearisomeness of your avocations, and think how you sacrifice your amusements, and your health . . . my soul sickens at its own guilt. . . . Indeed I long to see you, altho' I cannot help dreading it.'[7]

Anyone who is inclined to attribute Coleridge's flabbiness of character to his addiction to opium should notice that these hysterical letters were written before he had any recourse to narcotics.

His tendency to give way to mawkish sentiment in the face of an emergency is noticeable in his young married life, and again later, when he had to cope with matrimonial crises. About a year after he had married, he hoped to settle at Nether Stowey, under the Quantocks, where his friend, Thomas Poole, lived. He was relying on Poole to find him a cottage in the village. Poole, however, was doubtful whether Coleridge would prove a welcome resident, owing to his extreme political opinions, and he wrote to him accordingly. This comparatively small setback in his plans produced a distracted letter, which can be paralleled by others to the same recipient: 'The tumult of my spirits has now subsided; but the damp struck into my very heart; and there I feel it. O my God! my God! when am I to find rest! Disappointment follows disappointment; and hope seems given to me merely to prevent my becoming callous to misery! Now I know not where to turn myself. . . . Since I have returned, I have been poring into a book as a shew for not looking at my wife & the baby! By God, I dare not look at them. . . . Pardon me if I write vehemently—I meant to have

written calmly; but bitterness of soul came upon me. Mrs.
Coleridge has observed the workings of my face, while I have
been writing; and is intreating to know what is the matter—
I dread to shew her your letter—I dread it. My God! my God!
what if she should dare to think, that my most beloved friend
is grown cold towards me!'[8]

His infirmity of purpose became obvious at an early stage in
his marriage. As so often happened in later life, his good
intentions, elaborated in confident terms, soon went astray.
When he was proposing to Poole that he should live in a
cottage at Nether Stowey, he wrote: 'I mean to work *very
hard*—as cook, butler, scullion, shoe-cleaner, occasional nurse,
gardener, hind, pig-protector, chaplain, secretary, poet, re-
viewer, and omniumbotherum shilling scavenger—in other
words, I shall keep no servant, and will cultivate my
land-acre and my wise-acres, as well as I can.'[9] His plans were
further elaborated, as follows: 'To Mrs. Coleridge the nursing
& sewing only would have belonged—the rest I took upon
myself—& since our resolution, have been learning the
practice. . . . I should have devoted my whole head, heart, &
body to my acre & a half of garden land—& my evenings to
literature.'[10] All started propitiously, for difficulties in the way
of residing in Nether Stowey had been disposed of; and he
proudly informed a friend that 'both my hands can exhibit a
callum, as testimonials of their industry'.[11] But, within a year,
a friend visiting him noticed that the garden was full of weeds.

It was typical of Coleridge that he married without any
immediate prospect of being able to keep a family. Money-
matters perplexed and bewildered him; and he was never
throughout his life capable of maintaining a condition of
solvency. His financial troubles started within a few months of
his marriage, when he wrote to his kindly and generous
publisher, Joseph Cottle: 'The present hour, I am in a quickset
hedge of embarrassments, and whichever way I turn, a thorn
runs into me—The future is cloud & thick darkness—Poverty
perhaps and the thin faces of them that want bread looking up
to me! Nor is this all—my happiest moments for composition
are broken in on by the reflection of—I *must* make haste—I am
too late—I am already months behind! I have received my *pay*
beforehand!'[12] An early project for making money was by

means of a periodical, *The Watchman,* of which he was to be the organizer and main contributor. It soon came to a disastrous end, for he had no skill at the business side; and he wrote pathetically to Poole that he had lost and not gained by the venture. 'Meanwhile', he added, with a poet's natural turn for realism, 'Mrs. Coleridge asks about baby-linen & anticipates the funeral expenses of her poor mother.'[13]

After a period of nine months spent in Germany with the object of enabling him to produce a book on a German philosopher, and so to replenish the family finances, he returned to compose the great work; but it came to nothing. Next, he tried his hand at journalistic work in London for a brief period. Then, in 1800, he settled in the Lake District to be near Wordsworth, though he had told Poole that he would never leave him. Within a few months the climate at Keswick had an injurious effect on his constitution which had been undermined by the serious attack of rheumatic fever of his youth. A sharp recurrence of this illness followed on his getting wet through on a long walk; and this precipitated a temporary breakdown in health. He found that he could subdue the pain that racked him by means of regular doses of opium. It was at about this period that his addiction to narcotics became serious, though he had had occasional recourse to them as early as 1796. He evidently, like other addicts, had to increase the dose steadily, and was before long taking up to a hundred drops a day. His will-power, which had always been a weak point in his character, began, from this time, to be increasingly enfeebled.

As soon as his health permitted, he started to hatch new schemes for making a livelihood. He abandoned poetry, as he came to the conclusion that he never had the essential poetic genius; but we may suspect that he found that it required more concentrated effort than he was prepared to give it. He proposed to undertake a metaphysical investigation which gave no promise of monetary reward. He dallied with the study of the history of the Slavonic, Gothic, and Celtic languages; and, a little later, tried to involve Wordsworth in a scheme for chemical research, to be aided by a laboratory and a library of specialist books. This scheme was an even less promising money-maker than its predecessor; and he soon found it desirable to spend his winters in London to try and earn money from journalistic work. In this field, he was much aided by Daniel Stuart, the proprietor of the *Morning Post* and, later, of the *Courier*. Coleridge wrote Stuart a letter in regard to a scheme in which he and Southey would supply topical verses for publication in Stuart's newspaper. The letter reflects admirably on the respective qualities of Southey and himself, having, perhaps a broader application than Coleridge intended. He wrote: 'Southey & I do well together in this line; for I have always 50 subjects with all the ideas thereunto appertaining, but it is always a struggle with me to *execute*—and this Southey performs not only with rapidity, but takes great pleasure in doing it.'[14]

Most people in Coleridge's position would have felt bound to overcome a disposition to indulge themselves in the fanciful role of a carefree dreamer, superior to the necessity for concerning himself about money. But he was never able to divorce himself from this attitude. He made some ingenuous remarks on this subject when writing to his wife from London during one of the winters spent there, trying to improve his financial position. 'I have vexed & fretted myself that I did not send it [a draft of money for household expenses at Keswick] a fortnight ago—there was no earthly reason, why I should not. You know how hateful all money-thoughts are to me!—& how idly & habitually I keep them at arm's length.'[15]

He was as feckless and capricious in regard to his health as in regard to his responsibilities as a husband and father. Even after the practical warnings he had had of the seriousness of his physical limitations, he would undertake the wildest exploits on climbing or walking expeditions; and attacks of illness inevitably followed through failure to take elementary precautions. When he went on the famous Scottish Tour in 1803, he was, in his own view and that of his friends, in a precarious state of health. But, after he had divided from his companions, he walked half across Scotland, covering 263 miles in eight days. On another occasion, about the same time, he got soaked to the skin on a mountain top. A letter which he wrote to one of his many benefactors, Thomas Wedgwood, gives an impression of his incorrigibly irrational and irresponsible outlook: 'You ask, in God's name, why I did not return [from the climb up the mountain] when I saw the state of the weather? The true reason is simple, tho' it may be somewhat strange—the thought never once entered my head. The *cause* of this I suppose to be that . . . I never once in my whole life turned back in fear of the weather. Prudence is a plant of which I, no doubt, possess some valuable specimens—but they are always in my hothouse, never out of the glasses—& least of all things would endure the climate of the mountains. In simple earnest, I never find myself alone within the embracement of rocks & hills, a traveller up an alpine road, but my spirit courses, drives, and eddies, like a leaf in autumn: a wild activity of thoughts, imaginations, feelings, and impulses of motion, rises up from within me—a sort of *bottom-wind*, that blows to no point of the compass, & comes from I know not whence, but agitates the whole of me; my whole being is filled with waves, as it were, that roll & stumble, one this way, & one that way, like things that have no common master.'[16] This inflated, magniloquent bombast was all very fine, and may have served its purpose in impressing his correspondent; but he involved other people in his rashness; and his disregard of common prudence in this respect is but another example of his inability to impose on himself a reasonable degree of self-discipline.

Many of the weak points in his character are best exemplified against a background of his marriage and the history of his unhappy relations with his wife. Soon after his return from Germany, about four years after the date of his marriage, he went on a tour of the Lake District with Wordsworth; and at this time he met Sara Hutchinson, the sister of Wordsworth's wife-to-be. This outwardly unattractive young woman had in every other respect the qualities that appealed to Coleridge, in which his wife was to some extent deficient. Sara H. was placid, forbearing, and sympathetic. Especially was she sympathetic in regard to his literary exploits. Above all, she knew how to appreciate and applaud him. Like him, moreover, she had a lively sense of fun. Before he had known her long, he realized that he was in love with this Sara, and not with Sara, his wife, who was impatient of his frailties, especially his inability to earn a living. His wife not only failed to express her admiration of him; she made complaints about his neglect of her, and about his attachments elsewhere, particularly with the Wordsworths. Sometimes, it seems, she lost her temper at his aggravating habits; but she certainly had many grounds for complaint,

as we shall see from numerous instances of his selfishness and
his lack of consideration for her.

As the rift in his marriage was widening, and as his friendship
with Sara H. was growing warmer, he carried on a disingenuous
correspondence with his wife while at the same time writing
letters of affectionate intimacy to his friend. He had various
opportunities of seeing her when she was staying with the
Wordsworths at Grasmere. He pressed his wife most strongly to
countenance and approve his friendship with Sara H., and
pretended that his feelings were platonic, whereas he was
fully conscious that they were something more. His letters to
Sara H. contained remarks that leave little doubt about the
extent to which his tenderness for her had gone, such as: 'O
dear Sara!—how dearly I love you.' 'God bless my darling
Sara! . . . Bless you, my darling.'[17]

Coleridge's liability to become involved in such an intrigue
was largely due to his temperamental unsuitability to stand up
to the unintermitting stresses and responsibilities of matrimony.
He was not the man to relish the regularity and discipline of
married life. His friend, Daniel Stuart, writing shortly after
Coleridge's death, provides an amusing, and at the same time
discerning, picture of this aspect of the man: 'Coleridge could
not endure the cares of a family. Money was often required,
and hints were as often given that he might earn abundance by
his writings. In excuse for his retiring from his family, then at
Keswick, he said to me one day . . . that he was worried about
domestic affairs: that he was perpetually teased, among other
things about the cow; the cow this and the cow that, he making two
syllables of the word (kee-ow); the *kee-ow* was unwell; the kee-ow
was going to calve &c., he pronouncing the word peevishly.'[18]

When, however, he was away from home, he expressed
himself to be in a fever of anxiety about the health and welfare
of his children; and his letters to his wife contained frequent
passionate outbursts concerning the tortures of trepidation and
disquietude he was undergoing, accompanied by realistic
particulars of his own ailments. He was so terrified of bad news
that he used to leave letters he had received unopened for some
days. The basic explanation of all this extraordinary behaviour
is his concentrated interest in himself. When in Germany, he
wrote to his wife whom he had left in England: 'God bless you,

my love! write me a very, very long letter—write me all that
can cheer me—all that will make my eyes swim & my heart
melt with tenderness!'[19] Again, when he was in London three
years later, he wrote much in the same strain: 'My dear love—
write as chearfully as possible. I am tenderer, & more fluttery,
& bowel-weak, than most—I cannot bear any thing gloomy,
unless it is quite necessary.'[20]

There is no denying the fact that he was often inconsiderate
to his wife, trying though she may have been to him at times. He
never seemed to think that she needed a holiday. Not in-
frequently he went off himself on tours with Wordsworth and
other friends. Circumstances which might have kept most
husbands in the home did not confine him there. He was away
from home, in Wales, with his benefactor, Thomas Wedgwood,
when his daughter, Sara, was born. His wife had agreed that
this trip was necessary, or at least expedient, and he wrote to
her: 'O that I were now with you! I feel it very hard to be
away from you at this trying time—I dare not think a moment
concerning you in this relation, or I should be immediately
ill.' But he wrote again in a few days' time announcing that he
would soon be arriving at home with his travelling companion
as a guest, adding, as an additional instance of his deficient
sensibility, that his wife should not let the guest 'be any
weight or bustle on your mind'.[21]

But his lack of consideration in matters such as this is slight
in comparison with that involved in his disloyal behaviour
about Sara H. A month before his daughter was born, he wrote
a long letter to his wife which, for its deceitfulness, arrogant
effrontery, and patronizing airs, is without rival in all his
letters to her. This letter throws much light on Coleridge, the
man, especially his recurrent self-righteousness. It is, therefore,
quoted here at some length.

'My dear Love!' he wrote, 'let me in the spirit of love say two
things. 1. I owe duties, & solemn ones, to you, as my wife; but
I owe equally solemn ones to myself, to my children, to my
friends, and to society.Where duties are at variance, dreadful
as the case may be, there must be a choice. I can neither retain
my happiness, nor my faculties, unless I move, live, & love, in
perfect freedom, limited only by my own purity & self-respect,
& by my incapacity of loving any person, man or woman,

unless I at the same time honour & esteem them. My love is
made up $\frac{9}{10}$ths of fervent wishes for the permanent *peace* of
mind of those, whom I love, be it man or woman; & for their
progression in purity, goodness, & true knowledge. Such being
the nature of my love, no human being can have a right to be
jealous. My nature is quick to love, & retentive. Of those, who
are within the immediate sphere of my daily agency, & bound
to me by bonds of nature or neighbourhood, I shall love each,
as they appear to me to deserve my love, & to be capable of
returning it. More is not in my power. If I would do it, I
could not. . . . 2. Permit me, my dear Sara! without offence to
you, as heaven knows! it is without any feeling of pride in
myself to say—that in sex, acquirements, and in the quantity and
quality of natural endowments whether of feeling, or of intellect,
you are the inferior. Therefore it would be preposterous to expect
that I should see with your eyes, & dismiss my friends from *my*
heart, only because you have not chosen to give them any share
of *your* heart; but it is not preposterous in me, on the contrary I
have a *right* to expect & demand, that you should to a certain degree
love, & act kindly to, those whom I deem worthy of my love.'[22]

More than two years passed; and Coleridge had been to
Malta on a long visit, for the benefit of his health. On his
return, he felt determined to live separately from his wife;
their mutual aggravation was more than he could bear; and he
was still entrapped by his love for Sara H. After reaching
England, he delayed for some weeks before going to his home at
Keswick. But, when he went North from London, he first
called to see Sara H., before returning to his family, a very
significant order of events. He had written to his wife pretending
that he was detained in the South by business, and implying
that his real desire was to be at home. 'My heart aches so
cruelly', he told her, 'that I do not trust myself to the writing
of any tenderness either to you, my dear! or to our dear
children. Be assured, I feel with deep tho' sad affection toward
you; & hold your character in general in more than esteem, in
reverence.'[23] He was obviously hoping temporarily to evade the
issue by saying things which were plausible and, at the same
time, noncommittal.

It is difficult to find any justification for this kind of evasion;
and it may properly be qualified as hypocritical. In fairness,

however, to Coleridge, we should take note of some of the evidence in regard to Mrs. Coleridge's demerits as a wife, for she certainly gave him cause for a certain amount of irritation. Dorothy Wordsworth, a very percipient person, who would not have been consciously unjust to anyone, gave two impressions of Mrs. Coleridge, in 1801 and 1802. The earlier, which is mildly critical ran thus: 'She is much, very much to be pitied, for when one party is ill-matched, the other necessarily must be too. She would have made a very good wife to many another man, but for Coleridge!! Her radical fault is want of sensibility, and what can such a woman be to Coleridge? She is an excellent nurse to her sucking children (I mean to the best of her skill, for she employs her time often foolishly enough about them). . . . She is to be sure a sad fiddle faddler. . . .'[24] The later impression is decidedly unfavourable: 'Mrs. Coleridge is a most extraordinary character—She is the lightest, weakest, silliest woman! . . . So insensible and so irritable she never can come to good and poor C.!'[25] In considering the value of this latter opinion, we must remember that it may have been based to some extent at least on Coleridge's descriptions of incidents in his home life.

Coleridge himself supplied two interpretations of his wife's conduct, in letters to his friends in 1802. The first, to Southey, is coldly analytical. The second, to Thomas Wedgwood, is vivid and charged with deep feeling. To Southey, he wrote: 'Mrs. Coleridge's mind has very little that is *bad* in it—it is an innocent mind—; but it is light, and *unimpressionable*, warm in anger, cold in sympathy—and in all disputes uniformly *projects* itself *forth* to recriminate, instead of turning itself inward with a silent self-questioning. . . . Mrs. C. is so stung by the very first thought of being in the wrong that she never amends because she never endures to look at her own mind at all, in its faulty parts—but she shelters herself from painful self-enquiry by angry recrimination.'[26] (It is a pity that Coleridge seemed unable to analyse his own defects with equally penetrating efficiency.) To Thomas Wedgwood, he wrote: 'After my return to Keswick I was, if possible, more miserable than before. Scarce a day passed without such a scene of discord between me & Mrs. Coleridge, as quite incapacitated me for any worthy exertion of my faculties by degrading me in my own estimation. . . . If any woman wanted an exact & copious recipe, how to make a husband compleatly miserable, I could furnish her with one—with a probatum est, tacked to it.— Ill-tempered speeches sent after me when I went out of the house, ill-tempered speeches on my return, my friends received with freezing looks, the least opposition or contradiction occasioning screams of passion, & the sentiments, which I held most base, ostentatiously avowed—all this added to the utter negation of all, which a husband expects from a wife— especially, living in retirement—& the consciousness, that I was myself growing a worse man. O dear Sir! no one can tell what I have suffered. I can say with strict truth, that the happiest half-hours, I have had, were when all of a sudden, as I have been sitting alone in my study, I have burst into tears.'[27] Knowing, as we do, the extent to which he could dramatize and sentimentalize his experiences, we may assume that this description is exaggerated; but it doubtless has a basis of truth.

The inharmonious relations between husband and wife continued with but slight variation until their separation in 1806. In 1803, Coleridge had written to Poole: 'We go on, as usual—except that tho' I do not love her a bit better, I quarrel with her much less. We cannot be said to live at all as husband & wife, but we are peaceable housemates.'[28] At the time of the agreement for separation, Coleridge is quoted as complaining of his wife's 'self-encouraged admiration of Southey' and of 'her manifest dislike of me'.[29]

Unfortunately we have no letters of Mrs. Coleridge from which to gather her views about her husband's behaviour to her. There have, however, been preserved a series of letters from her to Thomas Poole, covering the years 1799 to 1834, which suggest that she was a sensible, and a reasonably cultivated and intelligent person. Various references to her in Southey's letters represent her as cheerful, lively, and somewhat eccentric, but one whose behaviour sometimes demanded more than a little patience. As a result of the evidence available to us, we are led to conclude that the wretched estrangement, which dragged on for many painful years, was due primarily to the egotism and moral instability of the husband, and to a less extent to the deficiencies of the wife.

Not long after their agreement to live separately, Coleridge spent some eighteen months as the guest of the Wordsworths at Grasmere. This lodging suited him admirably. He was treated not only with every consideration, but with immense forbearance and indulgence. Moreover, Sara H. was sometimes there to humour, flatter, and, quite undesignedly, to bewitch him. But, in spite of conditions which might seem propitious for his moral improvement, he continued his career of progressive demoralization. Dorothy Wordsworth, who had admired him and cherished his friendship for fifteen years, was now quite disillusioned, and told a friend: 'We have no hope of him. None that he will ever do anything more than he has already done. If he were not under our roof, he would be just as much the slave of stimulants as ever; and his whole time and thoughts, (except when he is reading, and he reads a great deal), are employed in deceiving himself, and seeking to deceive others. He will tell me that he has been writing, that he *has* written, half a *Friend* [the periodical that he was then promoting]; when I *know* that he has not written a single line. This habit pervades all his words and actions, and you feel perpetually new hollowness and emptiness.'[30]

For the next six years his slackness of purpose and inability to undertake responsibility became painfully marked. His famous quarrel with Wordsworth (see p. 85, above), though it had its origin in his abnormal behaviour as a guest, was perhaps as much Wordsworth's fault as his. But, when they were reconciled, and the Wordsworths wanted him to come from London to pay a visit and comfort them on the death of Wordsworth's little son, Thomas, he made no reply, though he had written a letter of condolence earlier on. His conduct was becoming so capricious that, if friendships were to continue, his friends had to exercise extraordinary tolerance.

It is not very easy to determine how genuine was Coleridge's devotion to his children. His feelings for them and his behaviour to them are worth considering in a general view of his character, as well as a means for assisting us to form an opinion about the sincerity of his attitude to his wife. His affection for his children was chiefly remarkable when circumstances were smooth and easy. If he became entangled in difficulties, he was inclined to think rather of himself than of them. When the children were small, his descriptions of them

were rapturous, and sometimes expressed in the florid, sentimental language characteristic of him. 'Hartley is all health &
extacy—He is a spirit dancing on an aspen leaf—unwearied in
joy, from morning to night indefatigably joyous.'[31] (He was so
pleased with the aspen-leaf metaphor that he used it on three
occasions, to three different correspondents.) 'From morning
to night', he said in another letter, 'he [Hartley] whirls about
and about, whisks, whirls, and eddies, like a blossom in a May-
breeze.'[32] Again: 'Hartley was breeched last Sunday, . . . O
bless him! bless him! If my wife loved me, and I my wife,
half as well as we both love our children, I should be the
happiest man alive—but this is not—will not be!'[33] The baby
Derwent aroused equal enthusiasm in him. 'Derwent, if I have
remained a long time without noticing him comes to me, &
says—Tiss!—He is such an angel!'[34]

When he was spending his winters in London, the question
arose of bringing back toys for Hartley. His affection for the
child was not then so obvious. In one year, he wrote to his
wife: 'I wish you would think of something that I may bring
Hartley—I have puzzled my head, & cannot think of any thing
that will at once delight him, & be durable.'[35] A year later he
wrote, evidently after having received a hint from his wife: 'I will
try and bring down something for Hartley; tho' toys are so outrage-
ously dear—and I so short of money—that I shall be puzzled.'[36]
The fact is, he was one of those parents who are prepared
to be uncompromising in the enjoyment of their children, but
who are not so sedulous in studying their interests and advantage.

A little later, when he had determined to go abroad for a
long stay, his expressions about the children were couched in
his most fulsome and unrestrained manner. He told his wife:
'I received your letter this morning—my eyes are still red with
crying over it, for joy & tenderness & sorrow of absence. O my
sweet Hartley! my darling—my own, very own Hartley! & my
stump! my pretty affectionate Derwent! . . . Be as minute about
the children as you can, never let any thing escape. You told
me nothing about sweet Sara. Tell me every thing—send me the
very *feel* of her sweet flesh, the very looks & motions of that
mouth. O I could drive myself mad about her!'[37] And, from
Malta, he wrote: 'O my children! my children! I cannot write
their names. Even to speak of them is an effort of courage.'[38]

But, when he reached England again, in August 1806, after a stay of many months abroad, he was afraid to go home, knowing that he could no longer live with his wife, and fully conscious that he was still in love with Sara H. Weeks passed; and it was only at the end of October, after having seen Sara H. in the North, that he reached his home at Keswick. We are bound to conclude that his affection for his children was not as intense as he represented it to be in his letters. He was prepared to wait more than two months after reaching England before seeing them, on some unconvincing excuses about being detained by necessary business in London. There seems to have been both truth and untruth in a letter which he wrote to his wife at the end of September, having waited several weeks in London before doing so: 'I love them [the children] so, that I retire back from the exceeding love I bear them, like a coward— I seem to myself too weak to bear the burden of my own heart.'[39]

After he had separated from his wife, he was content to disburden himself from his responsibility for his children's upbringing and education, and to leave the arrangements in the hands of the magnanimous Southey, in whose house his wife and children made their home. Owing largely to the extent to which his addiction to narcotics and stimulants had gone, he was always short of funds, because this depravity handicapped him from undertaking much steady mental exertion. Moreover, it was at one time said of him that his expenditure on opium and brandy alone used up most of his limited income. The school-fees of his sons and their expenses at the University had to be provided by subscriptions from friends and other means of a charitable kind. From time to time, he made some display of interest in his children's welfare; and, when Hartley reached the undergraduate stage, he had him to stay with him at Highgate during some of his vacations, where he himself was being lodged and cared for by a devoted medical practitioner, James Gillman.

In 1817, he wrote a letter to his wife, like many others of the Highgate period, full of aspirations and good intentions, and arranging for her to be credited with £50. 'For the rest I can only say that you or the children will have every shilling beyond my necessities.'[40] It would seem that he constantly aimed at sending part of his slender income to his wife, and sometimes succeeded. He claimed that he had paid Hartley's expenses when staying with him in vacations.

When, in 1820, Hartley's probationary Fellowship at Oriel College, Oxford, was not continued because the College authorities did not think well of him, Coleridge was highly indignant, and paid a fruitless visit to Oxford to try and retrieve matters. But he was even more pained because his luckless son did not come to him for comfort, but went North. 'My very name', he wrote to Derwent, 'appears not to have occurred to him. . . . Oh! if he knew how much I feel *with* him as well as how much I suffer for him, he could not so forget that he has a most affectionate friend as well as father in S.T.C.'[41] But, when, in 1822, poor Hartley had given way to drink, his father was ready to forward a plan to provide him with a post as assistant-schoolmaster in a village school near Keswick; and, thereafter, father and son never met again. In writing to his wife, in 1827, Coleridge mentioned Hartley, 'who is seldom, an hour together, out of my head, and still less *off* my heart'.[42] It is fair to add that, in 1829, he proposed to send to his wife £50 (the amount of a legacy received by him) 'to lay out, as she thinks needful, for dear Hartley'.[43]

Coleridge's later years, not unlike his earlier ones, were predominantly a history of good intentions, sometimes sincere, sometimes not, and mostly failing to reach fulfilment. When they failed, he regularly adopted the part of a luckless and aggrieved man of honour. He may have felt remorseful at failing in an obligation, but he soon forgot the matter; and the same farcical proceeding would shortly be re-enacted. He once wrote to his patient friend, Daniel Stuart, the newspaper proprietor, asking for a loan: 'Few things oppress my conscience so much, as my repeated non-performance of what I had engaged, and God knows! both meant and expected to have done for you; but in that instance the delicacy and generosity on your part toward me have always alleviated, often removed, the feeling.'[44] Another letter, to a publisher, some years later, asking for a loan and making similar protestations, is typical of his unfailing belief in the efficacy of good intentions. 'It is my intent', he declared, 'to devote the next six weeks undividedly to the Magazine, should I remain convalescent and without any serious relapse, and in order to thus be able to go to Ramsgate.

I

But for this I must seek some assistance from you—I venture to pledge myself, that no man on earth can accuse me of having received from him 5£ in advance, which was not liquidated by the promised work, or instantly returned—and I shall have deluded myself beyond all former experience, if the contents of my next parcel, which is all written, and requires transcription only, do not leave a balance in my favor, should you comply with my request to advance me 50£.'[45]

His son Derwent, as soon as he had grown up, received his particular confidences in regard to his literary and financial projects. When Derwent was twenty-one, his father wrote to him: 'I hope to make a little money within a month or six weeks: and if I can only prevent *my* debt to my more than disinterested friends [the Gillmans] from accumulating, in the course of the present year—and prevent your being in debt at all, I shall be tranquil, and hope for better times. Could I produce any work that should become popular, I might, I doubt not, sell the copy-right of an edition of my poems, biography etc. that have been out of print, for a sum that would go some way towards reimbursing my best friends, Mr. & Mrs. Gillman, whose very virtues do at times throw me into a gloomy mood.'[46] His letters include many examples of such hopeful schemes, whose non-fulfilment did not prevent a succession of pathetic repetitions of the same procedure. Although the pattern of his life at this period was doubtless not tedious or grotesque to him, it would seem monotonous and colourless to us if the man were not so remarkable, and if his behaviour did not provide us with so many interesting problems.

For many years during the period of his addiction to drugs, and even when this was reaching its most immoderate stage, about 1811, he maintained that he was morally blameless, and the victim of misfortune. At that time, he represented himself to his friend, John Morgan (who for many months was heroic in trying to restrain him from utter degeneracy) as an injured rather than a guilty person. Whether he sincerely believed this, whether he was deluding himself, or whether he knew that he was being dishonest, it is difficult to determine. He wrote to Morgan: 'I dare affirm that few men have ever felt or regretted their own infirmities more deeply than myself—they have in truth *preyed* too deeply on my mind, and the hauntings of regret have injured me more than the things to be regretted. . . . My present distracting difficulties which have disenabled me from doing what might have alleviated them, I must get thro' or sink under, as it may happen. Some consolation—nay, a great consolation—it is that they have not fallen on me thro' any vice, any extravagance or self-indulgence; but only from having imprudently hoped too highly of men. . . .'[47]

When, however, he reached the very nadir of his degradation, he relinquished his pretence of guiltlessness, as a relief, perhaps, to his weariness of spirit. He made a complete and characteristically fulsome avowal to his old friend, Joseph Cottle, his first publisher, to whom he was much indebted monetarily and otherwise. As might be expected from a man whose letters were often, as we have seen, couched in terms of unrestrained sentiment, parts of this *exposé* are written in that strain. But it does not seem necessary to assume that he was exaggerating his culpability, though there are likely grounds for supposing that he hoped that his pathetic condition would induce Cottle to afford him financial assistance. It will be noticed that the mention of his need for money is introduced obliquely towards the end of the letter.

'The object of my present reply', he said, 'is to state the case just as it is. First, that for ten years the anguish of my spirit has been indescribable, the sense of my danger staring, but the consciousness of my GUILT worse, far worse than all. I have prayed, with drops of agony on my brow, trembling not only before the justice of my Maker, but even before the mercy of my Redeemer. . . .

'Secondly, overwhelmed as I am with a sense of my direful infirmity, I have never attempted to disguise or conceal the cause. On the contrary, not only to friends have I stated the whole case with tears and the very bitterness of shame, but in two instances I have warned young men, mere acquaintances, who had spoken of having taken laudanum, of the direful consequence, by an awful exposition of the tremendous effects on myself.

'Thirdly, though before God I cannot lift up my eyelids, and do not despair of His mercy, because to despair would be adding crime to crime, yet to my fellow-men I may say that I was seduced into the ACCURSED habit ignorantly. . . .

'Suffice it to say, that effects were produced which acted on me by terror and cowardice, of pain and sudden death, not (so help me God!) by any temptation of pleasure, or expectation, or desire of exciting pleasurable sensations. . . . Had I but a few hundred pounds, but £200—half to send to Mrs. Coleridge, and half to place myself in a private madhouse, where I could procure nothing but what a physician thought proper, and where a medical attendant could be constantly with me for two or three months (in less than that time life or death would be determined), then there might be hope. Now there is none!! . . . You bid me rouse myself: go bid a man paralytic in both arms, to rub them briskly together, and that will cure him. "Alas!" he would reply, "that I cannot move my arms is my complaint and my misery." '[48]

If we admit that Coleridge must have suffered, from early manhood, pains which justified the use of narcotics in medicinal doses, he was not blameworthy provided he believed that these would make his life more tolerable. It is, however, doubtful whether he believed that a systematic indulgence in narcotics would be beneficial, for, as early as 1803, he told Southey that laudanum and brandy 'make me well during their first operation; but the secondary effects increase the cause of the disease'.[49] In so far as he was not blameworthy for his early addiction, some of the unhappy results flowing directly from it, such as his infirmity of purpose, may not be entirely his responsibility; and it might even be argued that secondary results, such as the unhappiness he caused to others, could not be specifically laid to his charge.

We have no need to be eager to adopt a judicial attitude in regard to these questions. We can be satisfied with as clear a view of this man of genius as the undisputed facts allow. In our efforts to gain this view, we are drawn in opposite directions. A man who is, time after time, displaying deplorable weakness of character, often to the detriment of others, arouses our exasperation, and even indignation. A man who is constantly suffering acute physical pain from no fault of his own, and who becomes involved in moral suffering as a result of attempts to subdue his physical suffering, arouses our compassion. If there is a doubt, in such a case, which of these two responses should prevail, the decision should be an easy one.

7

GEORGE GORDON, LORD BYRON
(1788–1824)
Reckless Brilliance

MANY men of genius have characters with notable in-congruities, characters that include both attractive and disagreeable features. Sometimes we lack sufficient evidence to enable us to be sure which of these predominate. Pope, for instance, is in this respect something of an enigma, for he made it his business to beguile his contemporaries about himself; and, in spite of modern investigations, has succeeded in still mystifying us today. No character could have had more striking contradictions than Byron's. But, with him, it is easy to gain a pretty clear notion of the balance of his qualities. Although he was much inclined to affectation, his contrivances were easily exposed; and anyone with a modicum of discernment could see through them. He was not of a calculating nature, like Pope.

The outstanding feature of Byron's disposition was his passionateness. He was frequently quite unable, or unwilling, to exercise self-control. Sometimes his excitable temper involved him in extravagant modes of expression. Nothing was held back; every thought, every feeling was evident and unmistakable. His impetuous manner is widely exemplified in his letters. Indeed, he was apt to write with such zest and verve that his self-revelation was profuse.

He has been dubbed an egotist; and he certainly merited that description more than most. But he was not so self-centred as to be unable to understand the reciprocities of friendship. Lytton Strachey characterized him both as incapable of friendship and so egotistical that his letters were concerned with one subject, and one alone, himself.[1] These assertions are hardly sustainable. In friendship he was unquestionably eccentric; he lacked sympathy and sensibility; and he often tried the patience of his friends. Nevertheless he was by no means without affection; and many of his letters prove him to be much more than a mere opportunist. His letters are vivid, racy, full of gusto, like their writer; and, in his earlier years, he sometimes asked his friends to tell him about themselves. He once concluded a letter to his friend, Thomas Moore, the poet: 'Write to me, and tell me of *yourself*. Do you remember what Rousseau said to someone—"Have we quarrelled? you have talked to me often and never once mentioned yourself." P.S. The last sentence is an indirect apology for my egotism,—but I believe in letters it is allowed.'[2]

His letters from abroad, comprising a big proportion of his correspondence, are full of highly entertaining descriptions of experiences and adventures; and this is evidence of his desire, perhaps only half-conscious, to give pleasure to his friends. From the nature of things letters written from a foreign land must be largely first-personal, since a man away from home and homeland must rely on his correspondents for help and counsel. But, where there was occasion for discussion of, say, literary subjects of common interest, he made use of it.

Moreover, a spirited and expansive letter-writer naturally assumes that he is entitled to indulge himself freely in self-expression without being classed as being self-centred.

Some of his letters to his wife, written immediately after their separation, as well as those written to her in later years, provide excellent examples of the way in which a variation in the tone of his language plainly declared his changing mood. As soon as it was obvious that his wife did not mean to live with him again, he wrote in agitated phrases which move rapidly from indignant and almost defiant protest to a profession of conciliation and tenderness. 'I have invited your return; it has been refused. I have requested to know with what I am charged; it is refused. Is this mercy or justice? We shall see. And now, Bell, dearest Bell, whatever may be the event of this calamitous difference, whether you are returned or torn from me, I can only say in the truth of affliction, and without hope, motive, or end in saying what I have lately but vainly repeated, that I love you, . . . and shall do, to the dregs of my memory and existence.'[3] There is no artifice or affectation in these words: his feelings are accurately portrayed. And, if we read between the lines of his letters to friends, written after he had gone to his exile abroad, we can find confirmation of his persistent love for his wife, and the lasting pain that the separation caused him.

As the years passed, his attitude changed from that of sullen resentment to that of mild embitterment. A letter which he wrote to his wife on matters of business accurately reflects this later mood: 'I acknowledge your note which is on the whole satisfactory—the style is a little harsh—but that was to be expected—it would have been too great a peace-offering after nearly five years—to have been gracious in the manner, as well as in the matter.'[4]

The breakdown of his marriage, and the rancorous attitude of his aristocratic acquaintances drove him from England, and left him with a lasting soreness in the most sensitive part of his nature, his pride. Though deficient in the ability to exercise steady will-power, he was ambitious for fame. His vanity was immense, and of the kind that depends for its satisfaction on attracting attention. Prominent among his means for attaining this end was his solicitude for his good looks and his figure, on which he lavished inordinate care. Indeed, this was the only

department of his life in which he displayed any notable
tenacity of purpose. His 'slimming' régimes were both strenuous
and unremitting.

He scarcely condescended to imply that he was more amply
endowed with brilliant and attractive qualities than other
people. He seemed to have an inherent haughtiness which
assumed that his fellow-men would defer to him, not so much
because he was their superior as because he was his illustrious
self. So fascinated was he by the limelight of celebrity that he
would, on occasion, perversely flaunt his vices. He delighted in
being talked about as much as he delighted in talking about
himself. If people displayed their stupidity in believing the
exaggerated stories he invented about his exploits, he gained a
particular pleasure.

His need to be conspicuous was paramount; and he found
that an admirable way of succeeding in this guise was by being
singular. Accordingly, he would often adopt an unpopular line
in conversation. If he could not have both admiration and
notoriety, he would at least have notoriety; and, when he talked
for effect, he did not mind if he lost the good opinion of the
few, provided he gained the attention of the many.

Among the various inconsistencies in his behaviour, one of
the most obvious is that between his appetite for popularity
and his supercilious demeanour. His ingrained arrogance
inclined him to aloofness and self-sufficiency; and, for considerable periods in his career, this aspect of him predominated.
Many of his letters disclose an antagonism between his need for
the comforts and consolations of friendship on the one hand, and
a proneness to solitary musing and a vague distrust of his
fellow-men on the other. This latter feature in his disposition
can be attributed in part to the unhappy circumstances of his
upbringing. In his childhood, his mother, a woman of coarse
mind whose conduct was wild and unpredictable, behaved
to him in a way well calculated to warp his nature, and so ruin
the prospect of his future happiness. She drove him to seek
solace, and place reliance, in himself alone, by reason of her
contemptuousness of the physical defect of his deformed foot
and other alleged imperfections. The effect of such brutal
treatment on him, as on any child with serious handicaps, must
have been profound.

His letters to his half-sister, Augusta, written at the age of
sixteen, give a painful picture of the unhappiness his mother
caused him. He spoke of his 'tormentor, whose *diabolical*
disposition . . . seems to increase with age', and of her 'out-
rageous conduct' which 'forfeits all title to filial affection'.
He wrote in more measured terms when he said: 'Her temper
is so variable, and, when inflamed, so furious, that I dread our
meeting; not but I dare say, that I am troublesome enough, but
I always endeavour to be as dutiful as possible.' At the age of
eighteen, he refused to live with her; and, at the age of twenty,
he declared he could never forgive her.[5] With our knowledge
of Byron's susceptibility to strong feeling, we may suspect an
exaggeration in some of these remarks; but there is independent
evidence of his mother's harsh treatment of him.

Doubtless his youthful experiences contributed to his
tendency to confront the world as a solitary contestant, relying
on himself alone to battle his way to fame. When he had
reached manhood, and after he had suffered some bitter experiences, especially the collapse of his social ambitions, combined
with the stigma of his exile in Italy, his predisposition to excessive
self-reliance was naturally aggravated. Among his consolations when abroad was his correspondence with his much-
beloved half-sister; but, in a mood of despondency, he could
harshly reject even so tender a sympathy as hers: 'as for me—
leave me to take care of myself. I may be ill or well—in high
or low spirits—in quick or obtuse state of feelings—like any
body else, but I can battle my way through. . . .'[6]

Nevertheless, like many other supposedly self-sufficient
persons, he was, in fact, much reliant on friendships, especially
in crises where sympathy was likely to be an anodyne. It was,
indeed, highly ironical that, with one exception, the occasion
on which he felt himself most in need of friends was the death
of his mother. In spite of all the discord there had been between
them, her death moved him deeply. But his particular need for
friendship at that time was attributable to the death, almost
simultaneously, of two close friends, Wingfield and Matthews.
He began to feel that his comradeships were crumbling. Soon
after his mother had died, he wrote to a friend: 'My dear
Scrope, if you can spare a moment, do come down to me—I
want a friend! . . . come to me Scrope, I am almost desolate—

left almost alone in the world.'[7] To another friend he wrote: 'My friends fall around me, and I shall be left a lonely tree before I am withered. Other men can always take refuge in their families; I have no resource but my own reflections. . . .'[8] And to yet another: 'You will write to me? I am solitary, and I never felt solitude irksome before.'[9] But how characteristic of the man that, when he succeeded in getting an old friend to stay with him, he found that he and his friend knew so much about each other that 'we have nothing *new* to say on any subject, and yawn at each other in a sort of *quiet* inquietude.'[10]

It was to his most intimate friend of that period, John Cam Hobhouse, that he disclosed his complex self in the face of his bereavements, and especially in regard to the loss of their common friend, Matthews: 'I am very lonely, and should think myself miserable were it not for a kind of hysterical merriment which I can neither account for nor conquer; but strange as it is, I do laugh, and heartily, wondering at myself while I sustain it. I have tried reading, and boxing, and swimming, and writing, and rising early, and sitting late, and water, and wine, with a number of ineffectual remedies, and here I am, wretched, but not "melancholy or gentleman-like".'[11]

Though Byron sometimes gave to others than Hobhouse the title of 'best friend', Hobhouse was the one who understood him best. They enjoyed the same absurdities, and could squabble without any serious results ensuing. Byron wrote to him with characteristic whimsicality in the later stage of his Grand Tour: 'After all, I do love thee, Hobby, thou hast so many good qualities, and so many bad ones, it is impossible to live with or without thee.'[12] In London once, he wrote to him: 'You can't conceive how I miss you', adding that there were so many things they would laugh at together 'that I yearn for you prodigiously'.[13] Later, at the end of a visit of Hobhouse to him in Venice, he wrote: 'I miss you damnably.'[14] And, near the end of his life, he again had Hobhouse as a guest in Italy. When they parted, he showed his affection for him in the old playful way: 'Hobhouse, you should never have come, or you should never go.'

Another friend for whom he had a genuine, lively, and lasting affection was Thomas Moore, the poet—a man whose talents, charm, and nobility of character made him a worthy subject of regard. Byron delighted in his company when they met in London in the years preceding his exile. 'Thomas', he once remarked to him, 'thou art a happy fellow; but if you wish me to be so, you must come to town, as you did last year; and we shall have a world to say, to see and to hear.' There was no one, he said, that he would rather turn to for consolation. And on Moore ending a London visit, he was, he felt, unable to describe how his heart sank at his departure.[15] Many of Byron's letters to Moore are proof of an unmistakable solicitude for his welfare, and for his success in the literary field. When Moore's famous poem, *Lalla Rookh*, was about to appear, he told him: 'Really and truly, I want you to make a great hit, if only out of self-love, because we happen to be old cronies; and I have no doubt you will. . . .' And when he had seen some preliminary extracts, he wrote: 'I suspect you have written a devilish fine composition, and I rejoice in it from my heart.'[16] Byron was not the man to indulge in sentimental expressions of affection; but it is easy to discern in his letters a genuine devotion to Tom Moore, if we duly discount the habitual breeziness of his manner of writing.

In the light of his correspondence with Hobhouse and Moore, no one should assert, as did Lytton Strachey, that Byron was incapable of friendship. And, of course, many other proofs could be adduced. Nevertheless, he had a freakish habit of speaking lightly of his friendships—evidently an outcome of his imagined self-sufficiency. He was apt to imply that Lord Clare, for whom he had formed a strong affection at school, was in a class alone, and that his other friendships were 'men-of-the-world' ones. This was certainly not true, though it is possible that he allowed his lofty pretensions to deceive him.

His intellectual arrogance disposed him to fancy that he was efficient at appraising the characters of his friends; and he took a pleasure in analysing them. This propensity must inevitably have diminished the warmth and spontaneity of his attachments. He even analysed the characters of his mistresses, which we might suppose that he would judge instinctively, or take for granted. Soon after he reached Italy, after having been deserted by his wife, he wrote to his publisher, John Murray, on whom he lavished many of his confidences: 'I am very well off with Marianna, who is not at all a person to tire me;

firstly, because I do not tire of a woman *personally*, but because they are generally bores in their disposition; and, secondly, because she is amiable, and has a tact which is not always the portion of the fair creation; and, thirdly she is very pretty; and fourthly—but there is no occasion for further specification.'[17]

Later on, he acquired a more permanent inamorata, the Countess Guiccioli: 'She is pretty, a great coquette, extremely vain, excessively affected, clever enough, without the smallest principle, with a good deal of imagination and some passion. She had set her heart on carrying me off from Venice out of vanity, and succeeded, and having made herself the subject of general conversation has greatly contributed to her recovery. . . . You may suppose what *esteem* I entertain for *her*. Perhaps it is about equal on both sides.'[18] As this description was given to his half-sister, Augusta, it is permissible to suspect that it is painted in not too glowing colours.

It is completely typical of Byron that his various liaisons prompted him to ponder deeply on the philosophy of irregular unions. Some remarks of his, on the disadvantages suffered by a mistress, comprise a masterly analysis. 'The humiliations and vexations a woman under such circumstances is exposed to cannot fail to have a certain effect on her temper and spirits, which robs her of the charms that won affection; it renders her susceptible and suspicious; her self-esteem being diminished, she becomes doubly jealous of that of him for whom she lost it, and on whom she depends; and if he has feeling to conciliate her, he must submit to a slavery much more severe than that of marriage, without its respectability.'[19] The factors are calmly assessed; but there are also, in the phraseology, evidences of emotion, disclosing to us a little of the impressions Byron derived from his own experience.

Some remarks of his, made when he was present on the occasion of Shelley's funeral on the Italian coast, are suggestive of the acumen he tried to bring to bear in dissecting the characters of his friends. 'Stop a moment', he said, 'let me see the jaw. I can recognize by the teeth anyone with whom I have talked. I always watch the mouth; it tells me what the eyes try to conceal.' This was the kind of skill he practised on his wife immediately before they were married. What a pity he did not practise it earlier, for there were few women who could have

made him a happy husband: it would have required a woman
with the stern qualities of a disciplinarian cloaked by the
amiability of a paragon and the tolerance of a saint. He wrote
to his dear Lady Melbourne, whom he described as 'the best
friend I ever had in my life': 'She [Annabella] seems to have
more feeling than we imagined; but is the most *silent* woman I
ever encountered; which perplexes me extremely. I like them
to talk, because then they *think* less. Much cogitation will not
be in my favour; besides, I can form my judgments better,
since, unless the countenance is flexible, it is difficult to steer
by mere looks. I am studying her, but I can't boast of my
progress in getting at her disposition; and, if the conversation
is to be all on one side, I fear committing myself, and those
who only listen, must have their thoughts so much about them
as to seize any weak point at once.'[20]

It is interesting to conjecture how real was the love of
Byron for the wife he so seriously tried to understand. The
evidence for the period during which they lived together is
inadequate; and there are no letters to help us at that stage.
Some biographers of Byron assume that he treated his wife
monstrously during the period of their cohabitation. But a considerable authority on the subject has recently expressed the
view that there is no reason to suppose that he was ever
deliberately unkind to his wife, in word or deed.[21] We are,
however, tempted to inquire how far he sustained his solemn
assurance that he would love her 'to the dregs of my memory
and existence'. It seems highly probable that a consideration
of various phrases in his letters written from Italy after the
breakdown of his marriage should lead us to the view that,
although he indulged both in recriminations and unbenevolent
remarks, he felt tenderly for her to the day of his death. He
could, it is true, refer to her as 'the Mathematician', an
expression meant to imply a cold and calculating person, or,
more broadly, as a 'virtuous monster' and 'a cold-blooded
animal'; but he admitted to Augusta that 'she—or rather the
separation—has broken my heart: I feel as if an elephant had
trodden on it. I am convinced I shall never get over it, but I
try.' And, on another occasion, in writing to Augusta about
the impasse caused in negotiations regarding the child of the
marriage, he concluded: 'God knows that it is wretched enough

—at least for me.'[22] There are also other little indications, including even passages that seem at first sight to suggest inexor-
ability, which tend in the same direction.

During his life in Italy, he often lacked congenial company;
and some loneliness was inevitable. He claimed that, from his
earliest youth, he had a passion for solitude. This is undoubtedly
an overstatement—part of his effort to achieve a reputation for
singularity. But an inclination to indulge largely in quiet
communing with himself may have been strengthened in manhood as a result of his intolerance, and of his setting too high a
standard for the satisfaction to be obtained from social relaxation. He was social enough at Cambridge, and made a number
of friends there; his Grand Tour, however, seems to have encouraged a tendency to aloofness. He wrote to his mother, as he
was nearing home: 'I don't suppose I shall be much pestered
with visiters; but, if I am, you must receive them, for I am
determined to have nobody breaking in upon my retirement:
you know that I never was fond of society, and I am less so
than before.'[23] As we have seen, some sudden bereavements
made him temporarily change his attitude, though he soon
returned to it; and many entries in his journal of 1813-14
seem to establish a genuine craving for seclusion. Nevertheless,
as some of the entries imply, his idea of a solitary life included
a considerable measure of social activity:

'Sheridan was in good talk at Rogers's the other night, but
I only stayed till *nine*. . . . I only go out to get me a fresh
appetite for being alone.'

'The more I see of men, the less I like them.'

'I hardly ever go out—and when I do, always regret it.'

'Hobhouse says I am growing a *loup garou*,—solitary hob-
goblin. True;—"I am myself alone." The last week has been
passed in reading—seeing plays—now and then visitors—
sometimes yawning and sometimes sighing, but no writing,—
save of letters. . . . Do I regret it?—um!—"Man delights not
me", and only one woman—at a time.'

'Last night, *party*, at Lansdowne House. To-night, *party* at
Lady Charlotte Greville's—deplorable waste of time, and
something of temper. Nothing imparted—nothing acquired—
talking without ideas:—if any thing like *thought* in my mind,
it was not on the subjects on which we were gabbling. Heigho!

—and in this way half London pass what is called life.'[24]

We can assume, then, from these indications of sociality that Byron's claim to the role of an anchorite is a little exaggerated. But, in so far as it is tenable, it can hardly have done much to forward his plan for attracting attention by his unconventional behaviour. Many years afterwards, in Italy, he wrote in his diary: 'At present, I can mope in quietness; and like being alone better than any company—except the lady's whom I serve.'[25] Here, again, there seems, from the circumstances, little likelihood of dissimulation.

On the other hand, many entries in the journal of 1813-14, from which the above-quoted extracts come, read like conversations with an imaginary person, and therefore have the appearance of the diversions of a lonely man, engaged in mitigating his self-enforced solitude. We cannot be sure; but in order to assist a conclusion, a few examples are given here of the confidences he seemed driven to make to himself in default of some sympathetic companion.

'I wish I could settle to reading again,—my life is monotonous, and yet desultory. I take up books, and fling them down again. . . .'

'This journal is a relief. When I am tired—as I generally am—out comes this, and down goes every thing. . . .'

'A wife would be my salvation. I am sure the wives of my acquaintances have hitherto done me little good. . . .'

'I wish I had a talent for the drama; I would write a tragedy *now*. But no,—it is gone.'[26]

We might, perhaps, suspect that his journal was written with an eye to eventual publication; but this seems unlikely, for many of the entries are trivial and unimpressive, such as: 'Sleepy, and must go to bed.' We can probably believe Byron when he declared that this journal was a means of obtaining solace by confiding in himself.

Sometimes he asserted that he was essentially gay and sportive, when in the right company. He told Moore that his reputation for melancholy often proved useful in keeping 'common-place acquaintance' at bay, but that he was in reality 'a right merry and conceited fellow'. Some years later, he wished Moore to tell an acquaintance that he was not 'the misanthropical and gloomy gentleman he takes me for, but a facetious companion . . . and as loquacious and laughing as if I were a much cleverer fellow'.[27] When it suited him, he adopted the part of a man suffering from a constitutional melancholy that he could only overcome by remarkable efforts of will-power. During various periods in his life, he remarked in a diary, he suffered from extreme depression in the early morning; this in addition to his being throughout his life 'more or less ennuyé'.[28] There was undoubtedly a measure of affectation in all this. Once, when he had been particularly gay and brilliant in society, he mentioned to his wife how falsely he had been described as melancholy. She, a person of remarkably keen insight, protested to him that he was melancholy at heart, and only pretended to be gay.[29] There was doubtless truth on both sides. But, in spite of what they both alleged, he, in his passion for singularity, was quite capable of pretending that he was pretending to be gay, when he was really enjoying himself. The situation, however, was not often as complicated as that; and a letter he wrote to Hobhouse on board ship, on his way home from his Grand Tour, seems to support Lady Byron's view that much of his merriment was artificial. 'Dear Hobby', he wrote, 'you must excuse all this facetiousness, which I should not have let loose, if I knew what the devil to do, but I am so out of spirits, and hopes, and humour, and pocket, and health, that you must bear with my merriment, my only recourse against a Calentura [a tropical fever which induces sailors to jump into the sea].'[30]

It is clear that he was sufficiently unsociable to abominate ordinary mixed social parties, which, in his opinion, all resembled each other in being no more than unprofitable waste of time. It is even doubtful whether he could be unselfconscious enough to let himself go, and break out into irresponsible merriment even in a strictly male party. His friendships were handicapped by his excessively analytical mind; and his enjoyment of a jollification was evidently impeded in the same way. He described a convivial evening in which he had taken part as if he had been a detached spectator. 'Like other parties of the kind, it was first silent, then talky, then argumentative, then disputatious, then unintelligible, then altogethery, then inarticulate, and then drunk. When we had reached the last step in this glorious ladder, it was difficult to get down again without stumbling; and, to crown all, Kinnaird and I had to conduct Sheridan down a damned corkscrew staircase, which had certainly been constructed before the discovery of fermented liquors, and to which no legs, however crooked, could possibly accommodate themselves.'[31]

His letters from Italy, written in the prime of life, incline us to think that the kind of social activity which pleased him most was that of unsophisticated bohemianism. It could not be too free and easy or ungenteel. He claimed that he knew the natives intimately, and concerned himself closely with their everyday affairs. This method of life may not have been very profitable in the sense of yielding intellectual dividends, but it satisfied his basic need for candour and open-heartedness. Society in England had involved him in subtlety and affectation; but there was little point in attracting attention in a foreign country, where his compatriots were few, and where finesse would be lost on the natives. He doubtless found it a relief to discard his artificiality.

A story of the light-hearted way he confronted a major domestic crisis when living in Venice is proof of his suitability to a happy-go-lucky type of life. He wrote to his half-sister: 'As troubles don't come singly, here is another confusion. The chaste wife of a baker—having quarrelled with her tyrannical husband—has run away *to* me. . . . I am a little embarrassed with my unexpected acquisition. However, she keeps my household in rare order . . . ; we have turned her into a housekeeper.'[32] Another letter, written by him as a young man at Lisbon, depicts, in a jocular strain, both his zest for mixing with people as different as possible from those in London society, and his irrepressible high spirits: 'I am very happy here, because I loves oranges, and talks bad Latin to the monks, who understand it because it is like their own,—and I goes into society (with my pocket-pistols), and I swims in the Tagus all across at once, and I rides on an ass or a mule, and swears Portuguese; and have got a diarrhoea and bites from the mosquitoes. But what of that? Comfort must not be expected by folk that go a-pleasuring.'[33] A man who could be thus spirited and frivolous must have been excellent company when in the vein.

Most poets are warm-hearted; they would not be poets if they were not so; and Byron was no exception. His charitableness

K

was like himself, unconstrained. As a young man, at a time when his finances were considerably embarrassed, he lent, and then made a gift of, £1,500 to his friend, Francis Hodgson, who had become engaged to be married, and was anxious to pay his father's debts before entering upon matrimony. Byron appeared genuinely distressed that his action became known outside his intimate circle, and told Hodgson that the disclosure 'most fairly and fully' released him from any obligation for repayment.

When he was in Italy he had a creditable reputation for charity to the poor, and he is said to have spent a considerable proportion of his income in this way. Lady Blessington observed: 'He is peculiarly compassionate to the poor. I remarked that he rarely, in our rides, passed a mendicant without giving him charity, which was invariably bestowed with gentleness and kindness; this was still more observable if the person was deformed, as if he sympathised with the object.'[34]

His more energetic manner of interposing on behalf of unfortunates is illustrated by an incident he recounted in a letter to John Murray: 'I intended to have written to you at some length by this post, but as the Military Commandant is now lying dead in my house, on Fletcher's bed, I have other things to think of.

'He was shot at 8 o'clock this evening about two hundred paces from our door. I was putting on my great coat to pay a visit to the Countess G., when I heard a shot, and on going into the hall, found all my servants on the balcony, exclaiming that "a man was murdered". As it is the custom here to let people fight it through, they wanted to hinder me from going out; but I ran down into the street: Tita, the bravest of them, followed me; and we made our way to the Commandant, who was lying on his back, with five wounds, of which three in the body—one in the heart. There were about him Diego, his Adjutant, crying like a child; a priest howling; a surgeon who dared not touch him; two or three confused and frightened soldiers; one or two of the boldest of the mob; and the street dark as pitch, with the people flying in all directions. As Diego could only cry and wring his hands, and the priest could only pray, and nobody seemed able or willing to do anything except exclaim, shake and stare, I made my servant and one of the mob take up the body; sent off Diego crying to the Cardinal....

It seems that if I had not had him taken into my house, he might have lain in the streets till morning; as here nobody meddles with such things, for fear of the consequences— either of public suspicion, or private revenge on the part of the slayers. They may do as they please: I shall never be deterred from a duty of humanity by all the assassins of Italy, and that is a wide word.'[35] This letter, while significant of Byron's disregard of danger, also discloses his fondness for self-glorification, for the story he tells does not fail to draw attention to his intrepidity.

His kindnesses to fellow-authors in trouble amounted to more than the mere dispensing of money. He himself suffered some of the vexations of authorship, and was therefore qualified to have real sympathy for his colleagues. He was especially thoughtful about the difficulties of Coleridge; and he wrote to Moore about him: 'By the way, if poor Coleridge—who is a man of wonderful talent, and in distress, and about to publish two volumes of poesy and biography, and who has been worse used by the critics than ever we were—will you, if he comes out, promise me to review him favourably in the *Edinburgh Review*? Praise him I think you must, but you will also praise him *well*, of all things the most difficult. It will be the making of him. This must be a secret between you and me, as Jeffrey [the editor of the *Edinburgh Review*] might not like such a project; —nor, indeed, might C. himself like it. But I do think he only wants a pioneer and a sparkle or two to explode most gloriously.'[36] Unfortunately, this scheme went awry; and later he wrote to Moore: 'I am very sorry that Jeffrey had attacked him [Coleridge], because, poor fellow, it will hurt him in mind and pocket.'[37] There is a delicate sympathy, and completely altruistic goodwill shown here. About the same time, hearing that Coleridge was distressed for money, he sent him £100, at a period when his own creditors were pressing him closely.[38]

The considerable efforts that he made to help Leigh Hunt were not successful. Hunt's residence in Italy was supported by him to the extent of some hundreds of pounds. He told his friend Kinnaird that he was willing to give such help because Hunt had stuck by him 'through thick and thin when all shook and some shuffled in 1816 [i.e. when he was scorned by many at the time of the breakdown of his marriage]'. When his

attempts to help Hunt looked like failing, he wrote: 'I could not
see them [the Hunt family] in such a state without using the
common feelings of humanity, and what means were in my
power, to set them afloat again.'[39]

He had, it seems, a very poor opinion of such of the poetry
of Keats as he had seen. But when he heard that Keats had
suffered severely, and even been brought to his death-bed, as a
result of the cruel attack on his poetry that had been published
in the *Quarterly Review*, he wrote to Shelley: 'I am very sorry to
hear what you say of Keats—is it *actually* true? I did not think
criticism had been so killing. Though I differ from you essentially in your estimate of his performances, I so much abhor all
unnecessary pain, that I would rather he had been seated on the
highest peak of Parnassus than have perished in such a manner.
Poor fellow! though with such an inordinate self-love he would
probably have not been very happy.'[40]

He was stout in his defence of Shelley's character when many
of his colleagues in literature traduced him at the time of his
death. 'You are all mistaken', he wrote, 'about Shelley. You
do not know how mild, how tolerant, how good he was in
society.' And: 'As to poor Shelley who is another bugbear to
you and the world, he is to my knowledge the *least* selfish and
the mildest of men—a man who has made more sacrifices of his
fortune and feelings for others than any I ever heard of.'[41]
But, a little earlier, in Shelley's lifetime, he seems to have been,
to say the least, disingenuous in regard to the widespread
attacks on Shelley's character. If he was not actually deceitful
at this stage (on which there is some doubt), he was certainly
disloyal by reason of unworthy insinuations indulged in
conversation.

There is, moreover, a conspicuous instance in Byron's letters
which is inconsistent with Lady Blessington's view of him as an
essentially kindly man, and which discloses him as a perfidious
friend. At the time when he was living in Italy, he seems to
have come to the conclusion that his companion of earlier
days, Francis Hodgson, to whom he had shown great kindness,
and with whom relations had been close and cordial for many
years, was a time-server; and he wrote to John Murray, his
publisher, in terms that are not only spiteful but treacherous.
He said: 'I have read Parson Hodgson's *Friends* in which he

seems to display his knowledge of the subject by a covert attack or two on some of his own. He probably wants another living; at least I judge so by the prominence of his piety, although he was always pious—even when he was kept by a washerwoman on the New Road. I have seen him cry over her picture, which he generally wore under his left armpit. But he is a good man, and I have no doubt does his duty by his parish.'[42] Within the next eighteen months, however, we find Byron writing to Hodgson in most friendly fashion, having been prompted to do so by his half-sister, Augusta, and telling him that Murray had sent him the book, *Friends*, 'which I thought very good and classical'.[43] We must admit that Byron was double-faced in this conjuncture; and we shall have to draw attention later to an even more unpleasant characteristic of his, an occasional vindictiveness.

On the other hand, there is a critical test of a man's good nature which he passed triumphantly: he was consistent in his kindliness to subordinates and servants. With them, he could have remarkable patience; and, if they showed him devotion, he could reward it by genuine benevolence. His personal manservant, Fletcher, was evidently an exasperating fellow, unadaptable and sometimes inefficient; and yet Byron put up with him during years of his life abroad, for the reason that Fletcher was sincerely attached to him. From boyhood he was steadily solicitous for the welfare of an old family servant, Joe Murray. He would ask, in his letters, to be remembered to 'poor old Murray'; or would add: 'Don't forget to tell me how Murray is.' He made him an annual allowance; and, after his departure on his exile abroad, he told his solicitor to pay further moneys to him, 'poor old man'; and finally gave *carte blanche* for disbursements for his benefit.[44] There was, too, a fire-lighter, a woman, in his employ when he was a young man, who was old, and had noticeably unprepossessing features. When asked by a friend why he retained her in his service, he said: 'The poor old devil was so kind to me.'[45]

As with so many ardent characters, kindliness and bravery coexisted in Byron. His intrepidity is attested by many incidents in his career. One incident, related in a letter of his, is specially worth quoting, because it exemplifies the courage of both Byron and Shelley, each in his particular *genre*, at the same time. Byron wrote: 'He [Shelley] was once with me in a gale of wind, in a small boat, right under the rocks between Meillerie and St. Gingo. We were five in the boat—a servant, two boatmen and ourselves. The sail was mismanaged, and the boat was filling fast. He can't swim. I stripped off my coat—made him strip off his and take hold of an oar, telling him that I thought (being myself an expert swimmer) I could save him, if he would not struggle when I took hold of him—unless we got smashed against the rocks, which were high and sharp, with an awkward surf on them at that minute. We were then about a hundred yards from shore, and the boat in peril. He answered me with the greatest coolness, that "he had no notion of being saved, and that I would have enough to do to save myself, and begged not to trouble me". Luckily, the boat righted, and, baling, we got round a point into St. Gingo, where the inhabitants came down and embraced the boatmen on their escape, the wind having been high enough to tear up some huge trees from the Alps above us, as we saw next day.'[46] It would be easy to give other instances of Byron's fearlessness in the face of danger, both from the threats of nature and from those of man. His conduct in regard to the body of the dead commandant, quoted above, was an example of coolness in a situation which might well have become perilous. When he was in Greece, near the end of his life, some Greek sailors from the islands came into his room without invitation or permission, and insolently demanded the surrender of a prisoner. Byron had no intention of acceding to any such demand, whether supported by force or not. The sailors threatened force, but he pointed his loaded pistol at them with so much assurance that they blenched before him and withdrew.

His famous 'tumultuous passions' were doubtless not altogether to the disadvantage of his character, for without them he would not have been so exhilarating a companion. His generosity and good nature might have been less profuse; and his exploits, instead of being of the heroic type, as when he swam the Hellespont, from Sestus to Abydos, would have been on a more prudent scale. Other people could, perhaps, have done all these things, but not in his distinctive manner. On the other hand, uncontrolled emotions, being, as they unquestionably are, defective features in a man's character, must involve unpleasant traits, or at least grotesque disconformities.

Amidst a diversity of wild and irresponsible behaviour, Byron was able to impose on himself a measure of discipline in matters which seemed to him of essential importance. As we have remarked, his tendency to obesity was such a matter; and he exercised both restraint and resolution in combating the menace of an unbecoming figure. But the measures taken were all inordinate. He adopted the most injudicious of diets. For some long period he confined himself to vinegar and potatoes a combination of two ingredients well calculated, it would seem, to cancel each other out. At another time, his diet consisted of vinegar and water, and a little rice. Later on, it was six biscuits a day, with tea to drink. But he did not consider diet to be adequate treatment: he also used violent exercise. 'I have taken', he wrote as a young man, 'every means to accomplish the end, by violent exercise and fasting, as I found myself too plump. I shall continue my exertions, having no other amusement; I wear *seven* waistcoats and a great coat, run, and play at cricket in this dress, till quite exhausted by excessive perspiration, use the hot bath daily; eat only a quarter of a pound of butcher's meat in 24 hours, no suppers or breakfast, only one meal a day; . . . take physic occasionally. By these means my ribs display skin of no great thickness, and my clothes have been taken in nearly half a yard.'[47] After his return from his Grand Tour, during which he increased in weight, he dressed himself in a Turkish pelisse, and undertook a régime of boxing and sparring, so as to reduce his bulk. He broke away from these strenuous courses from time to time; and, when he did, it was in a characteristically abandoned fashion. He wrote in his journal: 'Stuffed myself with sturgeon, and exceeded in champagne and wine in general, but not to the confusion of head. When I *do* dine, I gorge like an Arab or a boa snake, on fish and vegetables, but no meat. I am always better, however, on my tea and biscuit than on any other regimen, and even *that* sparingly.'[48] A little later, he told Thomas Moore that he had nearly killed himself with eating a whole collar of brawn after he had already had an enormous dinner, with the result that he suffered from a prolonged attack of indigestion.[49]

With such outlandish habits, it is not surprising to learn that, at a period of his life as a young man, as well as in later life, he suffered from despondency, 'but accompanied with so violent a thirst that I have drank as many as fifteen bottles of soda water in one night, after going to bed, and been still thirsty—calculating, however, some lost from the bursting out and effervescence and overflowing of the soda-water, in drawing the corks, or striking off the necks of the bottles from mere thirsty impatience'.[50] At the end of the night his bedroom must have presented a dishevelled, indeed, a riotous appearance.

Much of his ungovernable temper was no more than a means of 'letting off steam', of which he certainly seems to have had an excess. This kind of behaviour generally affected no one but himself; but, quite often too, he behaved in a manner which involved his fellow-men. So violent could he be, and so adept was he at an encounter, that he frequently proved to be the successful party. He was thus inclined, as the years passed, to be increasingly disputatious. His irascibility and violence undoubtedly became more noticeable after the breakdown of his marriage. The tragic separation from his wife, the ignominy of his social ostracism, the unconventional life he led, all tended to induce a deterioration in his ability to exercise control of himself. His impetuous and high-handed manner is well illustrated in an incident which happened when he was out riding one day near Venice. The story, as recounted to Thomas Moore, might amuse us if we were not affected by disgust at his excessively arrogant airs. 'Last week', he wrote, 'I had a row on the road . . . with a fellow in a carriage, who was impudent to my horse. I gave him a swingeing box on the ear, which sent him to the police, who dismissed his complaint. Witnesses had seen the transaction. He first shouted, in an unseemly way, to frighten my palfry: I wheeled round, rode up to the window, and asked him what he meant. He grinned, and said some foolery, which produced him an immediate slap in the face, to his utter discomfiture. Much blasphemy ensued, and some menace, which I stopped by dismounting and opening the carriage door, and intimating an intention of mending the road with his immediate remains, if he did not hold his tongue. He held it.'[51]

His hot-headed impatience led him into transitory quarrels with John Murray, his publisher, and with John Hanson, his solicitor, though it is fair to say that both of them gave him a good deal of provocation. As to his stockbroker, he felt himself free to vent his towering passion on this harmless person without any attempt at restraint. He told Douglas Kinnaird, his patient and efficient business friend: 'You may give my compliments to Mr. Bland and tell him that I have no personal pique against him, for I do not even know him; but if the funds [i.e. Government securities] ever fail and I lose my property in them it is through *him* and his formalities, and by all that is dear to man I will *blow his brains out* and take what fortune may afterwards send me. I am perfectly serious, and pray tell him so, for as I have said so will I do.' This was no momentary outburst of temper, for he repeated his threat in another letter written a few days later.[52]

John Murray, his publisher, was well known for being dilatory and casual in his methods of correspondence; and Byron sometimes became exceedingly exasperated by him, and wrote to him in great indignation. More often, however, he treated him with a mixture of persiflage and playful intimidation. 'You sometimes', he told him, 'take the liberty of omitting [? part of] what I send for publication: if you do so in this instance, I will never speak to you again as long as I breathe.'[53] About the publishing of *Don Juan*, he wrote: 'Of Don Juan I hear nothing further from *you*—you chicken-hearted, silver-paper stationer, you! . . . You have . . . no more blood than a water melon.'[54] But he could express himself in a restrained manner to Murray, even under severe provocation, as when he wrote: 'All I desire is two lines, to say, such a day I received such a packet: there are now at least *six* unacknowledged. This is neither kind nor courteous.'[55]

After he had finally decided that he could not retain Murray any longer as his publisher, he received a letter from him which melted his heart, and he told Thomas Moore: 'The fact is, I cannot *keep* my *resentments*, though violent enough in their onset. Besides, now that all the world are *at* Murray on my account, I neither can nor ought to leave him; unless, as I really thought, it were better for *him* that I should.'[56]

On occasion, he could give way and apologise, and do so handsomely, which proves him to be less of the harsh and overbearing egotist that some of his letters would suggest. He told

Kinnaird: 'My letters were, I grant you, very impatient, but I regret very much that they should have "worked you".'[57] He was also capable of being submissive and amenable to advice, especially where it was a question of hurting harmless people's feelings. When Hobhouse protested about a passage in *Don Juan* which would have distressed Queen Charlotte, he agreed to omit it; and he assented to Kinnaird's taking it upon himself to disregard a request to forward a letter which he agreed, upon consideration, was a harsh one. To Murray, he wrote: 'You know very well that I did not approve of Keats's poetry, or principles of poetry, or of his abuse of Pope; but, as he is dead, omit *all* that is said *about him* in any *MSS*. of mine, or publication.'[58]

He prided himself on not being vindictive, but with incomplete justification. His letters to and about his wife, written from exile, are, it is true, inclined to become more good-natured as the years passed. Three years before he died, he told her: 'For my part, I am violent, but not malignant; for only fresh provocations can awaken my resentments. . . . I assure you that I bear you *now* (whatever I may have done) no resentment whatever.'[59] But a number of remarks of a caustic nature can be found in his letters regarding his wife's parents. His suspicion of a malevolent influence, exerted by his wife's mother, persisted for years. He once wrote: 'Lady Noel has, as you say, been dangerously ill; but it may console you to learn that she is dangerously well again.'[60] This was obviously, in part at least, playful. But he was capable, under peculiar provocation, of displaying a degree of vindictiveness that was discreditable, and quite inexcusable. Sir Samuel Romilly, a distinguished lawyer, who had acted in his legal capacity for Byron's wife's family at the time of the separation, committed suicide in pathetic circumstances, after the death of his wife. Byron thereupon wrote to John Murray in pitiless terms: 'I have at least seen Romilly shivered who was one of the assassins. When that felon, or lunatic (take your choice, he must be one and might be both) was doing his worst to uproot my whole family tree, branch, and blossoms; when, after taking my retainer, he went over to them; when he was bringing desolation on my hearth and destruction on my household gods, did he think that, in less than three years, a natural event—a severe domestic—but an expected and common domestic calamity,—would lay his carcase in the cross roads, or stamp his name in a verdict of lunacy? . . . But the wretch is in his grave. I detested him living, and I will not affect to pity him dead; I still loathe him—as much as we can hate dust—but that is nothing.'[61]

It is a relief to turn from this unhappy instance of implacability to the unfolding of his finer self at the conclusion of his life. When he found that he could take a leading part in the regeneration of Greece, he evidently at the same time experienced a profound regeneration in himself. We may be sure that he had had from his youth a latent ambition to undertake some constructive work that would benefit humanity, and perchance make him famous. This ambition remained firmly embedded in his consciousness. Seven years before he died, he told Thomas Moore that, apart from literature, 'I shall do something or other—the times and fortune permitting —that "like the cosmogony, or creation of the world, will puzzle the philosophers of all ages" '.[62] While he must often have felt that his life in Italy was empty and unprofitable, he suddenly had a full realization of the futility of a career pervaded by triviality and self-indulgence. His opportunity had come; and his transformation was quick and thorough. As the editor of some of his recently published correspondence, Sir John Murray, has remarked: 'There is a striking change in the tone of Byron's letters from this time forward: there is little of the banter and recklessness which characterize his earlier letters. As soon as he is brought face to face with real work and responsibility, his sound common sense, his clearness of vision, and his modesty as to his own capabilities are clearly evident.'[63] Self-interest which had previously been a leading motive in his plans and activities gave way to the much more attractive prospect of spending himself in a cause. And not only spending his energies, but spending freely of his money. In the preceding years, as a perverse result of inheriting a share in the property of his wife's family, he had become unexpectedly parsimonious. But, on reaching Greece, he all at once became prepared to give a large proportion of his fortune for the Greek cause. He even considered making available the proceeds of the sale of his Rochdale estate, amounting to some £34,000.

A few sentences from letters to friends, written within six

months of his death, can be used to illuminate his genuine ardour for devoting himself to the interest of Greece. His ever-dependable friend, Kinnaird, thought it proper to warn the impetuous Byron about excessive or ill-advised expenditure. Byron justified himself, and added that 'it is better playing at nations than gaming at Almacks or Newmarket'. And, later, he remarked: 'But let the Greeks only succeed, and I don't care for myself.' 'As I have embarked in the cause, I won't quit it; but "in for a penny, in for a pound". I will do what I can, and all I can, in any way that seems most serviceable.' 'We will do our best—and I pray you to stir your English hearts at home to more *general* exertion; for my part, I will stick by the cause while a plank remains which can be *honourably* clung to.'[64]

Byron's haughtiness, his reserve, his overbearing and satirical manner, his complete assurance that he was always in the right, his irrepressible eccentricity, his overweening desire to attract attention, are all reflected in his letters. So too are his pleasing features, such as a basic kindliness, generosity, fearlessness, and a vivacity that delighted his friends. In the same way that he was unrestrained in his less attractive qualities, he was unrestrained in his more attractive ones; and in the same way that he was unrestrained in his behaviour, he was so in revealing his qualities, both good and bad, in his correspondence. We have mentioned the incongruities of his character. No study of him, however elaborate, can explain them away; and the last phase of his life's story produces some surprises which render any attempt at simplification less feasible than ever. It is certain that Byron would have smiled at any such endeavour, and would have declared that the picture seemed as irrational to him as to anybody else. But, reckless and capricious madcap that he was, he would, we may guess, have hoped that his Grecian episode might be regarded as having redeemed for him an equivocal record of conflicting, and often misguided motives.

8

PERCY BYSSHE SHELLEY
(1792–1822)
Unconventional Idealism

THOUGH both Byron and Shelley were blessed, or cursed, with a profusion of ardent and vehement feelings, Shelley's temperament was less irresponsible than Byron's, for he always claimed to be guided by principle. Some people would assert that he was, in fact, guided by no other principle than that of licence; but this would be a harsh and undiscerning judgement, for he genuinely believed that, in his relations with women (and they were the controversial element in his career), he was subject to the paramount dictates of love, or of an ideal in which love was deeply involved. If love prompted him to become devoted to a new companion at the expense of an existing attachment, he would claim that he was not chargeable with neglecting the one whose star was in the descendant, for it was inherent in his philosophy that love must be obeyed. There are, however, so many people who cannot believe that anyone is at liberty to act on these tenets, that Shelley is sometimes characterized as a ruthless villain.

When a man's character is under critical review, there is no more pertinent and searching question to be asked than such a one as: Is he capable of habitual unkindness? If the answer is Yes, then there is no use attempting any defence of him in a court of morals. In Shelley's case, the question may be put in a more specific form:—Did his theory of the propriety, or indeed the necessity, of love leading where it wills (a theory bound to bring unhappiness in its train) lay him open to a charge of inhumanity? There is plenty of evidence to prove that he was fundamentally so tender-hearted a man, so overflowing with generous sentiments, that we can dismiss the possibility that he was wilfully regardless of other people's unhappiness. And yet a new love could have such overruling, all-absorbing significance for him that he seemed, on one or two occasions, to be heedless of the misery which his arbitrary behaviour was bound to entail.

Shelley's changing loyalties, from one woman to another, did not amount to inconstancy in the sense that it would with ordinary, sober-minded people. In his case, a new love was not so much an emotion aroused by a person, as one derived from a sublime, exalted theory that had captivated him. His first wife, Harriet Westbrook, prompted in him the ideal of chivalry. She needed to be rescued and succoured; and he believed the task would be an entrancing one, or at least he managed for some time to persuade himself into this belief. His second wife, Mary Wollstonecraft Godwin, symbolized his apotheosis of the beauties of the mind. Poetry, and the quality that calls for poetical expression, had then engaged his attention. In each change of loyalty, and there were several such episodes in his life, he was obsessed by an ideal; and the obsessions were so overmastering that the resultant effect on the persons involved in the drama was relatively unimportant to him.

A month before he died, he made a most revealing avowal in regard to this attitude of mind. He wrote in a letter: 'I think one is always in love [i.e. one always keeps falling in love] with something or other; the error, and I confess it is not easy for spirits cased in flesh and blood to avoid it, consists in seeking in a mortal image the likeness of what is perhaps eternal.'[1] In spite of his recognition of the evils inherent in his extreme sensibility, it is doubtful whether he, a man of intensely romantic feelings, could have avoided them. He would never have been so temperate as to be able to confine his compulsive ideals to the intellectual plane.

Not only was he fickle in his attachments to women, but, as an effect of his exuberance of mind, he sometimes found that it was not enough for him to be devoted to one feminine companion at a time. In this respect, as in some others, such as an ample degree of self-assurance when young, he resembled Coleridge, who, as we have noticed, claimed, in a perilous paradox: 'That we can love but one person, is a miserable mistake, & the cause of abundant unhappiness.' Coleridge was trying to justify his intimate love for two women at the same time; and he, like Shelley, found that, in practice, it was the attempt to love two women at once that was productive of 'abundant unhappiness'.

The expression 'blackguard' is occasionally attached to Shelley's name as a result of the supposedly inhuman and pitiless way he treated his first wife, and as a result of the extensive acceptance of the truth of malicious stories about his alleged illicit love for Claire Clairmont during the period of his second marriage. Some of his letters provide us with material which may help us to judge whether he was guilty of the charges of cruelty and immorality to which he was subjected during much of his life, or whether they were baseless calumnies. But, before proceeding to cite numerous passages from his correspondence, we may take note of a few instances of his notable kindness of heart. It is only proper that general evidence of his benevolence should be admitted in his defence. We can, no doubt, find instances of men who are, in some aspects of their life, gentle and benign, and in other aspects maleficent; but these instances must be very rare.

In the second year of his marriage to Harriet, while he was spending a bitter winter in Wales, workmen engaged on building a sea-wall nearby were suffering considerable hardships.

His friend, Medwin, wrote: 'I have often heard Mr. Madocks dilate on Shelley's numerous acts of benevolence, his relieving the distresses of the poor, visiting them in their humble abodes, and supplying them with food and raiment during the winter.' About a year after his second marriage, he was living at Marlow, where the local lace-makers were enduring conditions of privation owing to the failure of the market for their goods. Shelley's friend, Peacock, has left record that he went continually among the poor, and personally relieved their hardships. At both these times, his own finances were in an embarrassed state, when the giving of money must have involved some self-sacrifice.

His generosity in giving money to friends in need was, like that of other poets in the present gallery, conspicuous. His help to Leigh Hunt is deserving of special remark. Not only was it given when he was far from well-off, but he displayed a heroic forbearance in Hunt's persistent perplexities. In the last year of his life he wrote to Hunt: 'I send you by return of post £150, —within 30 or 40 of what I have contrived to scrape together. How I am to assemble the constituents of such a sum again, I do not at present see; but do not be disheartened—we will all put our shoulders to the wheel.' A month later, he was still trying to find means of raising more money for his friend; and, instead of showing signs of aggravation, he wrote to Hunt, telling him not to delay in letting him hear how he and his family were progressing.[2] Leigh Hunt himself wrote in his *Autobiography*: 'His [Shelley's] last sixpence was ever at my service, had I chosen to share it.'

Shortly before he married Harriet, he met, near his Sussex home, a Miss Elizabeth Hitchener, a village schoolmistress who was gaining a little local notoriety for her zeal as an advanced thinker, and as a pioneer in such causes as the political rights of women. The possession of these revolutionary views ensured his interest in this young woman, of unattractive physique, and some ten years older than himself. Soon after his marriage he undertook a considerable correspondence with her. He wrote her some forty-five letters, mostly long ones, covering a period of nearly a year, often expressed in language that, according to normal standards, would be regarded as compromising.

His relations with Miss Hitchener provide an early and

striking example of his need for the love of a woman so as to enable him to give expression to a particular intensity of feeling. In this instance, he was fascinated by the ideal of philanthropic knight-errantry, whereby he hoped to undertake the amelioration of the conditions of life of his fellow-men. The brusque and seemingly harsh manner in which he discarded Miss Hitchener, when he found that his embodiment in her of his new-found ideal was misconceived, must be taken into account in a study of his character. If the evidence is weighed, we may perhaps conclude that, as a result of his obsession, his head was so far in the clouds that he was not able to take a sensible view of the risks involved in his professions to Miss Hitchener. The facts must be briefly reviewed.

Perhaps as a result of his disappointment at Harriet's inability to respond to his romantic aspirations, his ardour for the relief of suffering humanity was intensified. Harriet was not qualified to give much constructive sympathy in this field, whereas Miss Hitchener, with her daring flights of fancy, seemed exactly the person in whom he could find a stimulating and enthusiastic collaborator. In the early stages of his correspondence with her, he expressed himself in tones of high-flown sentimentality which must have been unsettling to a spinster living in a remote country village, especially coming from a man whom she knew was the heir to a baronetcy. He wrote, for instance: 'My dearest friend (for I will call you so), *you* who understand my motives to action, which, I flatter myself, unisonize with your own, you, who can contemn the world's prejudices, whose views are mine, I will dare to say I *love*: nor do I risk the possibility of that degrading and contemptible interpretation of this sacred word, nor do I risk the supposition that the lump of organized matter which enshrines thy soul excites the love which that soul alone dare claim . . . Henceforth will I be yours—yours with truth, sincerity and unreserve.' The letter ends: 'Sister of my soul, adieu. With, I hope, eternal love, Your Percy Shelley.'[3] On another occasion, he described Miss Hitchener as 'the sunshine of my life'; he asserted that her writing was 'dear, sacredly dear, to me is every line of it'. Again, her letters were 'like angels sent from heaven on missions of peace'.[4] And he was, moreover, constantly pressing her to come and live in his household, so that

L

they could together contrive the reformation of society.

In the next stage of the correspondence, he expressed to her his need for intellectual sympathy, using a bombastic type of phraseology which reflected his impassioned mood: 'Let us mingle our identities inseparably, and burst upon tyrants with the accumulated impetuosity of our acquirements and resolutions.'[5] He told her that he was determined no longer to think without her as the partner of his thoughts;[6] and he wrote: 'My true and dear friend, why should we be separated? When may we unite? What might we not do, if together? If two hearts panting for the happiness and liberty of mankind were joined by union and proximity as they are by friendship and sympathy. What might we not expect?'[7] In urging her to come and live with Harriet, Harriet's elder sister Eliza, and himself, he was injudicious enough to lead Miss Hitchener to take an extravagant view of her potentialities. He went to such absurd lengths as to assert: 'I perceive in you the embryon of a mighty intellect which may one day enlighten thousands.'[8] He added folly to folly; he first discomposed her heart, and then proceeded, by these fantastic phrases, to turn her head.

The ardent language he used in these letters must have given the poor lady a totally misleading impression of his intentions; and this language, combined with the irresponsible remarks of the kind just quoted, undoubtedly helped to induce the embarrassing dissension that followed a few months later. But he went further in a compromising direction by attempting to justify to Miss Hitchener his marriage with Harriet, a course which would naturally give her increased reason to hope for the full possession of his heart. The letter in which this justification was made has, however, a wider interest, for it is clear that, in it, he tried unsuccessfully to vindicate the expedience of the marriage to himself. We must, then, take note that, more than two years before he decided to leave Harriet, he had begun to recognize the failure of his marriage to her. This proof of his protracted efforts to maintain a tolerable companionship with Harriet will be germane to our consideration of his behaviour in eloping with Mary. Meanwhile, as this letter also concerns his attitude to Miss Hitchener, the relevant part of it must be quoted here: 'I will explain . . . the circumstances which caused my marriage . . . these must certainly have caused much conjecture in your mind. Some time ago when my sister was at Mrs. Fenning's school, she contracted an intimacy with Harriet.—At that period I attentively watched over my sister, designing, if possible, to add to the list of the good, the disinterested, the free. I desired therefore to investigate Harriet's character; for which purpose I called on her, requested to correspond with her, designing that her advancement should keep pace with, and possibly accelerate, that of my sister. Her ready and frank acceptance of my proposal pleased me, and, tho' with ideas the remotest to those which have led to this conclusion of our intimacy, I continued to correspond with her for some time. The frequency of her letters became greater during my stay in Wales. I answered them; they became interesting. They contained complaints of the irrational conduct of her relations, and the misery of living where she could *love* no one. Suicide was with her a favourite theme, her total uselessness was urged in its defence. This I admitted, supposing she could prove her inutility, [and that she] was powerless. Her letters became more and more [gloomy]. At length one assumed such despair as induced me to quit Wales precipitately.—I arrived in London. I was shocked at observing the alteration of her looks. Little did I divine its cause; she had become violently attached to *me*, and feared that I should not return her attachment. Prejudice made the confession painful. It was impossible to avoid being much affected. I promised to unite my fate with hers. I staid in London several days, during which she recovered her spirits. . . . Blame me if thou wilt, dearest friend, for *still* thou art dearest to me; yet pity even this error if thou blamest me. If Harriet be not, at sixteen, all that you are at a more advanced age, assist me to mould a really noble soul into all that can make its nobleness useful and lovely. Lovely it is now, or I am the weakest slave of error.'[9]

Shelley's letters to Miss Hitchener illuminate his character in a variety of ways. They tell us how credulous he was, and how deficient in prudence and common sense. Not only is it obvious that he was insufficiently mature in mind to undertake the responsibilities of marriage, but in his unbridled enthusiasm for his utopian schemes for social regeneration, he had sentimentalized over and beguiled this humble, intelligent, aspiring village schoolmistress, and, in the result, made both her and himself ridiculous. In accordance with his persistent habit through life, he had wished to attach himself to a woman with whom he might identify his ideal. He had believed Miss Hitchener to be qualified for this role; and it was only when she came to live with him that he discovered that he had involved himself in a prodigious fiasco.

Miss Hitchener's partnership in Shelley's hare-brained plans for social amelioration necessarily entailed a serious disruption of her way of life. In order to come and live with the Shelleys, she had to relinquish her employment as a schoolmistress. Only a few weeks after she was admitted into a household of which she was expecting to be a member for an indefinite period, she was subjected to the ignominy of being asked to leave, partly, it seems clear, as a result of the contrivances of Harriet and her unscrupulous sister, Eliza. Harriet alleged that Miss Hitchener 'built all her hopes on being able to separate me from my dearly loved Percy';[10] but there is no adequate evidence to show that Miss Hitchener was a designing female, intent on capturing Shelley or his money. On the contrary, he borrowed a considerable sum of money from her. Her letters to him (preserved in the British Museum) seem to aim at close relations, but not necessarily at supplanting his wife.

The circumstances in which Miss Hitchener was extruded from the Shelley household disclose him in an unpleasant guise, and one that was not typical of him in his prime. We see him infuriated at his own folly, and ferociously venting his wrath by denigrating the victim of that folly. Soon after Miss Hitchener had been dismissed, he wrote to his old college friend, Jefferson Hogg, communicating his conclusions on the matter: 'The Brown Demon, as we call our late tormentor and schoolmistress, must receive her stipend. I pay it with a heavy heart and an unwilling hand; but it must be so. She was deprived by our misjudging haste of a situation, where she was going on smoothly: and now she says her reputation is gone, her health ruined, her peace of mind destroyed by my barbarity; a complete victim to all the woes, mental and bodily, that heroine ever suffered! This is not all fact; but certainly she is embarrassed and poor, and we being in some degree the cause, we ought to obviate it. She is an artful, superficial, ugly, hermaphroditical beast of a woman, and my astonishment at my fatuity, inconsistency, and bad taste was never so great, after living four months with her as an inmate. What would Hell be, were such a woman in Heaven?'[11]

As we have already remarked, Shelley married Harriet when actuated by a spirit of chivalry, so as to relieve her from supposed persecutions. It was not long before he realized that she lacked the ability to be an adequate intellectual companion to him; but he made a sustained effort to kindle in her a zest for literature and learning. Harriet's elder sister, Eliza, who came to live with them, was a handicap to any such endeavours. Indeed, she was more than a handicap, because she actively encouraged her sister to indulge in extravagances in dress and manner of living which Shelley much disliked. After exercising great patience for many months, he saw that his marriage was bound to come to grief under the noxious influence of Eliza; and he wrote a letter to Hogg which indicates that he had given up hope of eliminating Eliza from her place of influence. This letter reveals him in the same mood of savage hatred that he displayed in regard to Miss Hitchener. 'I am now', he wrote, in respect of Eliza's presence in the home, 'but little inclined to contest this point. I certainly hate her with all my heart and soul. . . . I sometimes feel faint with the fatigue of checking the overflowings of my unbounded abhorrence for this miserable wretch. But she is no more than a blind and loathesome worm, that cannot see to sting.'[12] Later in life, when he was discussing the breakdown of his marriage with his friend, Peacock, the latter was puzzled, and said: 'I thought you were very fond of Harriet.' Shelley neither affirmed nor denied this statement, and remarked: 'But you don't know how I hated her sister.'

Owing, no doubt, to Harriet's annoyance at Shelley's scornful treatment of her cherished and indispensable Eliza, she grew cool with him, and went to stay with her people in Bath—the time-honoured method of 'bringing a man to his senses'. Shelley became convinced that Harriet no longer loved him, and, although he made a pathetic appeal to her in some verses inscribed 'To Harriet, 1814', the appeal was without real hope. A fortnight before he eloped with Mary, he requested Harriet to come and see him in London, so as to discuss the situation. After an interview, he wrote her a letter, partly designed, it seems, to quieten her apprehensions, and partly to break the news to her that, although he wished to remain her close and faithful friend, he would no longer regard her as his wife. 'I repeat', he said, '. . . that my attachment to you is unimpaired. I conceive that it has acquired even a deeper and more lasting character, that it is now less exposed than ever to the fluctuations of phantasy or caprice. Our connection was not one of passion and impulse. Friendship was its basis, and on this basis it has enlarged and strengthened.'[13]

No one but Shelley could have conceived such an impossible project as that of retaining his wife as a close friend, but in no more intimate relationship. We might well suppose that this project would have been automatically cancelled by his elopement with Mary. But, a few days after their arrival on the Continent on their quasi-honeymoon, he wrote a letter to Harriet of stupendous ineptitude, implying an insensitiveness that would have been unbelievable in a normal person. 'I write', he said, 'to show that I do not forget you; I write to urge you to come to Switzerland, where you will at last find one firm and constant friend, to whom your interests will ever be dear—by whom your feelings will never be wilfully injured.'[14] This letter has much more value than its illustration of Shelley's *gaucherie*, for it provides excellent proof that he was so completely insusceptible to the orthodox standards of moral obligation that he cannot be fairly judged by those standards. Needless to say, Harriet did not accept his invitation; and after an absence lasting some six weeks, Shelley, Mary, and Claire Clairmont (Mary's half-sister who was foolishly asked to accompany them), having discovered that their finances were inadequate for an extension of their escapade, returned to London.

Shelley continued his endeavours to induce Harriet to accept the position of the much esteemed friend; and Harriet was justifiably indignant. During a correspondence between them in which Shelley wrote some eight letters, the exasperation increased on both sides. The first letter in this series enables us to gather how fantastically unconventional were his views on the obligations of married persons. He wrote to her: 'You think I have injured you. Since I first beheld you almost, my chief study has been to overwhelm you with benefits. Even now when a violent and lasting passion for another leads me to prefer her society to yours, I am perpetually employed in devising how I can be permanently and truly useful to you, in what manner my time and my fortune can be most securely expended for your real interests. In return for this it is not well that I should be wounded with reproach and blame: so unexampled and singular an attachment demands a return far different. And it would be generous, nay even just to consider with kindness that woman whom my judgment and my heart have selected as the noblest and the most excellent of human beings.'[15]

This letter was, naturally enough, not acceptable to Harriet; and she came to the conclusion that she must take legal advice, so as to enforce whatever rights she had. Shelley told her that, if she persisted in this course, 'it is obvious that I can no longer consider you but as an enemy, as one who under the mask of friendship and affection has acted the part of the basest and blackest treachery'.[16] When he heard that she had consulted an attorney, he wrote to her in harsh terms: 'I desire to renew no intercourse of whatsoever nature with you, whilst you act under the principles which you recently avowed: these you were formerly the foremost to stigmatise and abhor.'[17] His further letters, still severe and uncompromising, show some signs of his recognition of responsibility towards her. 'I am united to another; you are no longer my wife. Perhaps I have done you an injury, but surely most innocently and unintentionally, in having commenced any connexion with you.'[18] 'I shall watch over your interests, mark the progress of your future life, be useful to you, be your protector, and consider myself as it were your parent; but as friends, as equals, those who do not sympathize can never meet.'[19] The ruthlessness of these expressions seems all the more indefensible when we remember that Harriet was at that time with child by Shelley, a boy, who was born, in November, 1814, a few weeks after this lamentable altercation. He did, however, as soon as he was able to do so, settle £200 a year on her, out of an annual income of £1,000 which he had extracted from his father.

Amazing as Shelley's attitude to Harriet seems, judged by any ordinary standards, we must admit that, in proposing the impossible, he was perfectly conscientious. If allowance is made, and it is a very large allowance, for his eccentric outlook in regard to his marital responsibilities, it is difficult to indict him of cruel desertion. He was trying to make what he thought was a reasonable and necessary adjustment in the relationship between his wife and himself. She would not agree to his proposals; and he sullenly left her in the care of her father and elder sister. But, as has often been pointed out, it is not proper, in view of his unfeeling neglect of her welfare, to acquit him of all blame for her suicide which took place some two years later. Of course, he never anticipated the possibility of such a heart-rending sequel; but he should have done so, for he knew that suicide had been for her a subject of speculation, and that she was a person whose tendencies might easily involve her in some such disaster.

The genuine surprise and pain evinced by Shelley at the censure and obloquy he earned for himself, as a result of his desertion of Harriet and his elopement with Mary, must surely support the view that his action was conscientious. He was particularly enraged against his publisher-friend, Thomas Hookham, who espoused Harriet's cause. Soon after the failure of his attempts to reach an accommodation with Harriet, he was in such embarrassment for lack of money that he was in danger of being arrested for debt. The Hookhams were somehow implicated in his difficulties, and he wrote to Mary: 'My imagination is confounded by the uniform prospect of the perfidy, wickedness, and hardheartedness of mankind. . . . I care not for the Hookhams; I'll tear their hearts out by the roots, with irony and sarcasm, if I find they have dared to lift a thought against me.' And, later, he wrote: 'I will make this remorseless villain loathe his own flesh in good time; he shall be cut down in his season; his pride shall be trampled into atoms; I will wither up his selfish soul by piecemeal.'[20]

He was almost equally infuriated by the hypocritical attitude of Mary's father, William Godwin, who in his revolutionary book, *Political Justice*, had treated the marriage-tie as a slip-knot that could be released at will. Shelley had acted in strict conformity with the principles of that book; but Godwin, since his own daughter was involved in Shelley's experimentation, perversely treated him as a base seducer. Some time after the elopement, he wrote to Godwin in embittered language: 'In my judgment, neither I, nor your daughter, nor her offspring, ought to receive the treatment which we encounter on every side. It has perpetually appeared to me to have been your especial duty to see that, so far as mankind value your good opinion, we were dealt justly by, and that a young family, innocent and benevolent and united, should not be confounded with prostitutes and seducers. My astonishment, and I will confess when I have been treated with most harshness and cruelty by you, my indignation has been extreme, that, knowing as you do my nature, any considerations should have prevailed on you to have been thus harsh and cruel. . . . Do not talk of *forgiveness* again to me, for my blood boils in my veins, and my gall rises against all that bears the human form, when I think of what I, their benefactor and ardent lover, have endured of enmity and contempt from you and from all mankind.'[21]

It is true that Shelley's bitter resentment at the denunciation to which he was subjected was aggravated by the financial worries that afflicted him soon after his attachment to Mary. But two years later, a few days as it happened before he heard of Harriet's suicide, he wrote to Leigh Hunt a letter of gratitude for his sympathy, at the same time telling him how sorely he resented the attitude of reprobation and even hostility which was still adopted by most of his acquaintance. He said that he did not conceal from himself that he was an outcast from human society. 'I am an object of compassion to a few more benevolent than the rest, all else abhor and avoid me. With you, and perhaps some others (though in a less degree, I fear) my gentleness and sincerity find favour, because they are themselves generous and sincere: they believe in self-devotion and generosity, because they are themselves generous and self-devoted.'[22] We must surely recognize that these expressions are those of an honest man, with a genuine belief in his principles of behaviour, however wrong-headed and infatuated he may have been in fact.

The news of Harriet's suicide came upon him, as it would on anyone in the same situation, as a grievous blow. But he strongly persisted in his repudiation of responsibility. He wrote to Mary: 'It is through you that I can entertain without despair the recollection of the horrors of unutterable villainy that led to this dark, dreadful death.' He evidently referred to the ghastly fact that Harriet's body was found to be in an

advanced stage of pregnancy. He therefore proceeded: 'Everything tends to prove, however, that beyond the shock of so
hideous a catastrophe having fallen on a human being so nearly
connected with me, there would in any case have been little to
regret. Hookham, Longdill [his solicitor], everyone, does me
full justice; bearing testimony to the upright spirit and liberality of my conduct to her. There is but one voice in condemnation of the detestable Westbrooks.'[23]

More than four years later, that eminently self-righteous
man, Robert Southey, took the opportunity, in writing to
Shelley, to denounce his conduct. Shelley's reply, written at
more than a sufficient interval for his susceptibilities to become
less tender, declared his unremitting resentment at the charges
of immorality levelled against him. 'You accuse me,' he told
Southey, 'on what evidence I cannot guess, of *guilt*—a bold
word, sir, this, and one which would have required me to
write to you in another tone had you addressed it to anyone
except myself... You select a single passage out of a life otherwise not only spotless, but spent in an impassioned pursuit of
virtue, which looks like a blot, merely because I regulated my
domestic arrangements without deferring to the notions of the
vulgar, although I might have done so quite as conveniently
had I descended to their base thoughts—this you call *guilt*.
I might answer you in another manner, but I take God to
witness, if such a Being is now regarding both you and me,
and I pledge myself if we meet, as perhaps you expect, before
Him after death, to repeat the same in His presence—that you
accuse me wrongfully. I am innocent of ill, either done or
intended; the consequences you allude to flowed in no respect
from me.'[24]

Shelley once told his friend, Peacock: 'Everyone who knows
me must know that the partner of my life should be one who
can feel poetry and understand philosophy.' Like his other
loves, Mary represented an ideal. Harriet had failed to inspire
him to express himself in poetry, or to stimulate his appetite for
philosophic investigation. Mary, however, was capable of
filling this part. She was endowed with an admirably clear
mind, and with sufficient imagination and susceptibility to
poetical impressions to make his romantic conception of her
come true. She shared his love of literature and learning; she

was an ardent student; and she sympathized with his advanced views on politics and about the principles of behaviour. Soon after their elopement-honeymoon, he expressed to her in a letter his delight in her intellect: 'How hard and stubborn must be the spirit that does not confess you to be the subtlest and most exquisitely fashioned intelligence; that among women there is no equal mind to yours! And I possess this treasure! How beyond all estimate is my felicity!'[25]

Indoctrination with Godwin's principles of free love was, of course, fraught with danger for them both. Overmastering passion was legitimated; impetuosity in relations between the sexes was, if not implicitly encouraged, at least condoned. It was not long, therefore, before the happiness of Shelley and Mary was in peril. Mary gave birth to a seven-months child, which soon died. But, while she was waiting for it, Claire Clairmont, her half-sister, whom Shelley so rashly invited to accompany them on the elopement, frequently kept Shelley company on walks and visits. This may well have aroused Mary's jealousy. Contemporaneously, Shelley's old friend, Jefferson Hogg, who had tried to seduce Shelley's first wife during an early period of their marriage, was assisting Shelley with money. Mary's letters to Hogg at this time prove her to be suggesting to him intimacies utterly inconsistent with her unofficial marriage to Shelley.[26] Happily this phase soon passed; but, a few months later, Shelley had gone off house-hunting; and Mary suspected that Claire had taken the opportunity of keeping him company. Mary's dislike, and even suspicion, of Claire persisted. At the conclusion of their second Continental tour (May to September, 1816), Shelley was again looking for a residence; and Mary wrote to him: 'give me a garden, and *absentia* Claire, and I will thank my love for many favours'.[27] These possible failures, on both sides, to maintain proper standards of behaviour and obligation not only help us to understand the conditions under which Shelley's second marriage was launched, but also have some bearing on circumstances which arose much later on.

Three months after returning to England from the second tour, Shelley included the following paragraph in a tender and affectionate letter to Mary, from which an extract has already been quoted: 'How is Claire? I do not tell her, but I may tell you how deeply I am interested in her safety. I need not recommend her to your care. Give her any kind message from me, and calm her spirits as well as you can.'[28] These remarks are to be explained by the fact that Claire was shortly to give birth to a daughter. Before the second tour, she had succeeded in her ambition of becoming the mistress, or at least the temporary mistress, of Lord Byron; and she met him again on this tour. The daughter, born to Claire, to be called Allegra, was acknowledged by Byron as his child. All the time, Claire lived with Shelley and Mary; and she eventually accompanied them when they decided to settle in Italy (March, 1818), and was sometimes a member of their household in the years that followed. Shelley supported her during considerable periods, and made provision for her after his death.

The puzzle of Shelley's relationship with Claire, if puzzle it is, will presumably never be solved. She evidently represented to him something that Mary did not: perhaps she gave him a tenderness of sympathy of which Mary was not capable. He was, however, so soft-hearted a person that it is not impossible that the basis of their *camaraderie* was Claire's unhappiness, and her reliance on him for solace. It is certain that, from time to time, Mary was uneasy, with Claire occupying the position of one of the family. But, even if Shelley's behaviour to Claire was not conducted with exemplary discretion, his altruism towards her was heroic, and sustained over some six years. His affectionate patience with her querulous manner and her exasperating vagaries, clearly implied in many of his letters to her, is deserving of liberal praise, and tends to prove that their association was an honourable one.

In August, 1821, Shelley learnt from Byron that, as a result of a story hatched by a dismissed servant, friends had believed that Claire was his mistress. He immediately wrote to his wife asking her to express to the deluded friends her disbelief in the story. Shelley's own denial of any misconduct is fully stated in his letter to Mary. In view of the doubts felt in some quarters about Shelley's integrity in this matter, the way in which he expressed himself is of particular interest. He wrote: 'Lord Byron has also told me of a circumstance that shocks me exceedingly; because it exhibits a degree of desperate and wicked malice for which I am at a loss to account. When I hear such things, my patience and my philosophy are put to a severe proof, whilst I refrain from seeking out some obscure hiding-place, where the countenance of man may never meet me more. It seems that *Elise* [a dismissed servant], actuated either by some inconceivable malice for our dismissing her, or bribed by my enemies, or making common cause with her infamous husband, has persuaded the Hoppners of a story so monstrous and incredible that they must have been prone to believe any evil to have believed such assertions upon such evidence. Mr. Hoppner wrote to Lord Byron to state this story as the reason why he declined any further communications with us, and why he advised him to do the same. Elise says that Claire was my mistress; that is very well, and so far there is nothing new; all the world has heard so much, and people may believe or not believe as they think good. She then proceeds to say that Claire is with child by me; that I gave her the most violent medicine to procure abortion; that this not succeeding she was brought to bed, and that I immediately tore the child from her and sent it to the Foundling Hospital. I quote Mr. Hoppner's words— and that is stated to have taken place in the winter after we left Este. In addition, she says that both I and Claire treated *you* in the most shameful manner, that I neglected and beat you, and that Claire never let a day pass without offering you insults of the most violent kind, in which she was abetted by me.

'As to what Reviews and the world says, I do not care a jot, but when persons who have known me are capable of conceiv-ing me—not that I have fallen into a great error, as would have been the living with Claire as my mistress—but that I have committed such unutterable crimes as destroying or abandon-ing a child, and that my own! Imagine my despair of good, imagine how it is possible that one of so weak and sensitive a nature as mine can run further the gauntlet through this hellish society of men.'[29]

Mary at once wrote to the Hoppners: 'I am perfectly con-vinced in my own mind that Shelley never had an improper connexion with Claire—at the time specified in Elise's letter, the winter after we quitted Este. . . . Need I say that the union between my husband and myself has ever been undisturbed. Love caused our first imprudence, love which improved by esteem, a perfect trust one in the other, a confidence and affection which, visited as we have been by severe calamities (have we not lost two children?) has encreased daily, and knows no bounds.'[30]

Shelley's letters to Claire at the beginning and at the end of 1821 are, perhaps, more full of tenderness and solicitude than those of other years. But the impression they give is of a high-minded benevolence which could not descend to a guilty intrigue. In January and February, he wrote letters containing the following passages:

'I wish to heaven, my dear girl, that *I* could be of any avail to add to your pleasures or diminish your pain—how ardently, you cannot know; you only know, as you frequently take care to tell me, how vainly . . . I took up the pen for an instant only to thank you,—and, if you will, to kiss you, for your kind attention to me, and I find I have written in ill spirits, which may infect you. Let them not do so! . . . Yours most tenderly.'[31]

'A thousand thanks for your affectionate letter, which to me is as water in the desert.'[32]

'Adieu, dear girl—confide, and persuade yourself of my eternal and tender regard. Yours with deepest affection.'[33]

In December, he wrote:

'Do not think my affection and anxiety for you ever cease, or that I ever love you less although that love has been and still must be a source of disquietude to me.'[34]

'Mary desires me to say (not that she sees this letter or any of yours addressed to me) that she would have written to you—but she has been very unwell.'[35]

Although it would be unduly suspicious to imply any gross impropriety from these fervent expressions of affection, it is impossible not to be struck by Shelley's indiscretion in maintaining such intimate relations with a young woman of so highly emotional a temperament as Claire. He had complained bitterly of the mental anguish that he had suffered as a result of the censoriousness and disdain of many of his acquaintance, ever since his elopement with Mary; but he never seemed able to restrain the vehemence of his ardent affections, so as to avoid giving repeated grounds for the reprobation that caused him much unhappiness.

In some respects, however, increased age brought ameliora-tion. When he was young, at the period of his first marriage, for instance, his temperament was contentious, irritable and intolerant. But, as a result of the passage of years, and, far more so, as a result of the discipline of experience, some of these characteristics were modified, and others became virtually defunct. With occasional exceptions, he learnt to be temperate, restrained, tactful, and patient. His patience with so moody a subject as Claire is impressive; and it is especially notable in his behaviour both to her and to Byron in regard to the protracted quarrel about the custody and management of the child, Allegra. In Byron, he had to deal with a violent, domineering, and, in this matter, a harsh and unfeeling disposition, where a high degree of tact was required, which he seems to have exercised consistently.

Negotiations regarding Allegra lasted from 1818 until the child's death in 1822. At first, the dispute was concerned with Claire's permission to see the child after she was given into Byron's custody. Shelley addressed Byron on this subject, displaying mature wisdom and sagacity: 'You write as if from the instant of its departure all future intercourse were to cease between Claire and her child. This I cannot think you ought to have expected, or even to have desired. Let us estimate our own sensations, and consider, if those of a father be acute, what must those of a mother? . . . But, in truth, if she is to be brought to part with her child, she requires reassurance and tenderness. A tie so near the heart should not be rudely snapt. . . . Your conduct must at present wear the aspect of great cruelty, however you justify it to yourself. Surely, it is better if we err, to err on the side of kindness, than of rigour. . . .'[36]

Two years later, the controversy was proceeding approximately on the earlier lines. Shelley then wrote to Byron: 'I wish you had not expressed yourself so harshly in your letter about Claire—because of necessity she was obliged to read it; and I am persuaded that you are mistaken in thinking she has any desire of thwarting your plans about Allegra. . . . What letters she writes to you I know not; perhaps they are very provoking; but at all events it is better to forgive the weak.'[37] Again: 'You are conscious of performing your duty to Allegra, and your refusal to allow her to visit Claire at this distance you conceive to be part of that duty. That Claire should have wished to see her is natural. That her disappointment should vex her, and her vexation make her write absurdly, is all in the usual order of things. But, poor thing, she is very unhappy and in bad health, and she ought to be treated with as much indulgence as possible.'[38]

In April 1821 Shelley became inclined to support Byron rather than Claire in the controversy, presumably because Claire was being irritatingly contentious. He told Byron that Claire's views about Allegra seemed unreasonable, and that Mary and he were convinced that Byron's conduct in regard to Allegra had been irreproachable.[39] And, finally, a short time before Allegra's death in the convent where Byron had placed her as a pupil, Shelley told Claire that she was most foolish in her plans to kidnap the child.[40]

We can discern in these letters of Shelley's a warm-hearted, generous-minded man, and one having a capacity for calm forbearance and common sense. These latter qualities were particularly needed in dealing with Mary's father, William Godwin, who took advantage of his position by importuning Shelley for financial help. He had little idea how to deal with business matters, and was constantly embarrassed for lack of funds, as often as not verging on bankruptcy. Mary was a devoted daughter; and it is obvious that Shelley's compliance with Godwin's requests was chiefly due to her pressure on him, and his desire to propitiate her. Godwin repeatedly exhibited astonishing insolence in urging his claims on someone who was himself in need of money, and who could only raise it on exorbitant terms by encroaching on his expectations as heir to a large estate. Shelley's patience and magnanimity, in the face of Godwin's effrontery and his impudent and extortionate demands, were truly remarkable. If anyone feels doubtful about his unflagging devotion to Mary, that doubt can be set at rest by a due consideration of his relations with Godwin.

The two men quarrelled more than once, but Shelley never became unmannerly or acrimonious, though at times he employed a thinly veiled sarcasm which was not only excusable, but richly deserved. A few extracts from his letters to Godwin, dealing with Godwin's financial demands over a period of about five years, can throw a revealing and favourable light on his character.

In 1816, Shelley wrote to Godwin: 'Perhaps it is well that

you should be informed that I consider your last letter to be written in a certain style of haughtiness and encroachment, which neither awes nor imposes upon me. But I have no desire to transgress the limits which you placed to our intercourse, nor in any future instance will I make any remarks but such as arise from the strict question in discussion.

'Perhaps you do well to consider every word irrelevant to that question which does not regard your personal advantage.'[41] And, later in the same year: 'I lamented also over my ruined hopes, hopes of all that your genius once taught me to expect from your virtue, when I found that for yourself, your family, and your creditors, you would submit to that communication with me which you once rejected and abhorred, and which no pity for my poverty or sufferings, assumed willingly for you, could avail to extort.'[42]

But, later in 1816, his attitude moderated, and he went so far as to tell Godwin that he respected him as the philosopher who still to a great extent regulated his understanding; and he asked Godwin's pardon if he had been unjust to him or unduly indignant.[43] A year after this, having composed the quarrel between them, Shelley wrote to Godwin in cordial terms, again affording him more financial assistance than he prudently ought. 'Certain it is', he wrote, 'that nothing gives me a serener and more pure pleasure than your society, and that if in breaking an engagement with you [of a financial kind] I have forced an exercise of your philosophy upon you, I have in my own person incurred a penalty which mine has yet taught me to alleviate. It gives me pain too that I cannot send you the whole amount you want. I enclose a cheque to within a few pounds of my possessions.'[44]

But, by 1820, Shelley's abundant patience had again been strained to breaking point; and he informed Godwin: 'I have given you within a few years the amount of a considerable fortune, and have destituted myself for the purpose of realizing it of nearly four times the amount. Except for the *goodwill* which this transaction seems to have produced between you and me [an appropriate piece of irony], this money, for any advantage it ever conferred on you, might as well have been thrown into the seas. Had I kept in my own hands this £4,000 or £5,000 and administered it in trust for your permanent advantage, I

M

should have been indeed your benefactor. . . . You still urge the request of £500. You would take anything in the shape of it that would compel me to make the great sacrifices (if indeed *now* it be not impossible) of paying it from my income, without —you must allow me to say—a due regard to the proportion borne by your accommodation to my immediate loss or even your own ultimate advantage. . . . If you are sincere with me on this subject, why instead of seeking to plunge one person already half ruined for your sake into deeper ruin, do you not procure the £400 by your own active powers?'[45] He closed the letter by insisting that Godwin should not play upon his daughter's feelings at a time when her health was precarious, by writing her letters about his penury and his supposed rights to exact financial assistance from himself. It is typical of Godwin that, as a result of this letter, he evidently threatened not to write to his daughter at all. Shelley put him to shame by replying: 'I need not tell you that the neglecting entirely to write to your daughter from the moment that nothing could be gained by it would admit of but one interpretation.'[46]

Towards the end of his short life, Shelley's tendency to be disconsolate became increasingly marked. He was recurrently captivated by exalted ideals; and, when these miscarried, he suffered a corresponding degree of disillusionment. About a year before he died, his short-lived affection for Emilia Viviani had waxed and waned; and, at about the same period, he was much distressed by the diffusion of the scandal about Claire and himself, and he wrote to Mary: 'My greatest content would be utterly to desert all human society. I would retire with you and our child to a solitary island in the sea. . . . If I dared trust my imagination, it would tell me that there are one or two chosen companions besides yourself whom I should desire. But to this I would not listen—where two or three are gathered together, the devil is among them. And good, far more than evil impulses, love, far more than hatred, has been to me, except as you have been its object, the source of all sorts of mischief.'[47] There are a number of indications in Shelley's letters that he was not a social person in the ordinary sense; but he delighted in con- genial company, and his cynical remarks about the exclusion of close friends from his prospective way of life are not to be taken seriously.

The despondent moods that affected the last year or so of his life were doubtless due to some extent to an infiltration of self-reproach; but they were much more likely to be the effect of the workings of his restless and unsatisfied idealism. During part of this period, his relations with Mary were not altogether happy: they were, in fact, apt to be strained. She seemed to be unable to embody his visions of perfection in the same way that she had done in earlier years. She had, temporarily at least, lost her buoyancy, and became subject to attacks of depression; and two melancholy people living together are likely to fray each other's composure. Mary was not ordinarily disposed to be jealous; she had suffered the intrusions of Claire for many years without revolt; but Shelley's brief yet ardent attachment to Emilia Viviani disturbed her equanimity. Emilia had been incarcerated in a convent with a view to extorting her consent to an undesired marriage; and Shelley thought he saw in her a type of beauty he had been reading about in Plato. He proved to be over-susceptible to her calculated deployment of her charms, and her heartless attempts to insinuate herself between husband and wife. Mary evidently suffered some distress as a result of the poem, *Epipsychidion*, that Shelley addressed to Emilia, in which it is possible to interpret the warm, glowing sun as Emilia, and the chaste, cold moon as Mary.

The romantic episodes, between Shelley and Jane Williams, quite near the end of his life, were such as might feature in many coteries of literary people without serious harm ensuing. But the Emilia affair was more indiscreet. Why, we must ask, should Shelley, having suffered so grievously from love's toils, and having realized and regretted the resultant unhappiness, involve himself once more in such considerable vexations? And, more pertinent still, why having, as he must certainly have recognized, made women suffer from his vagaries in the practice of the art of love, should he wantonly continue to do so? The latter question, it is obvious, bears directly on any study of his character. He was, in fact, still subject to the same impulses which had earlier overcome his sense of discretion in his relations with women. Even after his daunting experiences, if a woman represented a compulsive ideal, he must make love to her so as to try to fulfil that ideal. Emilia enabled him to express the intensity of his compassion. Her pathetic situation inspired him to love and poetry; and he experienced also, no doubt, a chivalrous impulse similar to that which had drawn him to his unfortunate first wife.

He lived his life in his imagination: that is probably why he was so much enamoured of the sea. As a boy, and even as a young man, he often took pleasure in sailing paper boats on rivers, ponds, and lakes. These 'little argosies', as Maurois aptly calls them, gave rein to his imagination. So too, on a larger scale, did the navigation of the sea. A few days before his death, he wrote to a friend in England: 'I have a boat here. It cost me £80, and reduced me to some difficulty in point of money. However, it is swift and beautiful, and appears quite a vessel. Williams is captain, and we drive along this delightful bay in the evening wind under the summer moon until the earth appears another world. Jane [Williams] brings her guitar, and if the past and future could be obliterated, the present would content me so well that I could say with Faust to the passing moment "Remain thou, thou art so beautiful." '[48]

Those who designate Shelley as a sensual reprobate can never have shared the experiences of his soaring fancy, living and thinking, as he did, on a plane above that of mere mundane creatures. He was too closely identified with the sublimity of beauty and goodness, to descend to any conduct that was mean or unworthy. He may have been culpably heedless of the pain he caused to others; but he was heedless because he was actuated, indeed constrained, by arbitrary, and, as all sensible people must think, mistaken principles. It is obvious that, if such principles were generally adopted, society would be in a state of anarchy. But, if we ourselves were not to be his victims, we might decide that, from time to time, it would be worth some suffering to be caught up in the rapturous aspirations of a Shelley.

—— 9 ——
JOHN KEATS (1795–1821)
Sublime Intensity of Feeling

THROUGHOUT Keats's letters, many of which are more poetical than those of any other poet, we can discern a glowing genius, whose eagerness and ardour are often inspiriting, sometimes a little provoking, but manifestly appropriate to the temper of youth. The task of sitting in judgement on Keats, in the sense of assessing the substance of his character, is a more embarrassing one than similar tasks undertaken in this book. A man who lacked time to exploit his convictions, or to modify his tentative attitudes to life, should surely be judged with lenity. It cannot, however, be said that the conclusions to be drawn about his character must needs rest on unsatisfactory evidence. The brief years of his adult life include a sufficient number of dramatic incidents to provide him with ample opportunities to display his distinctive qualities.

His letters arouse our lively interest largely because of his zest for philosophizing. Far from taking life for granted, he was constantly trying to gain a genuine understanding of the problems of human relations, and of the proper function of poetry; and he delighted in telling his friends about the results of his speculations. In this respect, as in others, his letters are the product of an excitable mind; perhaps an over-active one. He plunged into a subject, and before it had been adequately pursued, he rushed headlong into another. He was seldom placid; but was inclined rather to be restless and fitful.

After a year or two of employment at the profession of poet, he found that his efforts to solve a variety of enigmas were apt to be both inconclusive and vexatious; and he soon came to recognize that he was trying to wrestle with intractable questions with inadequate intellectual equipment. It became obvious to him that the best way to tranquillize his mind was to cure this defect. He told a friend: 'An extensive knowledge is needful to thinking people—it takes away the heat and fever . . .'[1] And, about the same time, he wrote, with ingenuous frankness: 'I know nothing, I have read nothing, and I mean to follow Solomon's direction of "get wisdom—get understanding" —I find cavalier days are gone by. I find that I can have no enjoyment in the world but continual drinking of knowledge.' He proposed to himself a programme of 'application, study and thought', and he framed a project of 'retiring for some years for this purpose'.[2] But he had, in fact, been a voracious reader since his late 'teens, and many of his conclusions on puzzling issues were based not only on happy intuitions, but on profitable meditation, the outcome of a diversity of study. Unfortunately, he died too young to go far in carrying out his laudable intentions respecting a more extensive survey of philosophy, history, and art.

In many aspects of his life he was, like some other poets, liable to be painfully agitated as a result of the extreme susceptibility of his emotions. Where ordinary people's equanimity would have been no more than ruffled, he would find a situation well nigh intolerable. If people with whom he was

living, or with whom he was in close relationship were uncongenial, he could hardly bear to remain in their presence.
'When I am in a room with people', he said, 'if ever I am free
from speculating on creations of my own brain, then not myself
goes home to myself, but the identity [i.e. the personality]
of everyone in the room begins so to press upon me, that I am
in a very little time annihilated. . . .'[3] On another occasion, he
remarked that being 'surrounded with unpleasant human
identities' prevented him from enjoying that 'delicious diligent
indolence' that induced his inspiration so effectively.[4]

But he did not merely suffer discomfort and disquiet from the
influence upon him of uncongenial personalities; he was also
discomposed by the presence of people who prompted his
imagination in a painful way. When he was nursing his much
beloved brother, Tom, who was dying from tuberculosis, the
sight of the life of such a one hanging by so precarious a thread
worked grievously on his tender feelings. 'His identity', he wrote,
'presses upon me so all day that I am obliged to go out—
and although I intended to have given some time to study alone,
I am obliged to write, and plunge into abstract images to ease
myself of his countenance, his voice and his feebleness—so that
I live now in a continual fever . . .'[5] He described the same kind
of reaction a year later, when he was living in the same house
with a friend who was seriously ill. 'I confess', he said, 'I
cannot bear a sick person in a house especially alone—it
weighs upon me day and night. . . .'[6]

This emotional intensity naturally expressed itself in his
letters to his friends and relations, as will be noticed in many
extracts to be incorporated in this chapter. Often his letters
comprise an exuberant flow of intense thoughts tumbling over
one another in the 'indistinct profusion' that Shelley remarked
on in regard to *Endymion*. But, naturally enough, his emotion-
alism was most evident in his love-letters to Fanny Brawne,
from which one or two specially significant passages will be
quoted later on. Surely it is not surprising that a poet of Keats's
calibre, when carried away by a passion for the woman who so
completely enchanted and enraptured him, should speak to her
in extravagant language. After a short period in which he had
supposed that his art might suffer from a consuming love for
Fanny, he realized that she had captivated him entirely and

irretrievably; and he wrote her a letter in which he declared:
'You have absorb'd me. I have a sensation at the present
moment as though I was dissolving—I should be exquisitely
miserable without the hope of soon seeing you. . . . You have
ravish'd me away by a power I cannot resist; and yet I could
resist till I saw you [again]; and ever since I have seen you I
have endeavoured often "to reason against the reasons of my
love". I can do that no more—the pain would be too great.
My love is selfish. I cannot breathe without you.'[7]

We may sometimes regret that Keats must have worn himself
out by his excessive intensity of feeling; but we can hardly
impute blame to him on this account. As, however, this aspect
of his disposition is of such notable importance in an assessment
of his behaviour, we must consider some remarks by Matthew
Arnold respecting this letter of Keats. Matthew Arnold referred
to Keats's 'abandonment of all reticence and all dignity', and
to the letter's 'relaxed self-abandonment' as 'something under-
bred and ignoble, as of a youth ill brought up without the
training which teaches us that we must put some constraint
upon our feelings and upon the expression of them'.[8] Surely this
disparagement is unwarranted: Matthew Arnold, with his smug
superiority and lack of perspicacity, was incapable of understanding the fervent, overwhelming love of a highly romantic
youth; and, for similar reasons, he may have been unqualified
to appreciate the spirit of much of his poetry.

Some of the episodes in Keats's relations with Fanny Brawne
were, as everyone knows, almost unbearably harrowing,
involving a degree of strain that could not continue long without
a breaking-point. And, in other respects, his short life had more
than a fair share of distresses and anxieties. Still, we must not
think of his days as being predominantly vexed with painful
impressions, though he experienced much sadness, and
pondered over it a great deal. Pain and pleasure were, for him,
only divided by a narrow barrier; and it is satisfactory to
remember that his enjoyment was sometimes as keen as his
affliction. He took a voluptuous pleasure, on occasions when he
could afford it, in good food and drink. At parties, he was often
a sparkling and even hilarious companion. He mentioned,
among his 'palate-passions', the breast of a partridge and a bottle
of claret, and remarked that claret 'fills one's mouth with a

gushing freshness—then goes down cool and feverless'.[9] When some of his friends joined him in a 'claret feast', 'we all got a little tipsy—but pleasantly so—I enjoy claret to a degree'.[10] And, of the eating of a nectarine, he wrote: 'It went down soft, pulpy, slushy, oozy—all its delicious embonpoint melted down my throat like a large beatified strawberry.'[11] In many of his thoughts, as disclosed in his letters, and in much of his poetry, he was very near the angels; but it is a comforting reflection that he was also abundantly human.

If it is true that an essential feature of the best poetry is the expression of intense feeling, it is not surprising that Keats's reputation as a poet stands so high. He himself was enlightening on this subject in one of those pregnant asides that are frequently encountered in his letters. He told his brothers that 'the excellence of every art is its intensity, capable of making all disagreeables evaporate, from their being in close relationship with Beauty and Truth'.[12] It is obvious that anyone holding these views would not be satisfied with the superficial, merely descriptive type of poetry that had been prevalent for many years before his time. He himself put all the energy, all the thought, and all the passion of which he was capable into his poetry. He once wrote, in a moment of characteristic enthusiasm: 'The faint conceptions I have of poems to come brings the blood frequently into my forehead.'[13] Although an admirer of Wordsworth, Keats considered some of his poetry to be insufficiently profound, lacking in intensity of thought, not making, in fact, any valuable contribution to the interpretation of Beauty and Truth. He remarked, in regard to Wordsworth's *Gipsies*, that the scene was pleasantly described, but that there was little more to be gained from its reading than a satisfactory visual impression; and he added that 'it seems to me that, if Wordsworth had thought a little deeper at that moment, he would not have written the poem at all—I should judge it to have been written in one of the most comfortable moods of his life. It is a kind of sketchy intellectual landscape, not a search after truth.'[14] Similarly, in mentioning Lord Byron's poetry, he observed: 'There is this great difference between us. He describes what he sees. I describe what I imagine. Mine is the hardest task.'[15] A remark in a letter of Browning's about some poetry of Tennyson's is apropos here, as it helps to make Keats's

position plain. 'We look at the object of art in poetry so
differently! Here is an Idyll about a knight being untrue to his
friend and yielding to the temptation of that friend's mistress
after having engaged to assist him in his suit. I should judge
the conflict in the knight's soul the proper subject to describe.
Tennyson thinks he should describe the castle, and effect of the
moon on its towers, and anything *but* the soul.'[16]

Keats took the view that poetry, though characterized both
by sublimity and depth of meaning, should not be pretentious;
and, like all the best artistry, should combine verve with a
suitable measure of restraint. It should, in fact, instil its
essential truths by inducing a quiet contentment rather than a
fascinated bewilderment. 'Poetry', he remarked, 'should be
great and unobtrusive, a thing which enters into one's soul,
and does not startle it or amaze it with itself, but with its
subject.—How beautiful are the retired flowers! how would
they lose their beauty were they to throng into the highway
crying out "admire me, I am a violet!—dote on me, I am a
primrose".'[17] He implies here that poetry must be natural and
unaffected; and so natural was it to him, in a slightly different
sense, that, here and elsewhere in his letters, he could not
resist writing poetry in prose.

At the same time that it is unobtrusive, poetry must be
intense, because its object is to intensify the reader's interest in
life. It must heighten his awareness of life's potentialities.
Keats made this point clear when he told his brother and sister-
in-law (George and Georgiana): 'The great beauty of poetry
is, that it makes every thing, every place interesting.'[18] His
habit of writing his poetry in the heat of inspiration helps to
explain why some of it is liable to be criticized as uncouth and
insufficiently integrated. He was well aware of the pertinence
of this kind of criticism; but he felt that, if he had been more
careful, and more cautious, he would have lost the spontaneity
which was essential to his object, for his poetry would not have
succeeded in being intense and, therefore, in stirring the reader
to the depths of his being. He expressed this point of view
forcefully in discussing the unfavourable comments made on his
first book. 'In *Endymion*', he said, 'I leaped headlong into the
sea, and thereby have become better acquainted with the sound-
ings, the quicksands, & the rocks, than if I had stayed upon the

green shore, and piped a silly pipe, and took tea & comfortable advice.—I was never afraid of failure; for I would sooner fail than not be among the greatest.'[19]

Some of his letters effectively disclose his extreme activity of mind; its inability to be at rest. He eagerly embraced the challenge of any topics which could excite and entrance it.[20] But, in the last year of his active authorship, he began to feel that he had been maintaining too feverish a pace; and he told George and Georgiana: 'Some think I have lost that poetic ardour and fire 'tis said I once had—the fact is perhaps I have: but instead of that I hope I shall substitute a more thoughtful and quiet power. I am more frequently, now, contented to read and think—but, now & then, haunted with ambitious thoughts. Quieter in my pulse, improved in my digestion; exerting myself against vexing speculations—scarcely content to write the best verses for the fever they leave behind. I want to compose without this fever. I hope one day I shall.'[21] It should not be assumed that, in these sentences, he was projecting a radical change in his attitude to poetry, involving a loss of intensity or of depth of meaning. His intention, we may surmise, was rather that the intensity should be less agitating, less overpowering, of a kind that would be the fruit of steady contemplation rather than of emotional excitement.

It would be a mistake to exclude reference to the numerous passages in his letters which introduce poetical ideas, as being irrelevant to a discussion of his character, for they reflect the very essence of the man, his ardent spirit. Moreover, his frequent consideration of the subject of poetry in his letters, sometimes combined with this habit of blending poetry and prose into one means of expression, is illustrative of his delight in sharing his inmost thoughts with his friends. Some of these have a sombre cast, in keeping with an occasional mood. He told a friend: 'I am certain of nothing but of the holiness of the heart's affections and the truth of imagination—What the imagination seizes as Beauty must be Truth—whether it existed before or not—for I have the same idea of all our passions as of love; they are all in their sublime, creative of essential beauty.'[22] And again: 'This is the world [referring to some bad news]—thus we cannot expect to give way many hours to pleasure—Circumstances are like clouds continually gathering and bursting—While we are laughing, the seed of some trouble is put into the wide arable land of events—while we are laughing it sprouts, it grows, and suddenly bears a poison fruit which we must pluck.'[23]

He was not, however, predominantly addicted to despondency or to assuming a lugubrious air. Numerous inferences can be drawn from his letters to indicate that he was much sought after as a lively and entertaining companion; and, from the same source, we can understand that his whimsicality was a large feature in his ability to entertain. He used a particular brand of it to amuse suitable correspondents. Perhaps the best example occurs in a letter to two sisters of a friend of his, of about the same age as himself: 'Give my sincerest respects to Mrs. Dilke saying that . . . had I remained at Hampstead I would have made precious havoc with her house and furniture —drawn the great harrow over her garden—poisoned Boxer— eaten her cloathes pegs,—fried her cabbages—fricaceed (how is it spelt?) her radishes—ragouted her onions—belaboured her beat root—outstripped her scarlet runners—parlezvou'd with her french beans—devoured her Mignon or Mignonette— metamorphosed her bell-handles—splintered her looking glasses—bullock'd at her cups and saucers—agonized her decanters—put old Philips [the gardener] to pickle in the brine-tub—disorganized her piano—dislocated her candle-sticks . . . and astonished Brown whose letter to her on these events I would rather see than the original copy of the Book of Genesis.'[24]

The quality of unselfishness was clearly at the top of Keats's list of the virtues. But, although he could exhibit a remarkable record of unselfish behaviour, especially in his devoted care for his brother, Tom, he was far from making any claim to be a proficient exponent himself. He wrote: 'Very few men have ever arrived at a complete disinterestedness [his word for "un-selfishness"] of mind: . . . . From the manner in which I feel Haslam's misfortune I perceive how far I am from any humble standard of disinterestedness—Yet this feeling ought to be carried to its highest pitch as there is no fear of its ever injuring society . . . I have no doubt that thousands of people never heard of have had hearts completely disinterested: I can remember but two—Socrates and Jesus—their histories evince it.'[25] Of those persons he knew personally, his sister-in-law, Georgiana, the wife of his brother, George, seems to have been considered by him to have the best claim to a character distinguished by unselfishness. He told a friend: 'I like her better and better—she is the most disinterested woman I ever knew—that is to say she goes beyond degree in it.'[26] It is, indeed, remarkable that the age of this paragon was then seventeen: young people's characters sometimes developed early in those days.

Several instances of Keats's own practice of unselfishness will present themselves in the course of this chapter, so that it will be sufficient here to notice one outstanding incident. Haydon, the painter, who was a man some ten years older than Keats, and who had impressed him with his talents and gained his affection, was experiencing a severe struggle to maintain himself from the profits of his profession; and Keats's abundant goodwill impelled him to offer him help with a loan, when he was not in fact sufficiently in funds to do so. His letter to Haydon, the language of which gives a realistic impression of the exalted spirit in which the offer was made, includes the following passage: 'I will turn to a thing I have thought on more—I mean your means till your picture be finished: not only now but for this year and a half have I thought of it. Believe me, Haydon, I have that sort of fire in my heart that would sacrifice every thing I have to your service—I speak without any reserve—I know you would do so for me—I open my heart to you in a few words—I will do this sooner than you shall be distressed: . . .' And he then, with diffidence, suggested that Haydon might first try the rich lovers of art, because the money he had hoped to raise for this loan had been set aside in his mind so as to enable him to study and travel, for the improvement of his qualifications as a poet.[27] His quixotic self-sacrifice in this matter can be more fully appreciated when we find that he was almost without any ready money at this time, and that, two days later, he was writing to his publisher asking for a loan of £30, 'ten I want for myself, and twenty for a friend'.[28] His desire to give expression to his spirit of helpfulness was irrepressible, as may be gathered from the fact that he had already lent to needy friends about £200 out of his slender patrimony.

The ingenuousness of some of the expressions in his letter

to Haydon may strike us at first as odd, but should be recognized as due to his guilelessness. What is undoubtedly naïvety in several of his aspirations, as communicated to his friends, might be suspected in many other people to be self-righteousness. 'I find', he said, for instance, 'there is no worthy pursuit but the idea of doing some good for the world.'[29] Six months later, he wrote to another friend: 'I am ambitious of doing the world some good: if I should be spared, that may be the work of maturer years—in the interval I will assay to reach as high a summit in poetry as the nerve bestowed upon me will suffer.'[30] A sense of urgency evidently oppressed him; and he may have divined that there would not be time for a long-term programme. He saw his objective so clearly that he expressed it artlessly, without feeling the need for careful qualifications.

Doubtless his friends were completely sincere who, both before and after his death, alleged that his premature end was due to heart-break at the ignominy following from the personal attacks made on him by brutal reviewers. He certainly suffered severely in mind, especially after he became mortally ill. But it is widely agreed now that he put a bold front on these grievous setbacks to his ambitions. He was not the self-centred type of man who would allow his spirit to be thus broken. He naturally did not betray his more depressed moods in his letters to George and Georgiana, who had emigrated to America a few weeks after the publication of *Endymion*, and before the adverse reviews had appeared. The comments he made to them a little later on, about the attacks on him in the *Quarterly* and other reviews may, however, taken as a whole, represent his steady, considered attitude. He bore up bravely at first; and, in his famous phrase, asserted: 'I think I shall be among the English poets after my death.' And he continued: 'Even as a matter of present interest the attempt to crush me in the Quarterly has only brought me more into notice, and it is a common expression among bookmen "I wonder the Quarterly should cut its own throat".'[31] But after a few months his attitude changed somewhat. He still determined to continue in his profession of poet, and felt assured of his ultimate success; but he was much less confident of the incapacity of the hostile reviewers to poison the minds of the public. He told George and Georgiana, after this period of further deliberation: 'My poem [*Endymion*] has not at all succeeded—in the course of a year or so I think I shall try the public again—in a selfish point of view I should suffer my pride and my contempt of public opinion to hold me silent —but for your's and Fanny's [his sister's] sake, I will pluck up a spirit and try again. I have no doubt of success in a course of years if I persevere—but it must be patience—for the Reviews have enervated and made indolent men's minds—few think for themselves—These Reviews are getting more and more powerful, and especially the Quarterly . . . I was in hopes that when people saw, as they must do now, all the trickery and iniquity of these plagues, they would scout them, but no, they are like the spectators at the Westminster cock-pit—they like the battle, and do not care who wins or who loses.'[32] He had, in fact, continued writing poetry after the *Quarterly's* critique had appeared. In the month before the date of the above-quoted letter, he had written *The Eve of St. Agnes*; and, just before it, he had written *The Eve of St. Mark*. Moreover, he published a fresh volume of poems in the summer of the following year (1820). It is obvious, therefore, that he did not feebly succumb to the venomous and ruthless attacks of his enemies, but displayed a remarkable fortitude and resiliency. Nevertheless it is doubtless true that his powers of resistance during his last illness were weakened by the mental anguish he underwent a year before.

Keats's character was sufficiently well balanced to enable it to combine the loftiest ambition with an admirable modesty. The cruelty of Croker's review in the *Quarterly* was particularly indefensible in view of Keats's modest phrases in his Preface to *Endymion*, where he mentioned the obviousness of his great inexperience and immaturity. The genuineness of this modesty is attested by some remarks he made in letters to his publishers. Before publication, he told them: 'In *Endymion*, I have most likely but moved into the go-cart from the leading strings.'[33] In his personal relations he was equally modest. He discovered, as a result of the combination of reflection and experience, that he was often happiest in the company of his friends if he allowed them to believe they were in the right in an argument, even at the risk of seeming less clever than they. 'I am content to be thought all this', he remarked, 'because I have in my own breast so great a resource.'[34] His friend, Bailey, said that 'he was uniformly the apologist for poor frail human nature, and allowed for people's faults more than any man I ever knew, and especially for the faults of his friends'. There is a considerable amount of evidence for his large-hearted tolerance in his correspondence with his friends. He evinced it very ingenuously in a letter to Bailey: 'To a man of your nature such a letter as Haydon's must have been extremely cutting—What occasions the greater part of the world's quarrels? simply this, two minds meet and do not understand each other in time enough to prevent any shock or surprise at the conduct of either party—As soon as I had known Haydon three days I had got enough of his character not to have been surprised at such a letter as he has hurt you with. Nor, when I knew it, was it a principle with me to drop his acquaintance although with you it would have been an imperious feeling.'[35] On another occasion, he told his friend, James Rice, that it was quite unnecessary for him to apologize for a supposed offence against their friendship; and he gave him some instances of how easy he himself had found it to offend people without the least intention of doing so, adding: 'I have long made up my mind to take for granted the genuine-heartedness of my friends notwithstanding any temporary ambiguousness in their behaviour. . . .'[36]

Not only was he tolerant in his views of the defects of character which so often lead to breaches in friendship, but he was so keenly interested in the maintenance of good relations between his friends that he was prepared to adopt the part of mediator, and to try and repair such breaches. When Haydon, who seems to have been adept at quarrelling, was at loggerheads with Keats's friend, Reynolds, Keats wrote to his brother: 'Considering all things, Haydon's frequent neglect of his appointments &c., his notes were bad enough to put Reynolds on the right side of the question—but then Reynolds has no powers of sufferance; no idea of having the thing against him; so he answered Haydon in one of the most cutting letters I ever read, . . . the fact is they are both in the right and both in the wrong.'[37] He also discussed the same quarrel with Bailey to whom he asserted that a good procedure to adopt in the practice of friendship is 'first to know a man's faults, and then be passive'. He proceeded: 'Before I felt interested in either

Reynolds or Haydon—I was well read in their faults, yet knowing them both I have been cementing gradually with both. I have an affection for them for reasons almost opposite —and to both must I of necessity cling—supported always by the hope that when a little time—a few years shall have tried me more fully in their esteem, I may be able to bring them together—the time must come because they have both hearts— and they will recollect the best parts of each other when this gust is overblown.'[38]

He also planned to heal a breach between Haydon and Leigh Hunt.[39] He, in fact, displayed the Christian virtues of gentleness and placability, as well as that of peacemaker, to a remarkable degree. But, at the same time, he was not afraid to stand firmly and sternly for justice and the maintenance of proper behaviour; and he was prepared to reprehend defects in character when he considered it to be requisite or even appropriate. It did not take him long, after making friends with Leigh Hunt, to discover the weak points in that man's character; and he wrote somewhat caustically to his brother on the subject, concluding that 'in reality he is vain, egotistical, and disgusting in matters of taste and morals. He understands many a beautiful thing; but then, instead of giving other minds credit for the same degree of perception as he himself possesses —he begins an explanation in such a curious manner that our taste and self-love is offended continually. Hunt does one harm by making fine things petty and beautiful things hateful.'[40]

Happily, Keats, who put such a high value on friendship, had some of the most devoted friends that a man ever had. The notable and spontaneous kindnesses he received from them, especially in regard to his illness, and, earlier, that of his brother, Tom, were, as we might expect from his character, keenly appreciated by him. As we shall have occasion to notice, he was one of those rare recipients of benefits who knew intuitively how to make his obligation a source of satisfaction to the giver. He knew how to be appreciative; and he frequently told his relations, in his letters to them, about the helpfulness of his friends. Haslam, he described as 'a most kind and obliging and constant friend—His behaviour to Tom during my absence and since my return has endeared him to me for ever . . . .'.[41] Brown, he said had been very kind to him when he

N

most wanted his assistance.[42] 'Brown and Dilke are very kind and considerate to me.'[43] And, again, he mentioned Brown's 'generous and most friendly actions . . . towards me'.[44]

Ordinarily, he accepted the ungrudging practical sympathy of his friends without any sense of embarrassment. But he could not, he felt, go on accepting loans of money from Brown who had had to limit his own expenditure as a consequence. It was incumbent on him to find some remunerative occupation. Meanwhile, he was impelled to open his heart on this subject in a long letter in the course of which he told his generous helper: 'You have been living for others more than any man I know. This is a vexation to me; because it has been depriving you, in the very prime of life, of pleasures which it was your duty to procure. . . . I had got into the habit of looking towards you as a help in all difficulties. This very habit would be the parent of idleness and difficulties. You will see it is a duty I owe myself to break the neck of it.'[45]

Obligations in respect of kindness, in the history of Keats's life, were far from being on one side only. We have, for instance, already noticed his over-zealous anxiety to give financial help to friends in need. But his kindnesses were, from the circumstances of his case, mostly conferred on his brothers and sister. In different ways, he displayed extreme self-sacrifice for both his brothers. He himself, George, Tom, and Fanny were born in 1795, 1797, 1799 and 1803 respectively. By the year 1810, they were orphans; and the younger ones looked up to John as the eldest and cleverest, though George was the biggest, strongest, most practical, and, later, the most businesslike. Keats's little sister, Fanny, was placed in charge of a guardian; and, as she began to grow up, he took an affectionate, fatherly interest in her welfare, and evinced a lively sympathy in the details of her life, which was truly remarkable in view of his own commitments in starting a career. A few extracts from his letters to Fanny, beginning at the time when she was fourteen years old, and continuing for three years, speak for themselves in proving his genuine concern for her.

'You must tell me about all you read. . . . This I feel as a necessity: for we ought to become intimately acquainted, in order that I may not only, as you grow up, love you as my only sister, but confide in you as my dearest friend.'[46]

'Now, Fanny, you must write soon—and write all you think about, never mind what—only let me have a good deal of your writing.'[47]

'You have no one in the world besides me who would sacrifice anything for you—I feel myself the only protector you have. In all your little troubles think of me with the thought that there is at least one person in England who, if he could, would help you out of them.'[48]

'You did not say a word about your chilblains. Write to me directly and let me know about them—Your letter shall be answered like an echo.'[49]

'Tell me if you want any particular book; or pencils, or drawing paper—anything but livestock. Though I will not be severe on it, remembering how fond I used to be of goldfinches, tomtits, minnows, mice, ticklebacks, dace, cock salmons and all the whole tribe of the bushes and the brooks: but verily they are better in the trees and the water, though I must confess even now a partiality for a handsome globe of goldfish—then I would have it hold 10 pails of water and be fed continually fresh through a cool pipe with another pipe to let through the floor—well-ventilated, they would preserve all their beautiful silver and crimson.'[50]

The ardent affection which Keats bore for his brothers after he had reached manhood was remarkable. He told his friend, Bailey: 'My love for my brothers, from the early loss of our parents, and even for earlier misfortunes, has grown into an affection "passing the love of women".—I have been ill-temper'd with them, I have vex'd them—but the thought of them has always stifled the impression that any woman might otherwise have made upon me.'[51]

Soon after George and Georgiana emigrated to America, Tom's physical condition became desperate; and it was obvious to Keats that he could not live more than a few days. He made the communication of this news to George and Georgiana the occasion of an affirmation of the depth of his family feeling. 'Ours', he said, 'are ties which, independent of their own sentiment, are sent to us by providence to prevent the deleterious effects of one great, solitary grief. I have Fanny and I have you—three people whose happiness to me is sacred—and it does annul that selfish sorrow which I should otherwise fall into, living as I do with poor Tom who looks upon me as his only comfort—the tears will come into your eyes—let them—and embrace each other—thank heaven for what happiness you have, and after thinking a moment or two that you suffer in common with all mankind, hold it not a sin to regain your cheerfulness.'[52]

The long, journalizing letters that Keats wrote to George and Georgiana comprised all the interesting news about common friends that he could muster, accounts of his own doings, occasional bursts of humour, efforts at diversion, entertaining narrations, and, above all in value both to the recipients and to us, his inmost thoughts and most intimate philosophizing. He could only have undertaken a correspondence on this scale, sufficient in total bulk to fill a small book, if his affection for these two had been as great and as real as he alleged. 'My brother, George', he told a friend, 'has ever been more than a brother to me, he has been my greatest friend . . .'[53] And he told Georgiana, in a letter: 'I have a tenderness for you, and an admiration which I feel to be as great and more chaste than I can have for any woman in the world.'[54]

His attitude to the question of marrying, in the period leading up to his engagement to Fanny Brawne, is, of course, of profound interest. About four months before he met her, he told Bailey, in a passage in a letter already quoted, that the thought of his brothers 'has always stifled the impression that any woman might otherwise have made upon me'.[55] A month later, he told his friend, Reynolds: 'I have spoken to you against marriage, but it was general. The prospect in these matters has been to me so blank, that I have not been unwilling to die —I would not [be willing] now, for I have inducements to life —I must see my little nephews in America, and I must see you marry your lovely wife.'[56] And, in the same month, he wrote to his brother, Tom, in terms to which we can give considerable credence: 'With respect to women, I think I shall be able to conquer my passions hereafter better than I have yet done.'[57] Two months later again he told his friend, Reynolds, that he had been haunted by the physical form of a woman for two days, but that poetry had conquered. 'I feel escaped', he said, 'from a new strange and threatening sorrow—and I am thankful for it.'[58] This last letter may explain the apparent discrepancies between the two preceding ones. It might seem, from reading the first-quoted letter, that he was averse to matrimony because his primary and all-absorbing attachment was to his brothers; but that point of view, an inherently unlikely one, was, if ever really effective, only transient. The next three letters apparently represent different points of view in regard to his consecration of himself to poetry.

A few months before he became intimately acquainted with Fanny Brawne, a remark in a letter from George and Georgiana prompted him to deal at length with the reasons for his opposition to the idea of marriage. His brother and sister-in-law had exhorted him to marry, and thus to enjoy the same kind of happiness that they had found. But, in reply, he advocated for himself the joys of the solitary, or rather the independent life. By independence he meant freedom to devote himself to poetry without any impediment or encumbrance, as we shall see when he became involved in a struggle between the claims of poetry and the enchantment of Fanny Brawne. He wrote to George and Georgiana: 'Notwithstanding your happiness and your recommendation, I hope I shall never marry. Though the most beautiful creature were waiting for me at the end of a journey or a walk; though the carpet were of silk, the curtains of the morning clouds; the chairs and sofa stuffed with cygnet's down; the food manna, the wine beyond claret, the windows opening upon Winander mere, I should not feel, or rather my happiness would not be so fine, my solitude is sublime. Then instead of what I have described, there is a sublimity to welcome me home. The roaring of the wind is my wife, and the stars through the windowpane are my children. The mighty abstract idea I have of beauty in all things stifles the more divided and minute domestic happiness. . . . I feel more and more every day, as my imagination strengthens, that I do not live in this world alone but in a thousand worlds. . . . I melt into the air with a voluptuousness so delicate that I am content to be alone. These things combined with the opinion I have of the generality of women—who appear to me as children to whom I would rather give a sugar plum than my time, form a barrier against matrimony that I rejoice in. I have written this that you might see I have my share of the highest pleasures and that, though I may choose to pass my days alone, I shall be no solitary.'[59]

By December 1818 Keats had spent a considerable amount of time in the company of Fanny Brawne. But, in writing to George and Georgiana, he behaved as many young men do to their relations when half in love, he dissimulated, and described the lady to them as in some respects attractive, but as meaning no more to him than would any pleasant feminine companion. He portrayed her as 'beautiful and elegant, graceful, silly, fashionable and strange'. He twice remarked that they had had an occasional tiff. He also noticed that she had 'a fine style of countenance of the lengthen'd sort—she wants sentiment in every feature—she manages to make her hair look well. . . . Her shape is very graceful and so are her movements . . . but she is ignorant—monstrous in her behaviour, flying out in all directions, calling people such names that I was forced lately to make use of the term *minx* . . . I am however tired of such style, and shall decline any more of it.'[60] Anyone with but a moderate discernment in such matters could have concluded from these remarks that the pair would be engaged before many months had passed. Perhaps, by April 1819, he was beginning to wonder if he could afford to get married. His poetry was obviously unlikely to gain him a living; and he told George and Georgiana, not that he was contemplating matrimony, but that he meant to see what he could do in the way of making a livelihood by some other means than poetry, such as journalism.

It has been generally supposed that he became informally engaged to Fanny in June 1819; and, soon afterwards, he wrote to her from the Isle of Wight, to which he had gone for his health, to tell her with, we may suppose, more seriousness than playfulness, that he must protest against the loss of his independence. 'I have never known any unalloy'd happiness for many days together: the death or sickness of someone has always spoilt my hours—and now when none such troubles oppress me, it is, you must confess, very hard that another sort of pain should haunt me. Ask yourself, my love, whether you are not very cruel to have so entramelled me, so destroyed my freedom.'[61] A few days later, after having received a letter from her which caused his self-interest to recede, and his love for her to show more warmly, he wrote her a letter which is distinctive among his earlier letters to her, for it expresses anxious thought for her welfare, rather than implying preoccupation with the importance of his own career as a poet. 'I never knew before', he said, 'what such a love as you have made me feel, was; I did not believe in it; my fancy was afraid of it, lest it should burn me up. . . . I have so much of you in my heart that I must turn mentor when I see a chance of harm befalling you. I would never see any thing but pleasure in your eyes, love on your lips, and happiness in your steps. I would wish to see you among those amusements suitable to your inclinations and spirits; so that our loves might be a delight in the midst of pleasures agreeable enough, rather than a resource from vexations and cares. But I doubt much, in the case of the worst, whether I shall be philosopher enough to follow my own lessons: if I saw my resolution give you pain, I could not.'[62] These are admirably altruistic and chivalrous expressions, proceeding from a lover at his most noble. Alas! Keats never found an opportunity to substantiate them.

After a few weeks in which he had been strenuously devoting himself to the composition of poetry, he wrote to Fanny, in August 1819, in terms which amount to an admission that he had half forgotten her, because the vocation of poetry had so captivated and ensnared him that there was no room for any other thought in his mind. 'I must remain some days in a mist —I see you through a mist: as I daresay you do me by this time. Believe in the first letters I wrote you: I assure you I felt as I wrote—I could not write so now. The thousand images I have had pass through my brain—my uneasy spirits—my unguess'd fate—all spread as a veil between me and you. Remember I have had no idle leisure to brood over you—'tis well perhaps I have not. . . . My mind is heap'd to the full; stuff'd like a cricket ball—if I strive to fill it more, it would burst.' He acknowledged that he was being harsh, and he concluded the letter: 'O my love, your lips are growing sweet again to my fancy—I must forget them.'[63] This tendency to breach of faith was not just a fleeting whim, for, at the same period, he was writing letters to his friends which were hardly consistent with the proper convictions of an engaged man. He described the love of a man for a woman as 'cloying treacle on the wings of independence',[64] and spoke of poetry as 'all I care for, all I live for'.[65]

In September 1819 he received bad news from George, whose financial position had suddenly become desperate owing to an unsuccessful investment. He at once wrote to George pledging himself to such pecuniary aid as might be available to him in the near or more remote future. He said: 'Your wants will be a fresh spur to me. I assure you, you shall more than share what I get, whilst I am still young—the time may come when age will make me more selfish.'[66] And again: 'Rest in the confidence that I will not omit any exertion to benefit you by some means or other. If I cannot remit you hundreds, I will tens, and if not that ones.'[67] This is, indeed, strange language from a penniless, prospective husband who is, or should be, already wondering how to procure the requisite funds to enable him to get married.

In the same series of letters, combined into one omnibus letter, he not only omitted to tell George and Georgiana of his engagement to Fanny, presumably because that would have made nonsense of his quixotic offer of financial aid, but he also still wrote as if marriage was outside his whole philosophy. In an expansive moment that revealed only part of his mind, he admitted that he was passing through some pleasureless times. 'I have forgot how to lay plans for the enjoyment of any pleasure. I feel I can bear anything, any misery, even imprisonment—so long as I have neither wife nor child.'[68] He went even further in his affirmation of convinced attachment to celibacy; he deliberately gave a misleading impression of his recent experiences of being in love by making fun of such a state. In mentioning to George and Georgiana the circumstances of the engagement of their common friend, Haslam, he told them: 'He show'd me her picture by Severn. I think she is, though not very cunning, too cunning for him. Nothing strikes me so forcibly with a sense of the ridiculous as love. A man in love I do think cuts the sorriest figure in the world. Even when I know a poor fool to be really in pain about it, I could burst out laughing in his face.'[69]

The scheme which had been in Keats's mind earlier in 1819, to devote himself to journalism for a time, so as to make some money, became doubly desirable after hearing about George's depleted purse. He wrote to his friends in September outlining his plan to live in Westminster, as a favourable base for his purpose. But he did not then tell George and Georgiana of this plan, which involved, temporarily at least, giving up the writing of poetry, because that would have disclosed to them the extent to which any financial aid he could give them would be a matter of bitter self-sacrifice.

No sooner had he settled in Westminster, all ready to pursue his journalistic activities, than he found that his devotion to Fanny had revived, and was stronger and more compulsive than ever. He then wrote her the ecstatic love-letter from which we have already quoted, in remarking on his intensity of feeling —the letter in which he said 'I have no limit now to my love', and which ends: 'I cannot breathe without you' (see p. 172, above). Within a day or two, the journalistic project seems to have been abandoned; and he moved to Hampstead, and was making love to Fanny with at least as much ardour as at the time of their engagement four months earlier.

As yet, his health, though frail, had not broken down; he was feverishly in love, and desirous of marrying Fanny with the least possible delay. His trustee had available for him a sum of about £300 which he could have drawn upon and used to start a home, thus achieving a situation which would un-doubtedly have been beneficial to his health and peace of mind. But, instead of paying due regard to his own and Fanny's happiness, he acted in such a way that, if his mortal illness had not soon overtaken him, he would have imperilled his future by an act of self-sacrifice that was prodigious both in its heroism and its irrationality. His action lost much of its virtue because it sacrificed Fanny as well as himself; and Fanny was obviously not consulted in the matter.

George came to England for a few days in January 1820, in order to extract money from the family trustee for new financial ventures in America. With Keats's consent and approval he took back with him to the New Country all the money due to the two of them except £100. He took, therefore, some £700; and he promised to repay to Keats £200 as soon as he could manage to do so. Keats told George nothing about his engage-ment to Fanny even when George was frequently seeing him during his short visit. George stated some time afterwards that, when he was on this visit, he found his brother 'not the same being; although his reception of me was as warm as heart could wish, he did not speak with his former openness and unreserve;

he had lost the reviving custom of venting his griefs'. This, of course, is not to be wondered at, because Keats was passing through the agonizing process of seeing his happiness receding to a vanishing-point; he knew that his health was precarious, and his prospect of being united to Fanny, at last immutably dear to him, was more indefinite than ever. He was unable to confide in his brother for whom he was giving up so much, because George would certainly never have accepted the loan of his brother's money if he had known the real position of affairs. However, only a few days after George had left again for America, Keats's fatal illness began, on 3rd February 1820, with symptoms that made it likely, if not obvious, that he had at the most a year or two to live. It is doubtful, therefore, whether his keeping his money, instead of letting George borrow it, would have served to lengthen his life.

He undertook his heroic deception with the best of intentions. There can be no doubt that the lustre of self-sacrifice so enraptured him that he failed to recognize, not so much that he was not being fair to himself, for he was prepared to accept that situation, but that he was not being fair to Fanny. As we have seen, his inconsistent behaviour to her in the summer of 1819, though he tried to justify it to her and to himself on the ground of the overriding claims of his allegiance to his life's work, was plainly lacking in proper consideration for a young girl to whom he had just made love in the most vehement and unequivocal manner, and to whom, it is generally assumed, he was informally betrothed. On each of these two occasions the fault was due to his allowing his emotions to get the better of his judgement. His intense urge to fulfil his destiny as a poet, on the earlier occasion, and his passionate desire to help his brother when in need, on the later, beclouded his discernment, and involved him in mistaken and even blameworthy courses of action. One of the results of his sudden breakdown in health was a momentary ability to recognize his situation in its true perspective; and he wrote to Fanny in terms of affectionate solicitude. 'To see you', he said, 'happy and in high spirits is a great consolation to me . . . God alone knows whether I am destined to taste of happiness with you: at all events I myself know this much, that I consider it no mean happiness to have lov'd you thus far—if it is to be no further, I shall not be unthankful—if I am to recover, the day of my recovery shall see me by your side from which nothing shall separate me.'[70]

At this point the story of the shaping of Keats's character should end. It would have been better for the happiness of both of them if he had died then, because thenceforward for some months his view of Fanny was a distorted one. In the summer of 1820, although he was constantly asserting that his condition was improving, it was in fact steadily deteriorating. He lay for hours nursing all sorts of unjustifiable suspicions, and somehow managed to persuade himself that Fanny was callous, because she indulged in social activities, including attendance at dances, while he was laid by. He became obsessed with an irrational jealousy; and he even charged her with being unfaithful to him.[71] It is not fair to bring these letters in evidence in an assessment of his character. Owing, no doubt, to his precarious physical condition, his sensitive mind became tortured by his magnifying and misconstruing incidents which had no sinister significance whatever. He suffered, it seems, from transitory paroxysms of indignant but baseless suspicion which he was unable to control; and, later on, he sincerely regretted them. Shortly after the most reprehensible of his letters to Fanny, he explained to her: 'You complain of my illtreating you in word, thought and deed—I am sorry,— at times I feel bitterly sorry that I ever made you unhappy— my excuse is that those words have been wrung from me by the sharpness of my feelings.'[72]

It is impossible to imagine a serene and imperturbable Keats, the beauty of whose poetry seemed dependent on his emotions being kept at a high degree of tension. No poet, perhaps, can be too emotional, provided that he is not mawkish or fulsome. But no great poet can be conspicuous for the intensity of his poetry, and at the same time be a model of equanimity and sweet reasonableness as a lover. In other human relations, where his feelings were not worked up into a ferment, Keats's spirit of kindness and self-sacrifice was constant and pre-eminent. It is significant that the imperfections of his character arouse our pity rather than our reprehension. In one or two brief episodes, his heightened emotions involved him in behaviour that was unworthy and indefensible; and he was so carried away by his illusions as to be unable to understand how unjustly he was acting. But, in a general view of his character, we must conclude that he was a man of large-hearted principles who nearly succeeded in living up to them. There is much to be learnt from his noble interpretation of his part in the drama of life: indeed, Keats, the man, when at his most heroic, may be as inspiriting as Keats, the poet.

---- 10 ----

EDWARD FITZGERALD
(1809–1883)
Endearing Idiosyncrasies

I T is often difficult to enter into a discussion of a poet's
character without becoming involved in a good many
biographical particulars. We have experienced this in some of
the preceding chapters. If a career is signalized by momentous
events, its dramatic quality makes it all the more necessary to
observe the extent to which circumstances have influenced
the development of character. Sometimes, however, the situation is quite dissimilar. Few lives of eminent people have been
so unmarked by sensational incidents as that of Edward

FitzGerald. Consequently, after a briefly sketched background to the not very abrupt ups and downs of his career, his character can be surveyed with scarcely any dependence on chronology.

No one who knew him could fail to notice that he was steadily indisposed to come to any critical decisions. Naturally, therefore, after making some interesting friendships at Cambridge University, he found it easy to neglect the adoption of any profession, especially as he had sufficient means to satisfy his very modest requirements. He proceeded to lead a quiet scholarly life, often staying in the houses of relations in Suffolk; and, until he was past forty, he was well content to be unable to point to any kind of achievement beyond that of becoming a discerning student of literature, and giving much pleasure to his selected friends by means of his peculiar gifts of self-expression. Besides delighting them with the impressions flowing from an accomplished and original mind, and by a pervasive undercurrent of whimsical humour that characterized his letters and conversation, he offered them an affection that was both tender and decorous. In an age when it was not expected that everyone should do a day's work for a day's pay, he justified his place in society not merely with credit, but with distinction.

Shortly before he was forty, his father, a man of ample means, became bankrupt owing to an unfortunate speculation. As a result, Edward FitzGerald's income was much reduced; and he was forced to undertake some rigid economies. He suffered this considerable change of fortune with perfect resignation, or perhaps it would be more accurate to say with perfect unconcern, for luxuries meant little or nothing to him. He had eight years to live before his mother's death brought him a comfortable income; and he then, out of a fantastically mistaken interpretation of a moral obligation to a deceased friend, married that friend's daughter, Lucy Barton, a cultivated, but tactless woman, a little older than himself, who discomposed him with her loud and deep voice and notable lack of physical attraction. Above all, she irked him with her insistence on his compliance with her idea of the social proprieties. He had by then reached the age of forty-eight, and his disposition was that of an inveterate bachelor, with singularities that had become as pleasurable as they were ineradicable. No wonder that cohabitation was short-lived, and that, after some ten months of desolating aggravations, they agreed to separate.

FitzGerald suffered much mental distress as a result of this misfortune, for which he characteristically accepted most of the blame. His sensitive nature made him feel unnecessarily humiliated; and, shy as he was, he became shyer of company than ever. But, happily, the prospect of assuagement and consolation was at hand. He had recently undertaken the study of the Persian language, and was beginning to translate Persian poetry into English. His *Omar*, into which he put all the best of his genius, was published in a small edition two years after the fiasco of his marriage; and it is obvious from his letters that he had considerable expectations from this publication. Its success would have done much to compensate for the discomfiture he had recently experienced. Alas! his little book attracted no attention whatsoever. It was, in fact, a complete failure.

He was certainly sorely disappointed, but not in the least embittered; and he continued to find solace in his literary pursuits. But, when writing to a friend about the failure of *Omar*, he remarked that he was consoling himself with his 'little ship'.[1] He turned deliberately to a supplementary means of enlivening his hitherto rather humdrum, uneventful manner of life, so that his keen interest in human nature could be exercised without the strain—for strain it was, to him—of maintaining conventional standards of behaviour in society. He exploited his love for the sea, sailing-boats and sailor-men; and, thenceforward, spent much of his time for a number of years, especially in the summer, in cruising in his yacht, or in excursions in more modest craft, and in cultivating the close acquaintance of his small crew, of the boatmen on the River Deben at Woodbridge, and of the longshoremen at Lowestoft. Numerous references in his letters attest his profound satisfaction in the natural, or what is now often called uninhibited, ways of these simple folk. He soon learnt not to expect moral perfection, but he found much to delight him in their artlessness and integrity.

The character of a highly sensitive man like FitzGerald is apt to be a complex one, with a number of inconsistencies. His shyness and diffidence, for instance, would sometimes involve him in behaviour that was not true to his real nature. From his retiring disposition, he might be thought to be a man of hesitant and timorous opinions. But, in fact, as we shall see, his opinions were often original, and expressed both trenchantly and categorically. He was at one and the same time soft-hearted and rigorous, much in the same manner as Dr. Johnson, who could be genuinely affectionate and good-natured, and within a few moments, brusque and downright. FitzGerald was both social and unsocial. He would sedulously avoid formal parties of people of his own class, but could be found spending evenings with fishermen, yarning with them and sharing their jollifications. Like other poets discussed in this book, he abominated affectation, snobbery, and bombast. In this respect he may be aptly compared with Thomas Gray, who had an almost lover-like fondness for his intimates, but who had his stiff and forbidding side. Gray and FitzGerald had, in fact, strong affinities, sharing, among several other qualities, a racy facetiousness and a preference for sincerity to cleverness.

The robust humour that FitzGerald introduced so delightfully into his letters contrasts interestingly with the sentimental view of friendship which was so essential a feature in his make-up. His playful manner, which we are bound to judge chiefly from his writing, was never pretentious or elaborate; it just flowed off his pen in the course of his indulgence in light banter or in whimsical extravagances. He wrote, for instance, to an artist friend: 'I don't see much prospect of my going to Cumberland this winter: though I should like to go snipe-shooting with that literary shot James Spedding. Do you mean to try and go up Skiddaw? You will get out upon it from your bedroom window: so I advise you to begin before you go down to breakfast. There is a mountain called Dod, which has felt me up its summit [he was a heavy man at that period]. . . . Remember me to Grisedale Pike; a very well-bred mountain. If you paint ——, put him not only in a good light, but to leeward of you in a strong current of air.'[2] The James Spedding mentioned in this letter was an old Cambridge friend, a great scholar, with an abnormally high forehead. FitzGerald enjoyed teasing him about it, and described him to others as 'The forehead'. He once remarked to Frederick Tennyson: 'No wonder no hair can grow at such an altitude.'

Although generous and hospitable, FitzGerald's guests sometimes found that the arrangements for meals were somewhat casual. He himself was averse to the habitual eating of meat; and special plans had to be made for the tastes of others. He told his friend Cowell, who was proposing to come and see him: 'I will order a *fowl* to be killed: so if any of you drive over "toward the end of the week" (as you talk of) you shall at least have *that* to eat: if you want more you must have the parrot—if more the cat: if still more Ginger [the dog]—if most of all Mrs. Faiers [his landlady].'[3] This is obviously only a very rudimentary kind of fun; but it is good evidence that he was not the stuffy recluse that some people might suppose. He could, however, be a good deal more subtle with his humour when he pleased. As soon as he had bought his little yacht, he changed her name to *The Scandal*, because, as he observed, that was the staple product of Woodbridge. He then, with an extra turn of humour, had the dinghy to the yacht named *The Whisper*. This was surely not the man to become the prey to a wishy-washy kind of sentimentality.

Doubtless friends are as fond of each other nowadays as they were a hundred years ago, though they seem to disclose it less noticeably on paper; but FitzGerald expressed himself in particularly affectionate terms, even for those days. At the hard-bitten age of twenty-five, after telling his intimate friend of Cambridge days, John Allen, how longingly he had been waiting for a letter from him, he concluded: 'my friendships are more like loves, I think.'[4] And he added in another letter to Allen: 'I have nothing to say, when all is said, but that I love you more & more.'[5] At middle age, he told Thackeray: 'I truly believe there is no man alive loves you (in his own way of love) more than I do';[6] and some of Thackeray's letters to him are expressed in equally, and even more, affectionate terms, with such frequent and familiar salutations as 'My dear old Yedward', 'God bless you Teddibus', 'my Teddibus', 'my dear Teddikin'. FitzGerald corresponded regularly with Frederick Tennyson from his Cambridge period to the end of his life; and, three years before he died, he wrote to him: 'I must not let Christmas and the Old Year pass away without a loving word from me'; and he ended: 'I do remain what for so many years I have been, your affectionate, Old Fitz.'[7] Throughout his life his fondness for his close friends kept welling up within him, so that it was impossible for him to restrain himself from giving

o

it tender expression. Nor was the affection one-sided. Both Thackeray and Alfred Tennyson declared that they loved FitzGerald best of all their friends.*

At some stages of his life FitzGerald was so overcome with shyness that he neglected to take easy opportunities of meeting his friends, and even avoided doing so under some ridiculous impression that he might not be welcome. But he always remained earnest in his desire that he should be able to feel his absent friends, as it were, close to him. Just as Keats did, he liked to know that his correspondents and he were enjoying thoughts in common. He wrote to his friend, Bernard Barton, the Quaker minor-poet and friend of Charles Lamb: 'I have been looking over the old London Magazine. Lamb's papers come in delightfully: read over the Old China the night you get this, and sympathize with me.'[8] He told Frederick Tennyson many times that he was constantly thinking of him, adding on one occasion the words, 'with a kind of love I feel towards but two or three friends'.[9] When Edward Cowell, who encouraged him to study the Persian language, and helped him much in his preparation for *Omar*, had gone to India for some years, he wrote to him: 'You will believe I think of you much oftener than I write to you. Indeed I am constantly thinking of you both: constantly missing you.'[10]

Part of his plan for encouraging a sense of closeness between him and his absent friends was to give them realistic descriptions of his situation, his attitude of mind, and his activities. As a young man of thirty, he gave John Allen a most delightful and most informative description of his way of life: 'Here I live with tolerable content: perhaps with as much as most people arrive at, and what, if one were properly grateful, one would perhaps call perfect happiness. Here is a glorious sunshiny day: all the morning I read about Nero in Tacitus lying at full length on a bench in the garden: a nightingale singing, and some red anemones eying the sun manfully not far off. A funny mixture all this: Nero and the delicacy of spring: all very human however. Then at half past one lunch on Cambridge cream cheese: then a ride over hill and dale: then spudding up some weeds from the grass: and then coming in, I sit down to write to you, my sister winding red worsted from

---

* Tennyson would, of course, have put Arthur Hallam in a class by himself.

the back of a chair, and the most delightful little girl in the world chattering incessantly.'[11] This picture, it should be noticed, is of FitzGerald when staying with his sister in her comfortable country house.

Now and then he just described his actual physical situation at the time of writing, assuming that this would be sufficient to induce the desired sense of proximity. In a letter written on a Sunday morning, he said: 'Now before I turn over, I will go and see about Church, as I hear no bell, pack myself up as warmly as I can, and be off. So goodbye till twelve o'clock.— 'Tis five minutes past twelve by the stable clock: so I saw as I returned from Church through the garden. Parson and Clerk got through the service see-saw like two men in a sawpit.'[12] And again: 'I am going this evening to eat toasted cheese with that celebrated poet Bernard Barton. And I must soon stir, and look about for my great coat, brush myself, etc. It blows a harrico, as Theodore Hook used to say, and will rain before I get to Woodbridge. Those poor mistaken lilac buds there out of the window! and an old robin, ruffled up to his thickest, sitting mournfully under them, quite disheartened.'[13] Sometimes these realistic sketches were more laconic: '7¼ p.m. After a stroll in mine own garden, under the moon—shoes kicked off— slippers and dressing gown on—a pinch of snuff—and hey for a letter. . . .'[14] There was comfort to the writer, too, in these effusions: he could have added some such remark as: 'I tell you all these details because, in doing so, I have the assurance that I cannot strain your patience, and because you want to feel close to me as much as I want to feel close to you.' We, also, can value these revealing passages, for they give us some of the information about FitzGerald that we are most anxious to have. We want to be able to visualize him as much as he wanted his correspondents to do so.

Sometimes, in reading his letters, and noticing how often he seemed, in his eccentric way, to prefer closeness to his friends in imagination to closeness in fact, we may begin to understand why he took so much pleasure in the pastime of reminiscence. We may suspect that he was inclined to find this more restful and less exacting than confrontation. 'Do you remember', he wrote to John Allen, 'that day when we sat upon that rock that runs out into the sea, and looked down into the clear water below?'[15] He often felt like indulging in reminiscence when writing to Frederick Tennyson, who was out of England for long periods. He told him, for instance: 'Our trip to Gravesend has left a perfume with me. I can get up with you on that everlasting stopping coach on which we tried to travel from Gravesend to Maidstone that Sunday morning: worn out with it, we got down at an inn . . .—and numberless other turns of road and humour which sometimes pass before me as I lie in bed.'[16] He reminded another friend of long standing, Spring Rice, of a trip on a Margate steamer when 'a boy came round with penny black strings (do you remember?) to keep our hats from blowing away'.[17]

In spite of the shyness which was at the root of his principle of absent friendship, he was far from being a theoretical rather than a practical exponent of goodwill. The most remarkable feature of his many acts of kindness is his thoughtful, generous sympathy. A notable example of this is the help he gave to Tennyson when the latter, as a young man, was straitened for funds. His charity often involved the giving of himself, and not merely the giving of money. There are several instances, disclosed casually in his correspondence, of his going to London from Suffolk to visit distressed friends and acquaintances. His kind-hearted actions were multifarious. He went to London 'to see an old College friend who is gone mad, and threatens to drive his wife mad too, I think'.[18] Another visit was with the object of comforting 'two bereaved ladies, one of whom has just lost her husband'.[19] Still another was to an artist who was 'slowly dying in a garret with scarce a friend to go and see him.' He joined in providing money for the poor man's necessities.[20] This was not the same friend of whom he wrote some years earlier: 'I have bought a picture of my poor quarrelsome friend Moore, just to help him; for I don't know what to do with his picture.'[21] He had a delicate and sensitive feeling for people's needs, even in quite trivial matters. He remarked to a friend: 'Thank you for the partridges, which I believe I should have devoured myself had not my neighbour, Miss Bland, been unwell and "off her feed", so I sent them to her.'[22] With many people it might be supposed that the telling of these incidents implied a measure of self-complacency; but not so with FitzGerald; for he would have been so unconscious of any particular credit being due to him that it would never have occurred to him that he should be reticent in such matters.

His beneficence sometimes took unexpected turns. It would seem inherently unlikely that he should prove not only an indulgent but a companionable uncle to his small nieces. But so it was. He was much in demand; and we have a pleasant picture, in one of his letters, of him playing with these little girls, scrambling and sliding about in a gravel-pit 'till our legs ache'.[23] A little later, he wrote of the same children as 'most delightful, the best company in all the world to my mind'.[24] Doubtless, the qualities that attracted him to his sailor and farmer friends, naïvety and open-heartedness, also attracted him to his nieces.

It is difficult to gauge how far he was indifferent to literary fame. He certainly would have much enjoyed seeing *Omar* acknowledged as meritorious by the cognoscenti. But he was unwilling to exert himself at all extensively in the field of authorship, though it is clear from some youthful poems that he had a notable gift in that direction. His ingenious verses, which are inappropriately headed *The Meadows in Spring*, disclose a technique which is remarkably mature for an author of only twenty-two. Genuine modesty, rather than indolence, seems to have restrained him from devoting himself whole-heartedly to the profession of poet. When he was approaching middle age, his friend, Barton, pressed him to spread his wings. He replied: 'As to my doing anything else in that way, I know that I could write volume after volume as well as others of the mob of gentlemen who write with ease: but I think unless a man can do better, he had best not do at all; I have not the strong inward call, nor cruel-sweet pangs of parturition, that prove the birth of anything bigger than a mouse.'[25]

His authentic modesty, combined with ingenuousness, is evident in many of his letters where he disavows a high degree of genius, and yet qualifies his remarks by laying claim to considerable literary ability. For instance, he told Cowell: 'I am a very superficial scholar: having much neglected to learn at school; and having in the last ten years dug out of dictionaries and grammars just enough to give me some insight into the great authors—long dead. This kind of scholarship lies much on the surface—soon come soon gone: I believe that I have got some of the substance of these great authors into my head, and am able to estimate what room they fill in the learning of the world.'[26] In other words, he had, in the period leading up to his exploits in Persian literature, trained himself as a literary critic by a discriminating study of classical literature.

In the stage preceding the publication of *Omar*, his feelings about its merits were characteristic of him. He was afraid it would not please Cowell, or, alternatively, that it would not please publishers or public. 'Yet', he remarked to Cowell, 'it is most ingeniously tesselated into a sort of Epicurean Eclogue in a Persian Garden.'[27] When this little book was published in 1859, he wrote a pathetic letter to Cowell, in which there is again a mixture of mistrust of the outcome with a mild justification of himself and his authorship. 'No one cares for such things; and there are doubtless so many better things to care about. I hardly know why I print any of these things, which nobody buys; and I scarce now see any of the few [friends] I give them to. But when one has done one's best, and is sure that that best is better than so many will take pains to do, though far from the best that *might be done*, one likes to make an end of the matter by print. I suppose very few people have ever taken such pains in translation as I have: though certainly not to be literal. But at all cost, a thing must *live*: with a transfusion of one's own worse life if one can't retain the original's better. Better a live sparrow than a stuffed eagle.'[28]

He was consistently unpretentious about *Omar*; and, in discussing a third edition with his publisher in 1872, he expressed himself as being afraid that some projected amendments would seem like 'making too much fuss about a small thing'.[29] It was not until the last years of FitzGerald's life that the poem began to be acclaimed as a masterpiece. For the first fifteen years or more after publication, it remained of no consequence to anyone but a handful of friends; and for some years more it was only properly appreciated by a few hundred discriminating connoisseurs. By that time FitzGerald had become blandly stoical in regard to the subject; and with his unfailing modesty he wrote to his publisher in 1875: 'As to old Omar—I think he has done well, considering that he began his English life as an 'Enfant Trouvé'—or rather 'perdu' in Castle Street fifteen years ago. I wonder he has survived up to this time. We will leave [him] at present to smoulder away what life is in him—perhaps as much as in myself.'[30]

His notable lack of self-approbation was constantly evident. At the time when his income was reduced to small proportions as a result of his father's bankruptcy, his friends hastened to commiserate with him. His answers to such letters evince his modesty in two aspects. He told a friend: 'In all this matter however I do not desire, nor need, sympathy—many are my defects—but solicitude for money and luxury is not among them: and as I and all my family shall have *enough*, independent of this smash, when my mother dies, we should be *base* to fret ourselves now.'[31] And to Frederick Tennyson he wrote: 'It really gives me pain to hear you or anyone else call me a philosopher, or any good thing of the sort. I am none, never was; and, if I pretended to be so, was a hypocrite. Some things, as wealth, rank, respectability, I don't care a straw about; but no one can resent the toothache more, nor fifty other little ills besides that flesh is heir to. But let us leave all this.'[32]

As early even as his Cambridge days FitzGerald had the reputation of being shy, and, for that reason, disinclined to social activity. But this tendency became more definite soon after he left Cambridge. He wrote then to his friend, John Allen: 'Tell Thackeray that he is never to invite me to his house, as I intend never to go: not that I would not go out there rather than any place, perhaps, but I cannot stand seeing new faces in the polite circles. You must know that I am going to become a great bear: and have got all sorts of Utopian ideas into my head about society: these may all be very absurd, but I try the experiment on myself, so I can do no great hurt.'[33] He evidently meant this quite seriously, for he could never enjoy any social gatherings other than small and intimate ones. Twenty years after the date of the above-quoted letter, he wrote to Frederick Tennyson, when on a visit to London: 'Dear old Alfred [Tennyson] is out of town; Spedding is my sheet-anchor, the truly wise and fine fellow: I am going to his rooms this very evening: and there I believe Thackeray, Venables etc. are to be. I hope not a large assembly: for I get shyer and shyer even of those I know. Thackeray is in such a great world that I am afraid of him; he gets tired of me: and we are content to regard each other at a distance. You, Alfred,

Spedding and Allen are the only men I ever care to see again.'[34] Shortly afterwards he told the same correspondent that Alfred Tennyson 'never writes, nor indeed cares a halfpenny about one, though he is very well satisfied to see one when one falls in his way'.[35]

These apprehensions and misgivings, it need hardly be said, were baseless. His sensitive nature caused him to take offence at slights and discourtesies that were purely imaginary. His friendship with Thackeray continued with feelings of deep affection on both sides; and, two years after the date of the letter in which he said they were content to regard each other at a distance, Thackeray, on leaving England for a tour in America, wrote FitzGerald a most affectionate letter entrusting his daughter's welfare to him as one of his closest friends. As to Alfred Tennyson, FitzGerald should have realized that he was the kind of friend who was incapable of maintaining a regular correspondence, but whose friendship remained steadfast in spite of years of physical separation and casual intercourse. Moreover, the fault was as much his as that of Tennyson. Several years later, when FitzGerald was on a visit to London, he wrote to Cowell giving news of his eminent friends, such as Spedding, Carlyle, and the Tennysons; and he remarked: 'I cannot make up my mind to go and see any of these good, noble men: I only hope they believe I do not forget, or cease to regard them.'[36] A man who is so shy that he cannot call and see his dearest friends when within easy reach of them, should at least have the grace not to complain of their supposed stand-offishness.

From the time that he was a young man and was enjoying the exchange of heartfelt proofs of devoted friendship, in correspondence with two or three intimate friends, he began to surmise that his companionships would be most pleasurable, and least likely to be impaired, if pursued through the medium of letters. When he was only twenty-two, he cautioned Thackeray that the letters passing between them had been so warm in tone that renewed meetings might prove disappointing and even result in 'a flatness, then a disgust, and then a coldness'.[37] At that stage in FitzGerald's career, these suspicions were transient. Yet it is almost true to say that from middle life onwards, especially after the failure of his marriage, he relished his friendships more in his friends' absence than in their presence, though this remark is not applicable to his relations with his Suffolk cronies. When Cowell and his wife, to both of whom he was much devoted, returned from a stay of some eight years in India, he felt too shy to face a reunion. Instead of making an early plan for a meeting, he wrote vague letters to them suggesting a possible foregathering at some very indefinite future date. He was sufficiently ungracious as to tell Cowell that he had 'lost the talent of *going* to see—even older friends than you!'[38] 'You know I go nowhere; think of not having *seen* old Spedding for 5 years!'[39] After several months a meeting was arranged; and, the ice being broken, the friendship was resumed with all its old, easy intimacy. He confessed to another friend: 'It may seem odd to you at first . . . that I feel more nervous, I may say—at the prospect of meeting with an old friend, after all these years, than any indifferent acquaintance.'[40] This was more than self-mistrust; it was evidently a peculiar and complex attitude of mind for which psychologists may have a convincing explanation.

When FitzGerald was nearing seventy, Alfred Tennyson, being temporarily in Suffolk, called on him unexpectedly, their previous meeting having taken place twenty years before. The agitation of FitzGerald's emotions can be imagined; but he was soon able to calm himself, and they spent two happy days together. 'He stayed two days', he told a friend, 'and we went over the same old grounds of debate, told some of the old stories, and all was well.'[41] The last three words of this description are very significant. They imply a sense of misgiving that such a meeting might have proved embarrassing or even disillusioning.

This affliction of his, for his extraordinary shyness was no less than that, involved him in situations that were both pitiable and ridiculous. When his old friend, George Crabbe, the son of the poet, died, he suffered great perturbation in trying to determine whether he should go to the funeral. He wanted to pay his respects, but the thought of appearing at such a function was most painful to him. His miserable state of indecision is observable in his letter to the son of the deceased. 'In case I should not go to the funeral, it will only be from my nervous fear of making any figure in it. . . . If I go, it will be rather for the sake of the living. . . . In case I do go to the funeral, I can put up at the Castle, or at Mrs. Garrod's, can't I? I want to keep clear of Woodbridge and all friends. . . . My dear George, don't misunderstand me in case I don't appear on the day; and don't mistrust all my little professions of sympathy.'[42] In fact, he mustered up courage to go: he could be resolute when fundamental principles of behaviour were at stake.

It is a common failing of excessively nervous persons to run away in the middle of a conversation, when that is the last thing they really wish to do. In some strange way their composure crumbles, and suddenly deserts them. FitzGerald occasionally broke off conversations in this humiliating fashion. He told the story of one such instance with admirable realism, enabling us to sympathize with him cordially in his distress. 'Just as I was going out [from the Royal Academy] who should come up to me but Annie Thackeray, who took my hands as really glad to see her father's old friend. I am sure she was; and I was taken aback somehow; and, out of sheer awkwardness, began to tell her that I didn't care for her new novel! And then, after she had left her party to come to me, I ran off! It is true, I had to be back at Sydenham: but it would have been better to forgo all that: and so I reflected when I had got halfway down Piccadilly: and so ran back, and went into the Academy again: but could not find A.T. She told me she was going to Normandy this week: and I have written to tell her something of what I have told you. It was very stupid indeed.'[43]

His bashfulness and lack of self-confidence involved him in much more serious troubles than apparent rudeness. When he was a young man in the thirties, he was the ardent admirer of— indeed, it can be safely said that he fell in love with—Elizabeth Charlesworth, the daughter of a Suffolk parson, who, some years later married his friend, Cowell. She was one of the few women he ever met who could have made him happy, especially because they would have had intellectual interests in common. There was no reason whatever why he should not have married her, assuming her willingness, except that he suspected that he was too ingrained a bachelor to be a successful husband. As he told Frederick Tennyson a little later: 'If I were conscious of being stedfast and good-humoured enough, I would marry tomorrow. But a humourist [i.e. whimsical person] is best by himself.'[44]

We can do no more than make conjectures about the precise motives that impelled him to propose marriage to Lucy Barton; but it is a likely supposition that the same shyness that prevented him from proposing to Elizabeth Charlesworth was responsible for involving him in an obligation that caused him much un-happiness. A member of the Barton family, with special opportunities for knowledge, has reconstructed the situation in very convincing terms: 'When Barton's small estate had been realized, FitzGerald saw clearly that it did not provide enough to support her [the daughter, Lucy Barton]; and, faithful to the assurance he had given some months previously to his ailing friend, he impetuously offered to make up the deficiency from his own income. Such an offer her sense of propriety forbade her to accept. One can imagine the effect of her refusal upon a temperament so sensitive as FitzGerald's. He accused himself of having committed an indelicacy—a breach of good taste. His disordered fancy prompted him to believe that he had grossly outraged the feelings of his old companion's daughter by offering her money. The thought was intolerable to him. He must make amends at all costs. And so, heedless of the consequences, he proposed, and she—blind to the distraction of mind that had impelled him—accepted his offer.'⁴⁵ If, in fact, he had had the self-possession to be completely frank with Lucy Barton about his motives for helping her financially, he would have saved himself a great deal of misery. As it was, he became inextricably involved, and headed wildly for disaster, actually telling a friend, when announcing his forthcoming marriage that it was 'a very doubtful experiment. . . . I shut my eyes to the consequences. . . .'⁴⁶

Shyness and infirmity of purpose are obviously closely related; and FitzGerald's shyness, on the one hand, rendered him incapable of coming to a decision, and, on the other hand, made him liable to come to a stupid, ill-considered one when he eventually forced himself to take action. He was the most unbusinesslike of men. For about thirty years, he lived in lodgings, largely because it was easier to adopt that course than any other. But when he reached the later fifties, he felt that he had so often talked about buying a house, he must pull himself together and do so. In telling a friend about his problem he remarked that he was so afraid of making a blunder that 'I quite lose heart to decide'; and he added: 'I do really want, however, to get into a house of my own with my own servants (where and with whom, of course, I shan't do half as well as here [in lodgings]), and this for several reasons.'[47] When he had taken the great decision, and had bought a house and enlarged it, he did not move into it, but pretended to himself that he had destined it for the use of his nieces in summer. After so long a period in lodgings, he said, he was frightened at a change, 'yet it would be better to go. Meanwhile here I am.'[48] Eventually, after some years, he moved into two rooms of the house, and kept much the larger part of it for the benefit of his relations or guests.

There are numerous references in his letters to transactions in which he became involved owing to undue impulsiveness. He would go to London to buy a silver tea-pot and come back, considerably aggravated with himself, having bought a plated tea-service. He would lend his yacht to a friend, and immediately discover several excellent reasons why such a course was both inconvenient and imprudent. He would go long distances to inspect places of interest; and suddenly, owing to some petty aggravation, or to an irresistible longing for home, would hurry back without having carried out his original intention.

For many years he obtained a great deal of pleasure from the hobby of buying and selling oil-paintings by distinguished painters, or by painters that he would blithely assert to be distinguished. Among his motives for this seductive occupation was a sense of competition with two Woodbridge cronies who were also intent on the same pastime. In this, as in other kinds of business, he was impulsive and capricious; but he was happy in it, because he could be conscientiously light-hearted about his mistakes. It was just a game. His reports on his adventures in this field disclose the more jaunty, breezy side of his disposition. 'My Titian is a great hit: if not by him, it is as near him as ever was painted.' 'I am yet haunted with the ghost of a battle-piece (little in my way) at a shop in Holborn.' 'Frail is human nature. I thought I had quite got over picture-dealing, when lo! walking in Holborn this day I looked into a shop just to show the strength of my virtue, and fell. That accursed Battle Piece—I have bought it—and another picture of dead chaffinches. . . .'[49]

Twenty years later he was still at the same game, with equal imprudence and impetuosity. 'I have bought a Crome from Norwich, which is very good in its way; but I don't care about it, and indeed only bought it to see what we could make of it with a little warm water: which has restored it almost to what it originally was. I shall either sell or change it one of these days.

'The little moonlight Crome which I had bought when I last saw you is quite a failure: not *old* Crome at all, as I might have seen if I had only cared to look at the back, where his son's name is very legibly written. However, I thought it *old* Crome in my short view of it; so I must give up my connoisseurship.'[50]

His companions in this singular pastime were Bernard Barton (the father of Lucy Barton), a bank-clerk at Woodbridge and a minor poet, and Thomas Churchyard, a local solicitor and amateur artist. Another friend in the locality was George Crabbe, a parson, and son of the poet. The three of them formed, with him, a little coterie. These friends were ordinary, undistinguished, not specially clever people; and he was perfectly happy in their company. It never occurred to him that his own intellectual attainments deserved anything better. They were easy, comfortable, sincere folk; and those were characteristics likely to intensify his appreciation of them. He described Barton as 'a generous, worthy, simple-hearted fellow: worth a thousand better wits'.[51]

As a young man, FitzGerald had lived from time to time in the large country houses of his father and his sister; but he was not in the least tempted to cultivate the acquaintance of the squirearchy. He loathed their formal dinner-parties; and he despised the newly installed squires who had made quick fortunes in industry, and who despoiled their estates, notably by wholesale felling of trees for timber, and who recognized no responsibility for helping the community, especially the poor. He took pleasure, as he grew older, in the friendship of the best of the townsfolk of Woodbridge and the ordinary countrymen round about, for instance a stationer and bookseller, a merchant's clerk, and a corn merchant whom he described as 'a good fellow; a John Bull with sense, veracity, experience, and decision; better to me than all the colourless squires, who know nothing that I don't know better: and that's not much'.[52]

Probably FitzGerald's eccentricity has been exaggerated. His strange inability to meet his old friends after a considerable separation without painful apprehensions was a weakness rather than an oddity. His preference for homely country people to 'society' was due to his independent frame of mind, a commendable moral courage, and, some would add, his common sense. It was, perhaps, a mixture of moral courage, modesty, and convenience which caused him to behave in unconventional ways. He did not consider that superficial aspects of his behaviour were of any importance, or that other people should attach any importance to them; so he sometimes dressed in an unusual or grotesque manner, just because it suited his whim or the needs of the moment. If it was windy, he tied on his silk top-hat with a scarf, and did not mind, or perhaps did not know, how ridiculous he looked. If his boots hurt him, he took them off, and carried them in his hand. He was not, thereby, indulging in exhibitionism; he was merely exercising his conception of reasonable liberty of action, and a conscientious belief in the unimportance of such trivial matters. Like Dr. Johnson, some of his so-called eccentricity was attributable to physical factors over which he had no control. The reputation he acquired among the more disrespectful youngsters in his Suffolk neighbourhood, for being 'queer', is doubtless to be partly explained by such peculiar habits as that of lifting his feet unusually high when walking. This habit was the more likely to evoke derision because he often wore his trousers very short.

He evidently did not place much value on his life; and, if that was so, he was entitled to behave in a way which might seem imprudent and eccentric to people with other ways of thinking. The crew of his yacht were sometimes aghast at his rashness. One day, the captain warned him, when he was sitting on deck, that the weather was so rough that he might be washed overboard. He refused to go below, and told the captain, doubtless with reasonable politeness, to mind his own business. On another occasion, the boom knocked him off the deck into the water while he was reading. He was rescued, still holding the book in his hand; and he resumed his position on deck in his dripping clothes, and imperturbably continued reading, as before.

It would be quite out of character for him to be consciously eccentric, in order to obtain notoriety, like Byron. There is only one example, apparently, of which there is record, of his trying to scandalize anyone by his unconventional behaviour. In describing to Barton his activities while on a visit to London, he said: 'I spent one evening with Carlyle, but was very dull somehow, and [was] delighted to get out into the street. An organ was playing a polka even so late in the street; and Carlyle was rather amazed to see me polka down the pavement—He shut his street door—to which he always accompanies you— with a kind of groan.'[53] Perhaps the temptation of thus shocking Carlyle was irresistible. But it must be remembered that FitzGerald was an Irishman, and was, as he himself used to remark, naturally a little mad. It is easy to find Irishisms in his letters. But should he be classed as an eccentric? The description is not necessarily a disparaging one. We may freely admit that he came within the category if we consider eccentricity, as did John Stuart Mill, to be 'a mark of genius, mental vigour, and moral courage.'

FitzGerald was, however, extremely conservative in many ways, for instance in his opinion that 'there is not, and never was, such a country as Old England'. 'I am sure', he said, 'no travel would carry me to any land so beautiful, as the good sense, justice, and liberality of my countrymen make this.'[54] He was insular in the sense that he did not believe in travel. The principle of it seemed to him to be unsound. He once remarked that its benefits were delusive, for 'the *soul* remains the same'. He could learn all he wanted to know about foreign countries by consulting books and pictures; and he alleged that his practical experience, in fact very limited, confirmed his suppositions. 'If anything I have seen in my short travels,' he told a friend, 'had given me any new ideas worth having, I should travel more.'[55] Frederick Tennyson, to whom he expounded these notions, tried to persuade him to come and live with him in Florence for a while; and he was a little hesitant; but he characteristically made no decision, and therefore the project came to nothing. Even a tempting description of Cicero's villa failed to entice him, and he asserted that 'if I saw all these fine things with the bodily eye, I should but see them as a scene in a play, with the additional annoyance of being

bitten by fleas perhaps . . .'.[56] Here is a nice problem to engage
the attention of the student of FitzGerald's character. How
could a man with an imagination like that exhibited in *Omar*
reject these alluring opportunities to stimulate and recruit his
fancy, by advancing such frivolous pretexts? Perhaps *Omar*
itself gives an adequate answer to this question, for he managed,
in that poem, to steep himself in the local environment without
ever having been anywhere near it.

When a young man, he spent a considerable amount of time
in visits to London; but, as he grew older, he reduced his visits
to those of absolute necessity. 'I hate this beastly London more
and more. It stinks of churchyards and fish shops.' 'Oh for to
sit upon the banks of the dear old Deben, with the worthy
collier sloop going forth into the wide world as the sun sinks.'[57]
Again: 'More and more do I find myself fit only for the country,
and for country people: London is pestiferous.'[58] 'London is very
hateful to me. I long to spread wing and fly into the kind clean
air of the country. I see nobody in the streets half so handsome
as Mr. Reynolds [the Rector] of our parish: all clever, composed, satirical, selfish, well dressed.'[59] Much as he disliked the
smells and dirtiness of London, the aspect of it that aggravated
him most was the affectation and insincerity of its smart people.
The remarks he made on this subject are worth consideration
because they throw much light on his character, his fundamental preference for openheartedness over cleverness, and for
country people over Londoners. 'I was at a party of modern
wits last night that made me creep into myself, and wish myself
away talking to any Suffolk old woman in her cottage, while the
trees murmured without.'[60] 'London melts away all individual-
ity into a common lump of cleverness. I am amazed at the
humour and worth and noble feeling in the country, however
much railroads have mixed us up with metropolitan civiliza-
tion.'[61] 'One thing that always bothers me in London, &
among the Wits & Wise Men, is—that they can give such
admirable reasons for being wrong, while I can give none for
being right.'[62]

His easy, natural way with Suffolk country people, and
especially with its maritime folk, made them like and respect
him. It is probable that they would have respected him more if
he had been less indulgent with them. But, on the whole, he

may well have gained more pleasure in his relations with these simple-minded people by not trying to curb his abundant kindliness. In middle life, as we have already noticed, he undertook a new pursuit, that of cruising or sailing on sea or river. It must be admitted that he 'spoilt' some of his sailor-men friends and employees. He good-naturedly made a habit of dispensing grog and shag on board his own craft; and he used to carry a bottle of rum and rolls of tobacco in his pockets to ensure a welcome from longshoremen at Lowestoft. His friend, William Donne, who noticed this, remarked that he would sometimes spend his summer evenings under the lee-side of a fishing-boat, hearing and telling yarns.[63] He himself gave an extremely revealing description of his intimate relationship with his friends on the beach. 'We have grog & pipes in a little tavern kitchen: & sometimes in a sort of *net-house*, where (on a Saturday night) we sing songs too! . . . and I gain applause in "Pretty Peg of Derby O!" '[64] His shyness somehow evaporated in unconstrained situations like these. How different would have been his behaviour at a London soirée!

The salty flavour of the sailors' conversation gave him much delight. He told Cowell: 'I do little else, now summer is come, than be afloat on river or sea—asking how wind and tide are—what such a schooner or billyboy [barge] is, & whither going; and amused with my two men's jabber about winds & seas, & seeing them cook and eat their dinners etc.'[65] At about the same period, he also wrote to Cowell: 'I am happiest going in my little boat round the coast to Aldbro', with some bottled porter and some bread and cheese, and some good rough soul who works the boat and chews his tobacco in peace. An Aldbro' sailor talking of my boat said—"She go like a Wiolin, she do!" What a pretty conceit, is it not? As the bow slides over the strings in a liquid tune. Another man was talking yesterday of a great storm: "and, in a moment, all as calm as a clock".'[66] He delighted in noticing the characteristic lingo of his sailor friends, for instance: 'That old Jemima and Wiolet [Violet] are rare company-keepers.' (Two sailing-ships that consistently sailed in company.) 'I never knew the say [sea] in such a takin'; all flurries like.'[67]

Not long after he turned amateur sailor, he made the acquaintance of a master-hand at the herring-boats, Joseph

P

Fletcher, familiarly known as Posh. An imposing, romantic figure, a man to whose strength and courage was joined a strain of tenderness, he effectively captured the admiration and affection of FitzGerald. And, in a year or two, they had become partners in a herring-fishery business. Posh was to be captain of a new lugger which was largely paid for by FitzGerald. He described his protégé as 'a delightful fellow', 'my dear old lugger Captain'—'a fellow I never tire of studying—If he *should* turn out knave, I shall have done with all faith in my own judgment: and if he should go to the bottom of the sea in the lugger—I shan't cry for the lugger.'[68]

For some time the friendship between these two progressed most happily. FitzGerald took Posh about with him, and entertained him; and Posh, in his engaging way, provided good measure of diversion. Every circumstance in Posh's life aroused FitzGerald's intense interest. He eagerly seized on the opportunity of entering into the hopes and fears of a fisherman's family. The promotion of Posh's little boy to trousers was a matter in which he wholeheartedly shared in the family's jubilation. He told Cowell about Posh's many excellences, 'so big and strong and broad, so quiet and yielding at home: making way to his little wife, and taking his little sick boy to bed with him in the day-time. The other day he wanted to show me four *kits* his cat had presented him with: they were up in a loft; up which he climbs, like a cat, and brings the four little blind souls down nested like birds in the inside of his fur-cap. As he stood holding them very gently, and looking at them with blue eyes, I thought what a good statue it was.'[69]

A year or two after FitzGerald had entered into partnership with Posh, relations began to grow difficult; and gradually the friction increased, partly owing to Posh's unbusinesslike methods, and partly owing to his excessive addiction to alcohol. After the partnership had been in existence for three years, it was dissolved. The friendship was considerably strained, but remained unbroken. FitzGerald was certainly saddened by his experience; he evidently behaved to Posh not only with great patience and forbearance, but with a humility typical of his generous nature. At a stage when relations were awkward, he wrote to Posh: 'My dear Posh, Mr. Spalding was with me last night; and I asked him if I was justified in the scolding I have given you about buying the lugger and nets too; telling him the particulars. He would not go so far as to say that I was *wrong*; but he thought that you were not to blame either. Therefore I consider I *was* wrong; and, as I told you, I am very glad to find myself wrong, though very sorry to have been so; and I cannot let a day pass without writing to say so.'[70]

When he was nearing old age, FitzGerald's eyesight failed a good deal. Reading by artificial light became difficult; and he employed local boys to come in for an hour or two in the evenings to read to him from some novel by a notable author. The main object was, of course, to divert the employer, but it was typical of him that the interest and comfort of the reader should not be forgotten. FitzGerald had sometimes to exercise much patience; one of the boys used to stumble 'at every third word,' and get 'dreadfully tired,' as did the employer himself. Nevertheless, he made it his business to 'renovate' the boy with cake and sweet wine.[71] The extent to which he would consider the tastes and be interested in the personalities of his boy-readers is illustrated by a letter about another and later assistant. 'Last night I made my reader begin Dickens' wonderful *Great Expectations*: not considered one of his best, you know, but full of wonderful things, and even with a plot which, I think, only needed less intricacy to be admirable. I had only just read the book myself: but I wanted to see what my reader would make of it: and he was so interested that he re-interested me too. Here is another piece of Woodbridge life.'[72]

His solicitude for the welfare of his housekeepers was in-variable; and the standard of efficiency he demanded from them was low. It was symptomatic of him that he consistently avoided causing trouble to anyone who looked after him. His main, midday meal, when he was alone, was composed of vegetables, cheese, and pudding or an apple. In the evenings, something more simple still, perhaps toasted cheese, for which he had the strongest liking, and a glass of ale. He took occasion once to apologize to a friend for the culinary limitations of a housekeeper, remarking that she had 'no head for subtilties'. When one of these women was ill, he took lodgings for her at the sea-side until she was fully recovered. This was Mrs. Howes, who told one of his friends: 'So kind he was, not never one to

make no obstacles [i.e. to make complaints]. Such a joky
gentleman he was, too.' Some years after his kindness to Mrs.
Howes, he wrote: 'My good old housekeeper has been . . .
very ill . . . only now able to get about again. I have this
morning been scolding her for sending away a woman who
came to do her work, without consulting me beforehand: she
makes out that the woman wanted to go: I find the woman is
very ready to return.'[73]

Music was one of the greatest pleasures in his life. He was an
accomplished performer on the piano; and he had an accurate,
but not particularly admirable, singing voice which was only
heard among a few intimates, as with the Crabbes at Bredfield,
where he spent many happy musical evenings. He told
Frederick Tennyson, himself a musician, a good deal about his
delight in music; and, from these accounts, we can learn
about the man himself. When tired of reading, he said, 'I
take up my pipe, or sit down and recollect some of Fidelio on
the pianoforte'.[74] 'I hear little music but what I make myself,
or help to make with my parson's son and daughter. We,
with not a voice among us, go through Handel's Coronation
Anthem! Laughable it may seem; yet it is not quite so; the
things are so well defined, simple, and grand, that the faintest
outline of them tells. . . .'[75] 'I play of evenings some of Handel's
great choruses which are the bravest music after all. I am
getting to the true John Bull style of music. I delight in Handel's
Allegro and Penseroso. Do you know the fine, pompous, joyous
chorus of "These pleasures, Mirth, if thou canst give, etc."?
Handel certainly does in music what old Bacon desires in his
Essay on Masques, "Let the song be loud and cheerful, not
puling, etc." One might think that the Water Music was written
from this text.'[76]

A. C. Benson, in his Life of FitzGerald, is inclined to suggest
that he was a dilettante in the bad sense, in fact somewhat of a
slacker. FitzGerald's diffidence would not have allowed him to
defend himself against such a charge. In his younger days he
used to speak of his 'besetting indolence' and his lack of any
stirring ambition; and he often wondered whether it was not
somehow wrong that he should find life so pleasant. But he had
his ideal of duty to society, and conscientiously tried to carry
it out. He would hardly have been satisfied with being looked

upon, as Gray wished to be, as 'a private independent gentle-man, who read for his amusement'. At the beginning of his career he doubtless regarded himself as a prospective literary person who would have his uses, either by reason of his learning or his authorship. But it would have seemed absurd to him to have felt bound to work at regular hours, though in fact he often did. For much of his life he got up early in the morning and stood (always stood) at his desk reading or writing till midday at least. When we recollect his translation of Calderon's dramas, his translations of Greek plays, his various adaptations and compilations, his years of intensive study of the Persian language, his *Omar* and other poems from the Persian, his incomparable letters, and, finally, the steadily acquired habits of thought and the immense stores of knowledge that qualified him to be an original and discriminating literary critic, we have no need to rush to his defence.

It has been asserted that FitzGerald, as a critic, was too much affected by prejudice hastily acquired and doggedly main-tained. This is in both respects an exaggeration, though it is certainly true that many of his views about contemporary literature were expressed in unduly sweeping terms. No one could say that his character was lacking in variety who noticed the wide contrast between the gentle, soft-hearted traits in his disposition on the one hand, and, on the other, his uncomprom-ising literary judgements, as when he described some of Carlyle's writing as 'twaddle' and 'perfectly insane'. His old friend Spedding who knew him thoroughly and who was well qualified by learning and experience to express an opinion, characterized FitzGerald's verdicts in matters of this kind as 'strange and wayward . . . though original and often profound and luminous'.

FitzGerald was certainly downright in his depreciation of some of the work of his friends, Carlyle and Tennyson. Perhaps he knew them too well to be dispassionate. Carlyle's burning fanaticism distressed him. Of *Heroes and Hero-Worship*, he said: 'I don't like to live with it in the house. It smoulders.' A few years later, he wrote to Cowell: 'I have . . . spent an evening with Carlyle. . . . He smoulders about Ireland; at least, he smouldered to me; but I am told that he blazes at a breath of opposition, which I did not venture.'[77] And, a little later, he wrote to the same correspondent: 'Still, his raving is that of genius, and a sincere man too—*that* indeed is his madness—and I am touched, I say, by his passionate cries.'[78]

He was persistent in asserting that Tennyson's best poetry, indeed his only first-rate poetry, was written before 1842. He recognized that he was 'considered a great heretic' for abusing Tennyson's *The Princess*. Here again, his judgement may well have been unduly influenced by his intimate knowledge of the author, for he wrote to Cowell at the time of the publication of *The Princess*: 'I know nothing that would now restore him to his native and abdicated powers, but such an event as the invasion of England! That would shake him up from his inglorious pipe, petty digestive solicitudes, and make him burst the whole network of selfishness twined about him by so many years of self-indulgence and laziness.'[79]

When, many years later, Tennyson visited FitzGerald at Woodbridge for two days, a visit noticed earlier in this chapter, FitzGerald told him, in playful terms we may assume, that he had better not have written anything after 1842, adding that he had then ceased to be a poet and become a mere artist. There was a penetrating discernment in this comment which might well have ruffled the great poet, but Tennyson is said to have taken the remark in good part. He was well aware of, and well understood, the stubborn partialities of his faithful friend. On another occasion, in old age, FitzGerald was writing to Tennyson; and, after making some slight criticisms on his play, *Queen Mary*, he concluded: 'Still your old Fitzcrochet, you see, still! And so will be to the end, I suppose.'[80]

In those days, people were inclined to enjoy either Tennyson's poetry or Browning's: it was difficult to approve wholeheartedly of both. But FitzGerald, while sad about the loss of vigour and originality in Tennyson's later poetry, had no reservations in his condemnation of Browning. He often discussed books with his old friend Cowell to whom he remarked in 1862: 'Browning, you see, has published another of his hideous subtilties,'[81] a phrase that will give sly pleasure to those who hold similar views. And he wrote in 1869: 'I have made three vain attempts at vol. I of Browning—did I tell you? It seems to me an audacious piece of defiance to the public whom he has found so long blind to his merits.'[82] He also described this volume as 'a most impudent piece of cockneyism'.[83] Opinions such as these sound

very dogmatic and absolute, but they must not be taken more
seriously than they were meant; and he certainly enjoyed
shocking his friends by expressing startling views. Nor was he
inflexible, for, as we have noticed, he could modify the more
trenchant of his strictures on Carlyle's vehemence. If he found
that he had formed a mistaken view, he was prepared to admit
it. His feelings about Wordsworth's poetry were mixed. When,
as a young man, he was discussing Wordsworth's sonnets, he
allowed his dislike of sonnets in general to affect his opinion of
Wordsworth's poetry. 'The difficulty of the sonnet metre in
English is a good excuse for the dull didactic thoughts which
naturally incline towards it: fellows know there is no danger of
decanting their muddy stuff ever so slowly: they are neither
prose nor poetry. I have rather a wish to tie old Wordsworth's
volume about his neck and pitch him into one of the deepest
holes of his dear Duddon.'[84] But he had, in fact, a lurking
affection for Wordsworth, whom he sometimes referred to as
'Daddy'. When FitzGerald was an old man, he told a correspondent a story illustrating Wordsworth's delight in adula-
tion, and added: 'It is this conceit that diminishes Wordsworth's
stature among us, in spite of the mountain mists he lived
among.'[85] Nevertheless, a few months later, on reading certain
of Wordsworth's published letters, he described these as 'so
good, kindly, sincere, and modest that . . . [they] make me think
I ought to feel more filially to my Daddy . . .'.[86]

*   *   *

One of the chief justifications for the study of poets' characters is the help it gives in the appreciation of their poetry. In
the present book, poets' letters are used with the special object
of assisting in an understanding of them as men. There is also
available an opposite process. Those who wish to know all
they can about poets as persons may sometimes reinforce their
information by reading the poets' poetry. A fascinating book
could probably be written with the title 'Poets in their Poetry,'
for, while it is obvious that much poetry is often consciously or
unconsciously autobiographical, the extent to which inter-
pretative skill can be exercised is not quite so apparent.
FitzGerald, however, is one of the few poets who wrote a great
poem which does not, in a large measure, express what he

thought and believed. Although his translation from the Persian was a very free one, it could not be so free as to involve a modification of the main conception of the original work. There is much of FitzGerald's own self in *Omar*, but rather in the beauty of imagery than in the substance of the philosophy. Just as we can enjoy the poem without subscribing to its tenets, so it was possible for FitzGerald to interpret it, and even to elaborate it, without identifying himself with its principles. And we must remember that Omar himself, as FitzGerald points out in the introduction to his little volume, 'very likely takes a humorous or perverse pleasure in exalting the gratification of the Sense above the Intellect, in which he must have taken great delight, although it failed to answer the questions in which he, in common with all men, was most vitally interested'.

FitzGerald was not an orthodox Christian, but his defection did not amount to much more than a sceptical view of the theology of the Old Testament, and a settled perplexity about a future life. He would never have mentioned God irreverently, as did Omar. Readers of FitzGerald's letters cannot possibly regard him as one who approved of all the views Omar affected to maintain. It is ridiculous, in the face of the evidence, to imagine that he would wish to encourage selfish expediency and voluptuous self-indulgence. His altruistic benevolence and almost austere manner of life are beyond a doubt.

Just because his poetical ability was so considerable, it is a pity that his masterpiece did not consist of his own commentary on life's problems, instead of his interpretation of somebody else's. So discriminating a student of human nature, and so fine an exponent of chivalrous principles, could have thus gained our even greater admiration, and would not then have had to share that admiration with another. But there could never have been any reasonable hope of his undertaking so ambitious a project, because it would have involved a degree of self-confidence quite inconsistent with his essential attitude of mind.

NOTES

The key to the letters in the abbreviated references below will be found on pp. xi–xii; e.g. G=Correspondence of Thomas Gray. The Roman figures refer to the numbers of volumes, where pagination is not continuous throughout.

CHAPTER 1: INTRODUCTORY REMARKS

1. G. 927.
2. G. 843.
3. G. 1079.
4. CC. 510, 516.
5. S. 653.
6. S. 666.

CHAPTER 2: ALEXANDER POPE (1688–1744)

1. P. I, 280.
2. P. I, 326–7.
3. P. II, 339; also P. II, 501.
4. P. III, 384.
5. P. IV, 5–6; also P. IV, 156, 169.
6. P. IV, 364.
7. P. IV, 187.
8. P. III, 166.
9. P. IV, 102.
10. P. IV, 106.
11. P. I, 169.
12. P. I, 335–6.
13. P. II, 31.
14. P. II, 140.
15. P. II, 235.
16. P. II, 437.
17. P. III, 57–8.
18. P. I, 243.
19. P. I, 323.
20. P. II, 31.
21. *Thraliana*, ed. K. C. Balderston, p. 431.
22. P. III, 138.
23. P. II, 452.
24. P. IV; also P. III, 490.
25. P. IV, 193.
26. P. IV, 370.
27. P. IV, 179.
28. P. IV, 62; also e.g., P. II, 31.
29. P. I, 135.
30. P. I, 172.
31. P. I, 393.
32. P. III, 228.
33. P. IV, 180, 210, 331, 392; also R. Carruthers, *The Life of Pope*, pp. 358–9.
34. P. III, 357–8.
35. e.g. P. II, 224, 391; P. IV, 221.
36. P. II, 17.
37. P. II, 530.
38. P. I, 456.
39. P. I, 460.
40. P. II, 16–17.

CHAPTER 3: THOMAS GRAY (1716–1771)

1. G. 83–4.
2. G. 181–2.
3. G. 226.
4. G. 288; also G. 561.
5. G. 991.
6. G. 259.
7. G. 303–4.
8. G. 836–7.
9. G. 335.
10. G. 460.

11. *Two Quiet Lives*, p. 172.
12. G. 323.
13. G. 603–5.
14. G. 551–2.
15. G. 568.
16. G. 946.
17. G. 926.
18. G. 766.
19. G. 822.
20. G. 233.
21. G. 255.
22. G. 335.
23. G. 960.
24. G. 380.
25. G. 379–80.
26. G. 881.
27. G. 1091.
28. G. 575.
29. G. 333f., 710, 752f.
30. G. 751.
31. G. 830.
32. G. 1019.
33. G. 522.
34. G. 1017–18.
35. G. 498–9.
36. G. 584.
37. G. 692–3.
38. G. 377.
39. G. 66.
40. G. 589.
41. G. 1126.
42. G. 1148.
43. G. 1189.
44. G. 61.
45. G. 210.
46. G. 276–7.
47. G. 364, 533–4.
48. G. 760; cf. G. 600–1.
49. G. 457.
50. G. 976–7.
51. G. 1079.
52. G. 513.
53. G. 515.
54. G. 516.
55. G. 564.
56. G. 565–6.
57. G. 466.
58. G. 571.
59. G. 1018.
60. G. 372.

CHAPTER 4 : WILLIAM COWPER (1731–1800)

1. C. II, 176.
2. C. IV, 148.
3. C. III, 434.
4. C. II, 305–6.
5. C. II, 461–2.
6. C. II, 173; III, 325.
7. C. II, 330.
8. *Gentleman's Magazine* (1784), Part I, pp. 412–14.
9. C. II, 364.
10. C. I, 248.
11. C. I, 217; also C. IV, 107.
12. C. I, 172.
13. C. I, 215.
14. C. I, 212.
15. C. I, 248.
16. C. I, 363–4.
17. C. II, 344.
18. C. I, 483.
19. C. III, 35–6.
20. C. II, 463–4.
21. C. IV, 160.
22. C. IV, 167.
23. C. III, 34.
24. C. III, 46–7.
25. C. III, 388.
26. C. IV, 103.
27. C. II, 182–3.
28. C. I, 184.
29. C. I, 337.
30. C. I, 219.
31. C. II, 181.
32. C. III, 445.
33. C. IV, 143.
34. C. IV, 224.
35. C. IV, 251.
36. C. IV, 318.
37. *Literary Essays* (1948), p. 274.

CHAPTER 5 : WILLIAM WORDSWORTH (1770–1850)

1. See Herbert Read, *Wordsworth*, p. 139.
2. *Dorothy Wordsworth's Journals*, vol. 2, p. 333.
3. E. 242.
4. M. 7.
5. E. 332.
6. E. 327.
7. e.g. M. 738–9; also L. 447, and *Correspondence of H. C. Robinson with the Wordsworth Circle*, pp. 394, 447–8.
8. L. 1216–17.
9. E. 57; also E. 58–9.
10. E. 302.
11. E. 474 (note).
12. L. 657–8.
13. e.g. L. 803.
14. *Correspondence of H. C. Robinson* (as above), p. 601.
15. L. 1179.
16. E. 326.
17. M. 65.
18. E. 95, 165–6.
19. L. 571.
20. L. 1087.
21. L. 1079.
22. *Correspondence of H. C. Robinson* (as above), p. 272.
23. M. 126ff.
24. M. 198.
25. M. 669–70.
26. M. 620–1.
27. L. 514.
28. E. 251.
29. E. 274.
30. *Dorothy Wordsworth's Journals*, vol. 1, pp. 104, 147, 150.
31. E. 339–40.
32. L. 43–4.
33. L. 875–6.
34. L. 879.
35. M. 781–2.
36. M. 734–5; also L. 254.
37. M. 705.
38. L. 281–2.
39. L. 876–7.
40. L. 1212.
41. *Correspondence of H. C. Robinson* (as above), p. 5, note 3.

CHAPTER 6 : SAMUEL TAYLOR COLERIDGE (1772–1834)

1. *Letters of Charles and Mary Lamb*, ed. E. V. Lucas, Letter 52.
2. CC. 301.
3. CC. 308.
4. CC. 262.
5. *Southey's Letters*, ed. Warter, vol. 1, p. 253.
6. CC. 789.
7. CC. 63, 64, 74.
8. CC. 271–3.
9. CC. 266.
10. CC. 274.
11. CC. 301.
12. CC. 185.
13. CC. 208.
14. CC. 759.
15. CC. 889.
16. CC. 916.
17. CC. 828, 850.
18. *Gentleman's Magazine*, New Series, vol. 10 (1838), p. 27.
19. CC. 430.
20. CC. 880.
21. CC. 890, 898.
22. CC. 887–8.
23. CC. 1181–2.
24. E. 273.
25. E. 303.
26. CC. 832.
27. CC. 875–6.
28. CC. 1015.
29. M. 84.
30. M. 366.
31. CC. 615.

32. CC. 668.
33. CC. 774.
34. CC. 804.
35. CC. 786.
36. CC. 940-1.
37. CC. 1062.
38. CC. 1159.
39. CC. 1184.
40. UC. II, 206-7.

41. UC. II, 271-3.
42. UC. II, 405.
43. UC. II, 429-30.
44. UC. I, 408.
45. UC. II, 297.
46. UC. II, 278; also 221-7.
47. UC. II, 57-8.
48. L.C. II, 617-18.
49. CC. 930.

CHAPTER 7 : GEORGE GORDON, LORD BYRON
(1788-1824)

1. *Literary Essays* (1948), pp. 279-81.
2. BQ. 203.
3. BQ. 327.
4. BQ. 546.
5. BQ. 8, 13, 15, 47; BP. I, 45-6.
6. BQ. 410.
7. BQ. 106.
8. BQ. 120.
9. BP. I, 339.
10. BP. II, 41; also 121.
11. BQ. 107-8.
12. BQ. 82.
13. BM. I, 56.
14. BM. II, 66.
15. BQ. 259, 272, 289.
16. BQ. 395, 398, 413.
17. BQ. 387-8.
18. BQ. 465.
19. *Byron's Conversations (Blessington)*, pp. 125-6.
20. BQ. 306.
21. G. Wilson Knight, *Lord Byron's Marriage*, p. 249.
22. BQ. 344, 376-7, 407, 437.
23. BQ. 98.
24. BQ. 239-54; also 272.
25. BQ. 555.
26. BQ. 210-46.
27. BQ. 180, 397.
28. BQ. 555, 581.
29. BQ. 636.
30. BQ. 97.
31. BQ. 320.
32. BQ. 436-7.
33. BQ. 52.

34. *Byron's Conversations (Blessington)*, p. 32; also BQ. 574.
35. BQ. 545-6.
36. BP. III, 232-3.
37. BQ. 384.
38. BP. VI, 113.
39. BP. VI, 124-5.
40. BQ. 601.
41. BP. VI, 32, 99, 157; BQ. 689, 704.
42. BQ. 454.
43. BP. V, 142.
44. BQ. 6, 8, 73; BP. I, 22; IV, 76, 232.
45. See BQ. 247.
46. BQ. 449.
47. BQ. 27-8.
48. BQ. 227.
49. BQ. 275.
50. BQ. 581.
51. BQ. 414.
52. BQ. 591, 593.
53. BP. V, 73.
54. BP. IV, 337-8.
55. BP. V, 8.
56. BQ. 690.
57. BM. II, 229-30.
58. BQ. 656, 658, 661.
59. BQ. 682.
60. BP. V, 272.
61. BQ. 458-9; also BP. IV, 275, 319-20.
62. BQ. 396.
63. BM. II, 248.
64. BP. VI, 285, 287, 289, 293, 329.

CHAPTER 8: PERCY BYSSHE SHELLEY (1792–1822)

1. S. 976.
2. S. 933, 944.
3. S. 141, 144.
4. S. 168, 175.
5. S. 262.
6. S. 212, 225.
7. S. 228.
8. S. 244.
9. S. 149–50.
10. S. 365.
11. S. 367.
12. S. 419.
13. SLL. 24.
14. S. 425.
15. SLL. 31.
16. SLL. 35.
17. SLL. 38.
18. SLL. 41.
19. SLL. 43.
20. S. 429, 431.
21. S. 469.
22. S. 530.
23. S. 534.
24. S. 816–17.
25. S. 433.
26. *My Best Mary, Selected Letters of Mary Shelley*, ed. M. Spark and D. Stanford, pp. 22–24.
27. S. 528 (note).
28. S. 534.
29. S. 888–9.
30. *My Best Mary* (as above), p. 93.
31. S. 844–5.
32. S. 851.
33. S. 855–6.
34. S. 923–4.
35. S. 926.
36. SW. IX, 301–2.
37. SW. X, 172–3.
38. S. 821–2.
39. SW. X, 254–5.
40. S. 950.
41. S. 451.
42. S. 469.
43. S. 483–4.
44. S. 541.
45. S. 811–14.
46. S. 819.
47. S. 905–6.
48. S. 977.

CHAPTER 9: JOHN KEATS (1795–1821)

1. K. 139.
2. K. 133.
3. K. 227.
4. K. 312.
5. K. 215.
6. K. 363.
7. K. 435.
8. *Essays in Criticism, 2nd Series* (1921 ed.), pp. 103–4.
9. K. 301.
10. K. 324.
11. K. 393.
12. K. 70.
13. K. 227.
14. K. 55.
15. K. 413.
16. *Letters of Robert Browning*, ed. T. L. Hood, p. 134.
17. K. 95; also 107.
18. K. 414.
19. K. 221.
20. K. 87, 237.
21. K. 421.
22. K. 67.
23. K. 314.
24. K. 42.
25. K. 314–15.
26. K. 151.
27. K. 271.
28. K. 272.
29. K. 133.
30. K. 227.
31. K. 231.
32. K. 301–2.
33. K. 107.
34. K. 240.

35. K. 66.
36. K. 242.
37. K. 80.
38. K. 83–4.
39. K. 80.
40. K. 251.
41. K. 229.
42. K. 287.
43. K. 296.
44. K. 312.
45. K. 395–6.
46. K. 37.
47. K. 39.
48. K. 282.
49. K. 283.
50. K. 286.
51. K. 151.
52. K. 228–9.
53. K. 207.

54. K. 229.
55. K. 151.
56. K. 177.
57. K. 201.
58. K. 216.
59. K. 239–40.
60. K. 253.
61. K. 352.
62. K. 355–6.
63. K. 369–71.
64. K. 372.
65. K. 374.
66. K. 398.
67. K. 422.
68. K. 399.
69. K. 401.
70. K. 467–8.
71. K. 490–1, 497.
72. K. 500.

CHAPTER 10: EDWARD FITZGERALD (1809–1883)

1. FT., to Quaritch, 8 July? 1870.
2. F. I, 76.
3. FC., to Cowell, 21 July 1852.
4. F. I, 30.
5. FT., to Allen, 9 Sept. [1834].
6. *Letters etc. of W. M. Thackeray,* ed. G. N. Ray, vol. 3, p. 114.
7. FM. 259.
8. F. I, 143.
9. F. I, 255.
10. FC., to Cowell, 13 June 1851.
11. F. I, 59–60.
12. F. I, 145–6.
13. F. I, 153.
14. F. II, 151.
15. F. I, 46.
16. F. I, 145.
17. FC., to Spring Rice, 15 Oct. 1855.
18. F. I, 271.
19. FM. 228–9.
20. *W. B. Donne and His Friends,* ed. C. B. Johnson, p. 280.
21. F. I, 175.
22. FM. 152.
23. F. I, 99.

24. F. I, 179.
25. F. I, 105.
26. FC., to Cowell, 28 Jan. 1845.
27. F. I, 348.
28. F. II, 4–5.
29. FT., to Quaritch, ? 1872.
30. FQ. 32.
31. *A FitzGerald Friendship,* ed. C. B. Johnson and Hannay, p. 24.
32. F. I, 257.
33. FT., to Allen, 21 May 1830.
34. F. I, 257.
35. F. I, 263.
36. F. II, 20.
37. *Letters etc. of W. M. Thackeray,* ed. G. N. Ray, vol. 1, p. 165.
38. FC., to Cowell, 5 Oct. 1864.
39. FC., to Cowell, 25 May 1864.
40. FC., to Pollock, 17 Nov. 1871.
41. FK. 113.
42. FM. 47–8.
43. F. II, 143.
44. F. I, 185.
45. FB. 170–1.
46. FC., to Spring Rice, ? 21 Oct. 1856.

47. FM. 61.
48. FM. 79.
49. F. I, 108, 110, 132–3.
50. FM. 72–3.
51. F. I, 216.
52. FC., to Spring Rice, 27 July
1863.
53. FB. 94–5.
54. F. I, 68.
55. F. I, 83.
56. F. I, 118.
57. F. I, 169.
58. FC., to Cowell, 8 May 1847.
59. F. I, 157.
60. F. I, 192.
61. F. I, 164.
62. FC., to Cowell, 23 July 1862.
63. *W. B. Donne and His Friends*,
ed. C. B. Johnson, p. 238.
64. FC., to Spring Rice, 20 April
1861.
65. FC., to Cowell, 23 July 1862.
66. F. II, 20–1.

67. *Sea Words and Phrases.*
68. F. II, 94.
69. FC., to Cowell, after 18 May
and before 7 June 1867.
70. James Blyth, *Edward FitzGerald
and Posh*, p. 140.
71. F. II, 110.
72. FK. 126–7.
73. F. II, 338.
74. F. I, 92.
75. F. I, 265.
76. F. I, 153.
77. FC., to Cowell, 4 Nov. 1849.
78. FC., to Cowell, 17 Dec. [1867].
79. FT., to Cowell, 13 Jan. 1848.
80. *Tennyson, A Memoir*, vol. 2, pp.
182–3.
81. FT., to Cowell, 18 Jan. 1862.
82. FM. 100.
83. FC., to Cowell, 25 April ? 1869.
84. F. I, 87–8.
85. F. II, 195.
86. F. II, 199.

INDEX

PRINTED IN GREAT BRITAIN
BY THE CAMELOT PRESS LTD.
LONDON AND SOUTHAMPTON

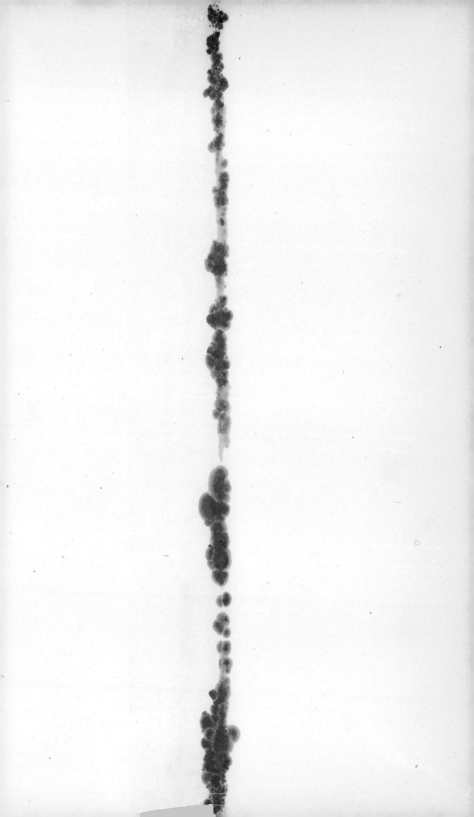